global

ADVANCED

coursebook

Lindsay Clandfield

Amanda Jeffries

Rebecca Robb Benne and Michael Vince

MACMILLAN

About Global

Lindsay Clandfield is a teacher, teacher educator and lead author of Global. He was born in England, grew up in Canada, taught at a university in Mexico, lives in Spain and has trained teachers from around the world. He is also the creator of the popular blog **Six Things** (www.sixthings.net), a collection of lists about ELT.

Amanda Jeffries is a teacher, teacher educator and author. She has taught in the UK and Chile specialising in teaching at advanced level and developing speaking and writing skills. As well as writing English language materials, she currently teaches at the University of Oxford, and is involved in setting up and running a range of teacher education projects.

Six quotes that inspired global

True education means fostering the ability to be interested in something.
Sumio Iijima, Japanese physicist

It is books that are the key to the wide world;
if you can't do anything else, read all that you can.
Jane Hamilton, American author

The English language is nobody's special
property. It is the property of the imagination …
Derek Walcott, Caribbean poet

The important thing is not to stop questioning.
Albert Einstein, German-American physicist

The mind is not a vessel to be filled,
but a fire to be kindled.
Plutarch, Greek historian

If you are going to write another
coursebook for the English
language, please try to do
something a bit different.
An English teacher who wishes
to remain anonymous

Global Advanced
by numbers:

10 units **168** pages **14** extracts from famous novels, plays and poems **46** vocabulary sections **37** explanations of English grammar **10** functional English lessons **16** accents from around the world in Global Voices **143** audio clips **30** video clips **240** interactive activities **100s** of curious and interesting facts

Content highlights

Global English
by David Crystal

Contents

EV – Extend your vocabulary   P – Pronunciation

Fact & Fiction

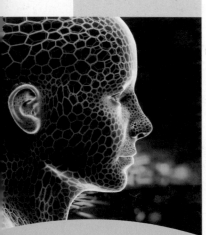

Speaking and Pronunciation

1 Work in pairs. Tell each other three facts about yourself that you think they do not know or could not guess, and one fact that is false. Your partner should ask questions to find out which statements are facts, and which is false. Then swap over.

2 With your partner, decide which words carry the main stress in each sentence.

1 I thought he was a student, but actually he's the teacher.
2 She thought I was from Spain, but in fact I'm from Mexico.

3 🔊 **1.01** Listen to check your answers. Then practise repeating the sentences with your partner.

4 Has anyone ever got a fact about you wrong? Have you got a fact wrong about someone else? Tell your partner.

5 Work with another pair. Introduce your partner. Include the true and the corrected facts from exercise 1. Use *in fact, actually,* or *in actual fact* to contradict the false information.

Reading

1 When you need information, do you normally use an encyclopedia or other reference book, or look online? Why?

2 Read *Six Wikipedia 'Facts'*. Five statements are true and one is false. Which one do you think is false? What made you think the others were true?

3 Read *Is Wikipedia part of a new 'global brain'?* on page 7. Which statement best reflects the writer's opinion? Find evidence for your view.

1 Sites like Wikipedia have removed the need for expert knowledge nowadays.
2 Professional experts still have a vital role to play in deciding about the accuracy and importance of facts.

4 Match the first lines below to paragraphs A–D in the text. Use the words in bold in the lines and in the text to help.

1 **But** is it really the case that we no longer need professional expertise?
2 **The internet** is often celebrated for giving a voice to anybody and everybody.
3 **Despite its weaknesses**, Wikipedia is still a great entry point for finding information and linking to other sites of interest.
4 With **this proliferation of user-generated content** has come the notion of a collective intelligence, or what some have termed 'a global brain'.

5 Explain the following phrases, as used in the text.

1 user-generated content (paragraph A)
2 citizen journalists (paragraph A)
3 peer review (paragraph B)
4 collective intelligence (paragraph B)
5 engineered content (paragraph B)
6 professional amateurs (paragraph C)

6 Choose the alternative you agree with most. Then discuss your ideas in pairs.

1 The idea of collective intelligence is *persuasive / intriguing / ridiculous.*
2 User-generated content *will probably / may / will never* replace the contributions of experts.

Six **Wikipedia** 'Facts'

1 The name *Wikipedia* derives from the Hawaiian word *wiki* meaning *quick* (the *Wiki Wiki Bus* in Hawaii is a fast airport shuttle bus). A *wiki* is a website that allows the easy creation and editing of web pages.

2 The first web-based wiki was created by Ward Cunningham in 1995 to enable computer programmers to share ideas online.

3 Wikipedia contains over 2.9 million English language articles, making it the largest encyclopedia ever assembled.

4 Wikipedia articles are written and revised by hundreds of thousands of unpaid volunteers, who may be academics, researchers, students or simply interested amateurs.

5 The website has an official non-bias policy, and articles must present a balanced view of a topic.

6 Articles are vetted for accuracy and appropriateness by a panel of experts on the Wikipedia Editorial Board.

Is **Wikipedia** part of a new **'global brain'?**

A _____ User-generated content on **sites** such as Wikipedia, YouTube® and MySpace, as well as **web tools** such as discussion groups, blogs, wikis and podcasts, have brought about an elevation of **the role of amateurs**. News organisations are crying out for 'citizen journalists', asking the public to help 'make the news' and offering money for eye-witness accounts and mobile-phone video clips, while TV companies trawl the internet looking for entertaining clips to televise.

B _____ **Such collective intelligence** is supposedly made up of an international community of ordinary people who contribute and peer review content to ensure that the highest level of knowledge on a particular subject is attained. The idea behind collective intelligence is that anyone can contribute to the knowledge pool on any chosen subject. And increasingly, collective intelligence is seen as preferable to professional expertise. Indeed, many in the blogosphere seem fundamentally suspicious of funded or 'engineered' content – that is, researched, credible, verified and edited content.

C _____ **And** are all opinions equally valid – or are some opinions simply more valid than others? Who acts as the filter? Surely the only way of achieving a coherent overview is to invite experts to sift through the content and judge what is quality and what is not? It is true that a small proportion of bloggers are authorities in their field or are 'professional amateurs', but this does not mean that we are witnessing the rise of a collective intelligence that will develop and disseminate ideas across the globe.

D _____ **There is undoubtedly a role** for user-generated content today. However, the new web world can surely only fulfil its true potential through more rigorous standards and filters on the quality of the content generated. Such content should not be elevated to the grandiose status of an emergent 'collective intelligence' – especially if that is at the expense of expert knowledge, which remains invaluable today.

Extend your vocabulary – collocations for going online

Read the collocations below and answer the questions with a partner.

- visit a *website / web page / blog*
- post a *blog entry / comment / photo*
- *download / upload* a file / an image / a video / information
- *click on / follow* a link
- update your *software / status / profile / blog*

Do you regularly access the internet? Why / Why not?

Are there any of these actions that you have never done?

Which, if any, have you done recently, and why?

Writing

You are going to write the introduction to an entry on one of the following topics for an online encyclopedia website:

- your town or region
- a favourite band, singer, composer or type of music
- a famous person from your country

1 Read the instructions for writers from the Wikipedia website below.

1 Which two criteria for acceptable articles are mentioned?
2 Do you think there is such a thing as 'a neutral point of view' or 'verifiable accuracy'? How can it be presented?

> Wikipedia has a neutral point of view. We strive for articles that advocate no single point of view. Sometimes this requires representing multiple points of view, presenting each point of view accurately and in context, and not presenting any point of view as 'the truth' or 'the best view'. All articles must strive for verifiable accuracy: unreferenced material may be removed, so please provide references. That means citing verifiable, authoritative sources, especially on controversial topics and when the subject is a living person.

2 Write your introduction. Then show it to a partner. Your partner should check that it meets the criteria, and ask questions to find out more information.

Fact & Fiction

Part 2

Reading & Speaking
The world's most adventurous museums

Listening
Interview about museums

Grammar
Present simple and continuous for facts and trends

Reading and Speaking

1 Work in pairs to discuss the questions.

> adventure   a fun day out
> boring information   experimental projects
> hands-on exhibits   historical artefacts
> specimens   temporary exhibitions

- Which of the ideas in the box do you associate with museums? Why?
- When did you last go to a museum?
- Which of the items above did you experience?

2 You are going to learn about some of the world's most adventurous museums and art galleries. Work in groups of four. Student A: turn to page 126. B: turn to page 129. C: turn to page 127. D: turn to page 131.

3 Tell the rest of the group about your museum. Then discuss these questions together.

- Which museum would you most, and least, like to visit, and why?
- Do you think museums like these can enrich our knowledge of the world? Why / Why not?

Listening

1 Work in pairs. Discuss whether you think these statements are true (*T*) or false (*F*).

1 Attendance at museums has declined recently.
2 Children are the largest growing age group for museum visitors.
3 Museums originated in the Renaissance.
4 Museums helped establish a scientific way of looking at the world.
5 Early museums all had similar exhibits.
6 The function of museums is changing in the digital age.
7 Museums should aim to engage people emotionally.
8 Museums will probably have disappeared in 100 years' time.

2 🔊 1.02 Listen to an interview with Professor Ken Arnold, Head of Public Programmes at the Wellcome Trust Museum, in which he discusses museums. Check your ideas for exercise 1. Does anything surprise you? If so, why?

3 Listen to the interview again and complete the gaps.

1 Yes, _____ more than ever _____, so more people are going to public cultural institutions these days than are going to sporting venues, and in recent years attendance at many museums has _____ risen steadily.
2 It can be hard to tell _____, but I think museums are increasingly appealing to young adult audiences.
3 _____ is this idea of facts that were publicly visible, that were verifiable by anyone who wanted to question them.
4 _____, museums can still effectively perform the same sort of function, but now not just for a few people.

4 Which of the expressions in the gaps are used …

1 to start an answer to a question?
2 to give an opinion?
3 to add emphasis?

5 Choose two questions to discuss in pairs.

- Think of a museum you know. What does it do to attract more visitors?
- Describe an interesting or unusual exhibit or temporary exhibition you have seen in a museum.
- If you could design a temporary exhibition, what would you choose to focus on?
- What do you think a museum might look like in 100 years' time?

Grammar

1 Match the grammar rules below with a phrase from the box.

> a temporary situation   a habit or routine
> a trend or new development
> an established fact

- Use the present simple tense to describe …
  - a _____, eg *Most museums do not charge an entrance fee.*
  - b _____, eg *I quite often go to exhibitions.*
- Use the present continuous tense to describe …
  - c _____, eg *Today, more and more young people are visiting museums.*
  - d _____, eg *The exhibits are currently being stored in the cellar while the museum is being renovated.*

Note the following uses of the present continuous:
- with *always* or *forever* to emphasise an emotional reaction to a regular activity
  *He's **always** coming late. They're **forever** putting on new exhibitions.*
- with certain state verbs which also have a dynamic, progressive meaning
  Museums are increasingly appealing to a younger audience.
  I'm loving having more free time these days.

2 Match each group of adverbials with one of the rules a–d.

1 nowadays, increasingly, these days, today
2 in general, normally, generally speaking
3 rarely, from time to time, every other week
4 at the moment, at present, currently

3 For each of the sentences, decide whether one or both alternatives are possible, and why.

1 Museum entrance fees *become / are becoming* more and more expensive.
2 I *work / am working* as assistant curator in the local museum.

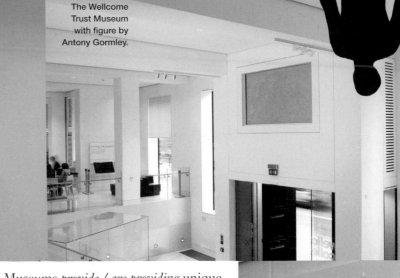

The Wellcome Trust Museum with figure by Antony Gormley.

3 Museums *provide / are providing* unique access to priceless treasures.
4 The local art gallery *tries / is trying* to raise funds to buy a new exhibit.
5 Public funding for museums and the arts is *reduced / being reduced* nowadays.
6 My friend *is always trying / always tries* to persuade me to go to exhibitions, but I'm afraid I *don't have / am not having* enough time.
7 The idea of visiting that exhibition *sounds / is sounding* less and less attractive.

4 Choose a suitable adverb to complete the sentences.

1 _____, we have a female prime minister in my country.
2 I _____ watch TV in the evenings.
3 I am _____ spending my weekends studying.
4 _____ people in my country speak good English.
5 It is becoming _____ difficult for young people to find a job in my country.

5 Write true sentences describing facts or trends connected with four of the following topics.

> air travel   cost of living   tourism   holidays
> learning English   leisure activities   spending patterns

Holidays: Most people in my country spend their holidays at home, but more and more people are going abroad for their holidays.

6 Read your sentences in small groups. What evidence do you have for your statements?

G **Grammar focus** – explanation & more practice of present simple and continuous for facts and trends on page 132

Speaking

fiction /ˈfɪkʃ(ə)n/ noun **
1 [U] books and stories about imaginary events and people. Books that give facts about real events, things or people are called non-fiction.

1 Work in pairs. Look at the definition of fiction and make a list of different types of books that could be classified as fiction or non-fiction. Which types of book do you generally prefer to read, and why? If you do not normally read, why is that?

2 Read *A good story*.
1 Choose six features you think are the most important.
2 Compare your ideas with a partner. Are there any ingredients in the list that you feel are not necessary?
3 Think of a well-known story or folk tale from your country, or one you remember from your childhood. Can you summarise the story in a single sentence?

Listening

1 Read about the frame story technique below. What exactly is meant by 'a story within a story'? Do you know the story of the *Arabian Nights*, or any of the tales within it?

2 ⊘ 1.03 Listen to the first part of the frame story of the *Arabian Nights*. How are these characters connected in the story?
1 Shahrazad   3 The King's Vizier
2 The King   4 Dunyazad

3 With a partner, try to put the events below in order 1–7. Can you remember any reasons given for the events?
a Shahrazad vowed to marry the king. ____
b The king met Shahrazad. ____
c Shahrazad told the king a story. ____
d The vizier became sad. ____
e Shahrazad's sister came to meet her. ____
f There were no young women in the kingdom. ____
g The king decided to meet Shahrazad the next night. ____

4 Listen again to check your answers.

5 In your opinion, which of the following does the story mainly illustrate, and why?
The power of:
• intelligence   • rulers
• love   • fiction

6 Shahrazad is said to have collected thousands of stories, having 'read books and histories, accounts of past kings and stories of earlier peoples'. If you had to tell a favourite story to save your life, which one would you tell, and why?

A **good** story...

has an intriguing plot
grabs your attention from the start
has a happy ending
is short and simple
has characters you can empathise with
teaches you something about life
has vivid descriptions
can be summarised in a single sentence
is like real life   is entertaining
has a powerful message
ends with a bang

The Frame Story

One of the earliest techniques in fiction is the frame story. A frame story is a narrative in which a main story is told in order to set the stage for a series of other shorter stories, each of which is a story within a story. The technique goes back thousands of years and can be found in stories from all over the world. One of the most famous frame stories in world literature is the *Arabian Nights* (also known as the *Thousand and One Nights*).

Vocabulary and Pronunciation

1 Read two sentences about the story. Which of the underlined adjectives is gradable?

The king was somewhat <u>surprised</u> when Dunyazad arrived to see her sister.

When Shahrazad offered to see the king, her father was absolutely <u>astonished</u>.

2 Complete the rules using the groups of words in the box.

> a rather, somewhat, a little, a bit, slightly
> b very, quite, pretty, fairly
> c absolutely, utterly, completely, totally

1 Gradable adjectives (eg *good*, *big*, *surprised*) can be qualified by adverbs such as _____.

2 Gradable adjectives with a negative meaning (eg *difficult*, *expensive*) can also be qualified by _____.

3 Ungradable adjectives (eg *wonderful*, *enormous*, *astonished*) can be qualified by adverbs such as _____.

3 Read more sentences about the story, and delete the gradable alternative.

1 The king was absolutely *furious / enraged / angry / incensed* to learn of his wife's betrayal.

2 He was completely *heartbroken / upset / distraught / devastated* so he ordered her execution.

3 The citizens were utterly *horrified / shocked / appalled / speechless* at the king's brutality.

4 Shahrazad's decision to see the king left her father feeling totally *mystified / puzzled / bewildered / baffled*.

5 The vizier was absolutely *pleased / overjoyed / delighted / euphoric* when Shahrazad's life was spared.

4 Find adjectives from exercise 3 with the following stress patterns.

1 O   3 Oo   5 ooO   7 Oooo
2 oO   4 ooOo   6 Ooo

5 🔊 1.04 Listen to check your answers. With a partner, take it in turns to read out the sentences in exercise 3, choosing one of the alternatives.

6 Look at the example of another way to describe emotional reactions in a story. Write some more sentences about the story using the ideas in exercise 3, and one of the words below.

The vizier learnt <u>to his utter amazement</u> that Shahrazad had not been killed.

> amusement   annoyance   astonishment
> bemusement   delight   dismay   fury
> horror   relief   sorrow

Writing

1 Work in pairs. You should each choose one of the opening lines from a tale from the *Arabian Nights*. Take it in turns to write sentences to develop the stories. Include descriptions of emotional reactions.

1 There was once a poor, elderly fisherman with a wife and three children, who was in the habit of casting his net exactly four times each day.

2 Once in the land of Egypt there was a woman who loved money so much that she could not find a husband rich enough to satisfy her.

3 In a certain town of Persia there lived two brothers, one of whom was named Kassim and the other Ali Baba. Their father at his death left them a very moderate fortune, which they divided equally.

4 Once upon a time there was a wealthy merchant who possessed many animals, as well as the gift of understanding the language of birds and beasts.

2 When you have finished, read your stories to another pair. Which do you prefer, and why?

Fact & Fiction

Reading

1 What do you think of when you hear the phrase 'science fiction'? Then tell the class. Do you enjoy science fiction books and films? Are they more 'fiction' than science?

2 Look at the interactive quiz below by NASA, The American Space Agency. Do you think the sentences are just science fiction? Tick (✔) the ones you think are based on scientific truth.

> **A** We now have evidence that some form of life exists beyond Earth, at least in primitive form. _____
>
> **B** Our solar system is not the only one: we know there are many other suns with planets orbiting them. _____
>
> **C** We currently have the technology necessary to send astronauts to another star system within a reasonable timespan. The only problem is that such a mission would be overwhelmingly expensive. _____
>
> **D** There is no gravity in deep space. _____
>
> **E** Some organisms can survive in space without any kind of protective covering.
>
> _____

3 Read *Just science fiction?* and match paragraphs 1–5 on page 13 to sentences A–E in exercise 2. Underline the information or phrases that helped you match them.

4 Check your answers to exercise 2. Which of the science facts did you find the most surprising?

5 Discuss these ideas with a partner.

- What would it mean for mankind if other star systems could provide potential new living spaces?
- Why do so many people insist that we are not alone in the universe?
- Given the rapid pace of change today, what will science fiction have to come up with to keep ahead of actual science research?

Extend your vocabulary – prefixes

1 Look at the words from the text. What do they mean? Match the prefixes in bold to the correct meanings:
1 **tele**scope   3 **extra**terrestrial
2 **ultra**violet   4 **inter**stellar

between	beyond
extremely	over a distance

2 Combine these words with one of the prefixes above. Explain the words to a partner.

active	changeable	judicial	modern
ordinary	shopping	sonic	

3 Find out the meaning of these other prefixes. Use a dictionary and find an example word for each one.

anti	hyper	multi	post	sub

Listening

1 🔊 1.05–1.09 Listen to five opinions and dialogues. Which one of these three questions are all five speakers reacting to?

1 Is there life on other planets?
2 Is space exploration a waste of money?
3 Would you like to go into space?

2 Listen again. Which speakers are in favour and which against?

For each speaker or pair of speakers (1–5) note down their reaction and reasons.

3 What's your answer to the question they are discussing?

JUST SCIENCE FICTION ?

1 _____
SCIENCE FACT
Improved telescopes and detectors have led to the detection of dozens of new planetary systems within the past decade, including several systems containing multiple planets.

2 _____
SCIENCE FACT
In a European Space Agency experiment conducted in 2005, two species of lichen were carried aboard a Russian Soyuz rocket and exposed to the space environment for nearly 15 days. They were then resealed in a capsule and returned to Earth, where they were found in exactly the same shape as before the flight. The lichen survived exposure to the vacuum of space as well as the glaring ultraviolet radiation of the Sun.

3 _____
SCIENCE FICTION
While many scientists speculate that extraterrestrial life exists, so far there is no conclusive evidence to prove it. Future missions to Mars, Jupiter's moon Europa and future space telescopes such as the Terrestrial Planet Finder will search for definitive answers to this ageless question.

4 _____
SCIENCE FICTION
Even the unmanned Voyager spacecraft, which left our solar system years ago at a breathtaking 37,000 miles per hour, would take 76,000 years to reach the nearest star. Because the distances involved are so vast, interstellar travel to another star within a practical timescale would require, among other things, the ability to move a vehicle at or near the speed of light. This is beyond the reach of today's spacecraft – regardless of funding.

5 _____
SCIENCE FICTION
If this were true, the Moon would float away from the Earth, and our entire solar system would drift apart. While it's true that gravity gets weaker with distance, it can never be escaped completely, no matter how far you travel in space. Astronauts appear to experience 'zero-gravity' because they are in continuous free-fall around the Earth.

Grammar

1 Match the examples a–f to the correct rules. Which words have been left out? Which sentences sound informal?

a *We have some sort of duty to find out if we are alone in the universe. Or at least **try to**.*

b *'I'd go into space, you know, if I got the chance.' – 'I think I **would** too.'*

c ***Know** what I mean?*

d ***Don't know** really. Haven't really thought about it.*

e ***You know** what?*

f *'The government could have used that money to help people in need instead.' – 'Yeah, they **could have** …'*

We often leave out words in order to avoid repetition. This is natural in everyday spoken and written English.
- the main verb and its object can be left out after an auxiliary verb _____
- an infinitive clause can be reduced to the word *to* _____
In spoken English, where the context is clear, unnecessary words can also be left out. This makes the sentence sound much more informal.
- at the beginning of a sentence, subject pronouns can be left out before all verbs _____
- in questions, the auxiliary verb can be left out (except before *I* and *it*) _____
- in questions where the subject is clear, the subject pronoun can also be left out _____

2 In these sentences words have been added to replace another phrase. What has been replaced?

Is space exploration a waste of money?
*I don't think **so**.   I hope **not**.*

3 Look at the dialogues. Put brackets round what can be left out, or cross out and replace with *so* or *not*. Sometimes there is more than one correct answer.

1 A: Is that a shooting star?
   B: It might be a shooting star. Hmm, but then again it might not be a shooting star.
2 A: Is he going to go on about scientific progress again?
   B: I hope he isn't going to go on about that again.
3 A: Do you believe in extraterrestrials?
   B: Yes, I think I do believe in extraterrestrials. You can't believe everything scientists tell you.
4 A: Do you fancy going to see the new sci-fi film? I think it's still on.
   B: Yes, I'd love to see the new sci-fi film.

4 Work in pairs. Student A: turn to page 126. Student B: turn to page 129. Ask and answer your questions.

G **Grammar focus** – explanation & more practice of ellipsis on page 132

Glossary
lichen *(noun)* – a small soft plant that grows on surfaces such as trees and walls

Warm up

Work in pairs. Discuss the following for your town or area:

- a good meeting point in the town centre
- a good place to meet up for lunch or coffee
- a good place for a night out with friends
- three interesting things to do with a friend at the weekend

Listening

1 🔵 1.10–1.12 Listen to three conversations in which people are making arrangements to meet. For each conversation, note down …

1 the relationship between the two speakers.
2 what they are arranging to do.
3 where and when they arrange to meet.

2 Listen to the conversations again and answer the questions.

Conversation 1
1 Why is the woman *tied up this Sunday*?
2 Why is it *a shame*?

Conversation 2
1 What time does Clare's coach get in?
2 Why might Rob arrive a little later?

Conversation 3
1 What plans does the man mention for before and after lunch?

3 🔵 1.13–1.14 Now listen to two conversations where people are describing plans for the weekend. Make notes on what each person is going to do.

Language focus

Read sentences from the conversations. Underline the expressions used to describe plans and arrangements. Then match each sentence to one of the categories.

A Clear intentions   C Formal timetabled events
B Fixed arrangements   D Possible plans

1 I've arranged to meet Sarah. _____
2 I'm helping her move house next Sunday. _____
3 My coach gets in at 4.30. _____
4 I'll be there as soon as I can. _____
5 I'm going to be working. _____
6 I'm due in court at half past two. _____
7 I might take some of my friends along. _____
8 We're going to have a lovely meal. _____
9 We'll probably go to the nursery. _____
10 I'm planning to go to London. _____
11 I'm thinking of visiting my mother-in-law. _____
12 Maybe I'll do some gardening. _____

Ⓖ **Grammar focus** – explanation & more practice of future forms on page 132

Pronunciation

1 Look at the questions. Do you think the speaker's voice goes up or down at the end of each sentence?

1 Are you doing anything on Sunday?
2 Is tomorrow any good for you?
3 What are your plans for the weekend?
4 What are you up to this evening?
5 Would you like to meet up for coffee?
6 Do you fancy coming round for supper?

2 🔵 1.15 Listen to check your ideas. What is the rule? Listen again and repeat.

Speaking

Work in pairs. Ask and answer about your partner's plans at different times in the coming week.

- Invite him/her to do some of the activities you discussed in the Warm up and make firm arrangements to meet.
- Swap roles and have similar conversations.

Useful phrases

- That sounds great! I'd love to
- I'd love to, but I'm afraid …
- I can't do 1.00 – can we make it a bit later?

Global English

English: just the facts?
by David Crystal

People often conclude the point they're making with the words '… and that's a fact!' It's a fact that the Earth is round and that Aleksandr Solzhenitsyn won the Nobel Prize for Literature in 1970. Facts are demonstrable, verifiable, unarguable. But with language, there are remarkably few of them!

How many people speak English around the world? Estimates vary enormously: some say around 1,500 million; some say 2,000 million or more. The uncertainty partly results from the lack of information about language use in many countries. Census forms rarely distinguish different functions – listening, speaking, reading, writing – or ask about a person's ability in each. But the uncertainty also reflects a question of definition: how fluent do you have to be to count as a speaker of English? At what point in a learning curve does someone dare to say: 'Yes, I speak English'? There can never be facts about global totals, only guesstimates.

How many varieties of English are there around the world? We talk happily about British English, American English, Caribbean English, and so on, and note the sounds, grammar, vocabulary, and discourse patterns which we find distinctive in each area. But there is never uniformity. Caribbean English, for example, breaks down into different varieties, such as Jamaican English and Trinidadian English. Then we find there are several differences in the way people speak English in Jamaica, depending on their location and their social status. Some of the differences are very marked; some are very slight. We find people disagreeing about whether two ways of talking are the same dialect or not. So, how many varieties are there worldwide? There are no facts here either; only opinions.

How many words are there in English? Nobody knows, because not even the largest dictionaries have tabulated all the technical terms that are found in such domains as botany and zoology, and many English-speaking areas of the world haven't had their local vocabulary surveyed. In 2009 there was a claim that on a particular day that year, the number of words in English would exceed a million. That was pure fiction; English reached one million words years ago.

New words are coming into English all the time, especially on the internet (*blog*, *twitter*, *unfriend*). Old words are falling out of use, especially as technology becomes outdated (*tranny*, *betamax*, *sputnik*). We can be sure about one point: whatever the total was yesterday, it will be different today. And that's a fact.

Warm up

Work in pairs. Read the questions, then discuss why it might be difficult to determine the answers.

- How many words are there in English?
- How many English speakers are there in the world?

Reading

1 Read *English: just the facts?* How does the author answer the two questions from the Warm up?

2 Read the text again. Which statements can you infer from the text? Mark them with a tick (✔).

1 You cannot dispute a fact such as 'the Earth is round'.
2 Every country in the world does a census to find out about language use.
3 Trinidadian English is a variety of Caribbean English.
4 The author believes that people don't know there are different varieties of English.
5 The author believes we should have a dictionary that collects all the words in English.
6 *Tranny* and *betamax* are words connected to technology.

3 Complete the sentences with the correct form of the word in brackets. All the words are in the text.

1 The class has made _____ (*demonstrate*) progress since term began.
2 The two politicians are bitter enemies, but in fact are _____ (*remark*) similar.
3 The _____ (*uniform*) of computer operating systems in the company makes transfer of data easier.
4 Her English showed a _____ (*mark*) difference after spending two weeks abroad.
5 We are going to _____ (*table*) the information so that we analyse the data more easily.

Speaking

Look at the following new words in English that are connected to technology. Which words or phrases do you know? Which ones do you think will become obsolete in 30 years? Discuss with a partner.

app	blog	hot spot	LOL	to google	to unfriend
twitter					

Dear Mr Spencer

a I am writing to apply for the position of Team Manager to support people with a disability, as advertised on your website. I believe I possess the necessary skills and personal qualities to do the job successfully, and I can bring to the post a proven track record in successful team management.

b As you will see from the enclosed CV, I hold a master's degree in The Mediation of Social and Intercultural Conflicts from the University of Florence. Since then I have undertaken further practical training in conflict mediation, followed by a theoretical exam to register at the Dutch Mediation Institute.

c In addition to my skills as a mediator, I have extensive experience of team management. From 2007 to 2010 I was employed as a project manager and programme leader at the Office of Discrimination Affairs, a non-profit organisation based in The Hague. This work entailed coordinating different projects in the field of discrimination prevention. I was in charge of financing and overseeing the final outcomes of the projects; and I was also the first point of contact for private donors and organisations involved in funding the organisation.

d Prior to my work at the Office of Discrimination Affairs, I worked as a volunteer guide on holidays for people with a disability, which taught me how to take the initiative, and take the lead in a crisis. Moreover, I am creative and able to inspire others with innovative ideas. In my free time, I enjoy studying philosophy and travelling (I have lived in both Italy and the UK as well as my native country, the Netherlands.). I am a native speaker of Dutch and I am fluent in Italian as well as English. This has not only broadened my outlook, but also enabled me to adapt easily to new environments.

I am available for interview at any time in the next two weeks. I look forward to hearing from you.

Yours sincerely
Hilde Faber

Reading

1 Read Hilde's letter. Match each paragraph to one of the headings.

1 Skills, personal qualities and interests
2 Qualifications
3 Reasons for applying for the job
4 Work experience

2 Find in the letter more formal ways of saying the words and phrases in italics.

1 the *job* of Team Manager
2 I *think I have* the necessary skills
3 I *have a* master's degree
4 *I've done more* training
5 I have *a lot of* experience of team management
6 *Before* my work at the Office of Discrimination Affairs
7 This has *taught me new things*.
8 *hope to hear from you soon*

3 Do you think Hilde is suitable for the job? Why / Why not?

Writing skills: formal letter conventions

Say if the statements are true (*T*) or false (*F*) for a formal letter. Correct the false statements.

1 Put your name and address in the top right-hand corner.
2 Put the title, name and address of the recipient in the top left-hand corner.
3 To state the subject, write <u>Re: noun (eg job application)</u> before the salutation.
4 Write *Yours sincerely* with *Dear Sir / Madam* and *Yours faithfully* with *Dear Mr / Ms Bragg*.
5 If you are writing an open letter to unknown recipients, start *To whom it may concern*.
6 Start *My name is ..., and I am writing* to ... / *in connection with ... / in response to ...*
7 Do not use contractions (eg *don't, he's*).
8 Put your signature below your name.

Linking ideas: addition

1 Look at these extracts from the letter which each link two ideas. Without looking at the letter, decide which word is missing from or would improve them. Then read the text again to check your ideas.

1 *In addition my skills as a mediator, I have extensive experience of team management.*
2 *I have lived in Italy and the UK.*
3 *I am fluent in Italian as well English.*
4 *I take the lead in a crisis. I am creative.*
5 *This has not only broadened my outlook also enabled me to adapt easily to new environments.*

Study skills

2 Add *not only* and *also* to the sentences below, making any other necessary changes. What is the rule for the position of *not only* and *also*?

1 I am a native speaker of Swedish and I am fluent in Norwegian.
2 I can work under pressure and I enjoy challenges.
3 I hold a degree in languages and a diploma in translation.
4 I have qualified as a nurse and have undertaken further training in midwifery.

3 Rewrite each sentence in two different ways using the words and phrases in brackets.

1 As well as playing golf, I am a coach for the local boys' football team. (*moreover; not only*)
2 I am a good team player. Furthermore, I am a good listener. (*in addition to, both*)
3 Besides playing the flute, I sing in the choir. (*in addition, not only*)

Preparing to write

1 Complete some of the expressions below to make them true for you.

2 Read your sentences to a partner. Ask and answer questions to get further information.

Giving personal information

- I have a *diploma / professional qualification / degree / master's degree / doctorate* in ...
- I have *trained as ... / undertaken training in ...*
- I have *extensive experience / a proven track record of ...*
- Since ..., I have *worked as ... / been employed as ... / studied ...*
- Prior to that, I *worked / studied ...*
- I am able to *take the initiative / motivate others / handle pressure.*
- I possess good *time management / IT / communication / interpersonal* skills.
- I am *flexible / tactful / enthusiastic / a good team member / well-organised / a good listener.*
- I *am a native speaker of / am fluent in / have a (good) working knowledge of ...*
- In my free time I enjoy ...

Writing

Write a letter to apply for a job you would like. Follow the same structure as Hilde's letter.

Setting goals

1 Complete the sentences below.

I am learning English because _____.
I am learning English in order to _____.

2 Compare what you have written with a partner. Then discuss these questions.

- In what situations do you use, or will you use, English outside the classroom?
- What skills or abilities do you need in these situations?
- What do you enjoy about learning English, and what do you find difficult?

3 Read some characteristics of an advanced user of English and rate each one.

1 = I can do this confidently
2 = I need more work on this
3 = I need a lot more work on this

An advanced user of English ...
- can speak confidently about complex subjects.
- can express him/herself appropriately in social or professional contexts.
- can use the right level of formality or informality.
- pronounces English clearly and intelligibly.
- can understand the gist of written texts quickly.
- can understand detail and implicit meaning in texts.
- can understand most of what he/she hears in most situations, even when it's not well structured.
- can use English grammatical structures accurately.
- can express his/her ideas using a wide range of vocabulary and expressions.
- can write clearly, accurately and appropriately in a range of genres.

4 Work in pairs. Tell your partner about two areas that you are pleased with and two you would like to improve. Discuss how you could work on weaker areas.

5 Complete the sentences below to set realistic priorities for your study time.

1 I can dedicate ...
- _____ *minutes / hours* per *day / week* on reviewing work done in class.
- _____ *minutes / hours* per *day / week* to improve my _____. To do this, I will _____.
2 I will evaluate my progress and review my goals every *week / two weeks / month.*

Light & Dark

Listening and Speaking

1 Work in pairs. Look at the painting by Vermeer and the installation by Olafur Eliasson, and answer the questions.

1 What is the focal point (the place your eyes are drawn to) in each one?
2 What else can you see in the foreground and the background?
3 What is happening in the painting? Do you think there might be a story behind it? If so, what?
4 Which of these words would you use to describe the light in each one?

| bright | cold | dazzling | deep | dim |
| faint | harsh | rich | soft | warm |

5 What do you think the installation could represent?
6 What is the mood in each one? Which do you prefer, and why?

Olafur Eliasson, born in Copenhagen in 1967, is a Danish-Icelandic artist famous for his sculptures and installations that make use of water, air and light.

2 🔊 1.16 Listen to a description of the painting. Use your finger to follow the details that the speaker mentions and answer the questions.

1 How does the speaker answer the first four questions in exercise 1?
2 Did listening to the description change your view of the picture at all? If so, how?

3 Work in pairs. You are going to describe a painting to your partner. Student A: turn to page 126. Student B: turn to page 129.

Johannes (Jan) Vermeer (1632–1675) was a Dutch painter who specialised in domestic interior scenes of middle-class life. He is now acknowledged as one of the world's greatest painters.

Cloths of Heaven

William Butler Yeats

Had I the heavens' embroidered cloths,
Enwrought with golden and silver light,
The blue and the dim and the dark cloths
Of night and light and the half-light,
I would spread the cloths under your feet:
But I, being poor, have only my dreams;
I have spread my dreams under your feet;
Tread softly because you tread on my dreams.

Glossary

Had I *(verb)* – If I had

Enwrought *(verb) (archaic)* – woven decoratively

Pronunciation

1 Read the sentence below and say where you think the speaker will pause.

Woman with a Balance is one of Vermeer's finest paintings.

2 🔊 **1.17** Listen to check your answers. Does the speaker's voice go up or down at the end of each phrase? Which word or words are stressed?

3 Look at the rest of the script on page 154 and predict the places where the speaker will pause. Listen to check the answers. Then read alternate sentences with a partner.

Reading and Vocabulary

1 Work in pairs. Read *Cloths of Heaven* and answer the questions.

1 Who do you think the poem is written to?
2 What does the poet want to offer, and what does he offer?
3 What is meant by 'golden and silver light' and 'the half-light'?
4 What do you think the last line means?

2 Which of the sentences below refer to real light and which to metaphorical light?

1 Scientists hope the discovery of this gene will *shed light on* the hereditary nature of the disease.
2 She travelled to India in search of *enlightenment*.
3 The government has *given the green light to* the proposal.
4 *In the light of* the latest revelations, the government has decided not to renew their contract.
5 We could just make out the outline of the house *by the light of* the moon.
6 The project has already taken six months, but I can see *the light at the end of the tunnel*.
7 New facts have *come to light* which suggest that our earlier hypothesis was wrong.
8 We had a very *illuminating* discussion, but *in the cold light of day* I reject his arguments.
9 When midnight struck, the whole sky was *lit up* by the firework display.
10 I thought he was an honest person, but I'm afraid his behaviour has led me to see him *in an altogether different light*.

3 Match the words and phrases to the light metaphors in italics in exercise 2.

approved   informative   understanding
looked at later and in a calmer way
help us understand better
emerged   considering   in a new way
signs that a situation is going to improve

4 Work in small groups. Discuss one or more of the following topics. As you speak, try to use as many as possible of the words and expressions in exercise 2 in a natural way.

* a surprising story you read in the news or heard from a friend
* a recent English lesson
* a new discovery or piece of research
* an interesting conversation you had recently

William Butler Yeats (1865–1939) was an Anglo-Irish poet and one of the major figures of 20th century literature. He was awarded the Nobel Prize for Literature in 1923.

Light & Dark

Speaking

1 How important is sunlight to you? Do you enjoy sunbathing? Why / Why not?

2 Work in pairs. A: turn to page 126 and B: turn to page 129. Read information about the Sun.

Vocabulary and Reading

1 Delete the alternative that does not collocate with the word in bold.

1 **solar** system fuel panel eclipse power
2 **nuclear** power waste warming weapon power station
3 renewable non-renewable fossil solar nuclear low **energy**
4 greenhouse carbon exhaust solar zero **emissions**

2 Discuss the photos on page 21 with a partner using some of the collocations in exercise 1. What renewable energy projects do you know about?

3 Read *The Solar Solution* and answer the questions.

1 Why is solar power …
  a convenient in tropical areas?
  b better than current alternatives?
  c cheaper for poorer people?
  d 'empowering' for the poor?
  e good for the planet?
2 Explain the meaning of the expressions in italics in the text.
3 Match each word in the box with one with a similar meaning.

affluent	curtail	dwelling	generate
halt	home	inexhaustible	limitless
produce	wealthy		

4 In which ways is solar power already being used? What are the possible advantages and disadvantages?

- generating electricity
- water heating
- heating and air conditioning
- charging electronic devices
- lighting
- transport

The Solar Solution

Imagine yourself in a mud hut in sub-Saharan Africa, or a simple <u>dwelling</u> somewhere in the tropics. As the sun sinks behind the horizon, your world is instantly plunged into gloom, and your activities <u>curtailed</u> or severely limited for long hours throughout the night. Unlike the <u>affluent</u> cities of the developed world, where sunset is the cue to flick a switch to light up the <u>home</u>, many developing countries lack the infrastructure to provide electricity via the national grid. Here, chores and schoolwork must be done by the dim, flickering light of a candle, or by the light of a kerosene lamp, which is both toxic and expensive, as well as being the cause of numerous accidents.

Yet in sunny latitudes a radically simple, safe and <u>limitless</u> source of energy is already *at hand*; the age-old power of the sun, harnessed by means of photovoltaic solar panels, is steadily revolutionising the lives of some of the poorest people on the planet. In the developed world, where the demand for energy is disproportionately high, *a huge outlay* is required to install panels large enough to <u>produce</u> all the electricity consumed by the average household. But where energy consumption is lower, these panels are relatively inexpensive to produce and install, and provide a practical means of <u>generating</u> electricity. As a result, people are literally empowered to gain access to *the benefits of civilisation* that are taken for granted in <u>wealthy</u> nations: lighting; household appliances such as cookers, fridges and pumps; and mobile phones and computers that allow people to link up, communicate and do business, and thus stand a chance of competing in global markets.

It is *a staggering fact* that in just one hour the sun is capable of producing enough power to fuel the world's current annual energy consumption. In the coming decades, solar power could be the key to reducing our current dependence on fossil fuels and solving the problem of *dwindling resources*. Moreover, if the world's governments can collaborate to create and implement energy policies on a global scale, and switch to renewable energy sources, it may be possible to reverse, or at least <u>halt</u>, *the impending catastrophe* of massive climate change. The <u>inexhaustible</u> power of the sun, which first gave life to our planet, might one day be its salvation.

Grammar

1 Complete the predictions about solar power from the text and answer the questions.

> a *Solar power _____ be the key to reducing our current dependence on fossil fuels.*
> b *It _____ be possible to reverse, or at least halt, ... climate change.*
> c *The inexhaustible power of the sun, ... _____ one day be its salvation.*
>
> 1 Does the writer think that these developments are certain, probable or possible?
> 2 Which of these words could also be used in the gaps to make future predictions, and how would they change the meaning?

> can   may well   will   would

2 Explain the choice of verb forms in the pairs of sentences below.

> 1 a *In 2030 the government **will build** ten new nuclear power stations.*
>   b *By 2030 the government **will have built** ten new nuclear power stations.*
> 2 a *This time next year we **will install** solar panels in our offices.*
>   b *This time next year we **will be installing** solar panels to generate energy.*

3 Read more predictions, and choose the alternative that is nearest to your opinion. Then answer the questions.

> a *Global warming **will definitely / will probably / may / will probably not / will definitely not** become more of a problem in the near future.*
> b *In the coming decades we **will / may well / could / probably won't / definitely won't** be investing more in renewable energy sources.*
> c *Oil is **bound to / likely to / unlikely to / bound not to** run out in my lifetime.*

> d *It is **inevitable / highly likely / possible / highly unlikely / inconceivable** that global temperatures will rise if we do not curb greenhouse emissions.*
> e *There's **no doubt / a strong chance / a possibility / little likelihood / no way** that we will have discovered new sources of oil by the middle of the century.*

> 1 Where does the auxiliary go in sentences with *probably* and *definitely*?
> 2 Underline the expressions in a–c that say *when* something will happen.

4 Read the predictions below, and rewrite them to reflect your opinion, eg:

There is unlikely to be a major nuclear accident in the foreseeable future.
I think <u>there may well be</u> a major nuclear accident <u>in the near future</u>.

- The world's governments will definitely find ways to halt climate change in the near future.
- There's no way we will ever be able to dispose of nuclear waste safely.
- There's a strong chance that thousands of species of plants and animals will soon become extinct on account of global warming.
- There's little likelihood that we will need to reduce our energy consumption in the short term.
- In the long term, humankind will probably need to emigrate to a different planet.

5 Compare opinions on some of the statements in exercises 3 and 4 in a small group. Who is the most and the least optimistic?

G **Grammar focus –** explanation & more practice of future predictions on page 134

Photos show: a low energy bulb, a solar-powered biosphere and wave-powered turbines

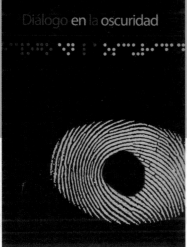

Diálogo en la oscuridad

Reading

1 'The only way to learn is through encounter.' What do you think this sentence means? Think of two situations in which this could be true.

2 Read about *Dialogue in the Dark*, an international exhibition. What are its aims? How does it relate to the statement in exercise 1?

Dialogue in the Dark

The brainchild of German entrepreneur Andreas Heinecke, *Dialogue in the Dark* is an awareness-raising international exhibition, housed in different centres around the world. It is designed to give sighted people an insight into the experience of being blind and of otherness, thus provoking a change in perspective. Taking as its maxim the philosopher Martin Buber's statement that 'the only way to learn is through encounter', it aims to evoke in the visitors extraordinary and powerful emotions that are mentally challenging, and thereby effect a profound change in the quality of their human interactions. Since it opened in 1988 it has had over six million visitors from more than 25 countries, and has employed over 6,000 blind people.

3 Read *An exhibition to discover the unseen*.
1 Which of the five senses (touch, taste, smell, sight and hearing) are mentioned?
2 Do you think the writer's experience matched the aims described above?

4 Match the highlighted words and phrases in the text with their meanings below.
1 souvenir or reminder
2 totally involved
3 almost fall while walking
4 separate
5 lacking
6 join up to make a complete picture
7 joining together aggressively
8 search clumsily

5 Which of the following emotions did the writer experience, and why?

confusion	embarrassment	fear
interest	sickness	surprise	worry

6 Find evidence in the text for the following statements about the visit.
1 The visit took place on a boat.
2 The writer employed new strategies to identify objects.
3 She found it hard to identify the location of noises.
4 She smelt things that were not really there.
5 She had to buy a drink in complete darkness.

7 Work in pairs. Discuss the questions.
• What do you think the writer might have written in her Braille message?
• Which of your five senses would you hate to lose the most, and why?

Vocabulary and Writing

1 Complete the sentences with words from the text to describe sounds.

I heard …
1 cars *whooshing by*.
2 birds _____.
3 bicycle bells _____.
4 dogs _____.
5 car horns _____.
6 water _____.

2 Can you imitate the sounds? Could anything else make them?

3 🔊 1.18 Listen to the sounds and try to identify the source, as in the example.
1 a *balloon* popping
2 a _____ rumbling
3 a _____ buzzing
4 a _____ creaking
5 a _____ banging
6 a _____ squeaking
7 a _____ crackling
8 a _____ going off
9 a _____ clicking

An exhibition to discover the unseen

As I entered the exhibition boat [which was] docked at the Amsterdam harbour, I was thrown from bright sunshine into complete darkness. A voice out of the black introduced its owner: 'I am blind and today I am your guide to my world.' Amidst nervous giggling, stumbling about and bumping against each other, our guide proceeded to lead us through a world devoid of visual stimuli. Disorientation does not begin to describe this unique experience of suddenly being robbed of your major sensory organ. The silly giggling soon gave way to feelings of dizziness, light nausea and wholehearted fascination. We were taken down corridors and into different rooms, asked to touch and identify different objects, to describe the space we were in, and how the objects in it were placed, relative to one another. Things I touched did not make sense at first, as my brain struggled with the unfamiliar task of having to piece together discrete touch sensations, felt consecutively, in order to identify the whole: something our brain normally takes in at a single glance.

We were led into a simulation of a busy street, where the noise of cars whooshing by, of bicycle bells ringing and car horns honking left me feeling insecure and apprehensive. Would the noises have sounded as threatening and as loud if I could see? There were other sounds I couldn't easily place without clues from our guide. I realised then how much sight contributes to how and what we hear. Another strange sensation was how often I was mistaken in locating the direction sounds were coming from. During our stroll in an imaginary park (birds chirping, dogs playfully barking in the distance) I could have sworn that the sound of water clattering onto marble stones came from my left. I was dead wrong. But what personally surprised me the most was the smell illusions I was having while immersed in this world of darkness. I smelt car exhaust in the busy street; I smelt flowers in the park; I smelt the distinct odour of fresh water clattering to the ground … It was as if my senses were ganging up to compensate for the one I had left behind, with no regard for a reality check.

Towards the end of this tour, our guide thankfully brought us to a bar (pitch black, of course), where we had to fumble for our wallets and the right coins to pay for our drinks, and make sure our fingers didn't mislead us in counting back the change for those who only had paper bills. On our way out, we were invited to write a text on a Braille typewriter and take it home, as a memento of this extraordinary exploration of life without light.

---

4 Which of the sounds could also be made by the following?

a fire	a floorboard	a hammer
an alarm clock	a pen	
conversation	new shoes	thunder

5 Choose one of the topics below, and write a few lines about it. Then read your description to a partner. Can they guess the place?

- Describe sounds you heard on your journey to the class today.
- Imagine you were in a completely different place. Describe the sounds you might encounter.

Useful phrases

- I heard a door *bang* / *banging*
- I can hear the *sound* / *noise* of a baby crying
- I heard *the rumble of thunder* / *the buzz of conversation*

Language note:
I heard a door bang = a single sound
I heard a door banging = a continuous or repeated sound

Speaking

Work in pairs. Imagine you are one of the following, and discuss the questions. If you have one of these disabilities, describe your real experiences.

blind or partially sighted	deaf or hard of hearing
a wheelchair user	

- How would you have come to your class today? What difficulties might you have had getting into the classroom? How could you have overcome them?
- What difference would it make to your ability to take part in the class now? What would you need to do?
- How far do you think your learning institution, workplace or leisure centre caters to the needs of people with a disability?

Light & Dark

Part 4

Speaking & Listening
Through the Tunnel

Extend your vocabulary
Ways of describing fear

Grammar
Narrative tenses

Speaking
Difficult experiences

Speaking and Listening

1 Think about a time when you were in one of the places in the box. Discuss the questions below with a partner.

> a cellar   a dark tunnel
> a deserted street at night
> an underground cave
> in the countryside at night

- Why were you there?
- What did you do?
- How did you feel, and what was the experience like?

2 You are going to listen to the last part of a short story called *Through the Tunnel* by Doris Lessing.

1 Read a synopsis of the story so far. What is the meaning of its title?
2 You will hear these words in the story. With a partner, predict what might happen.

> banged   blackness   blood   count   crack   dizzy   drown   fuss
> gasping   goggles   lungs   roof   shaking   trembling

> Jerry, an 11-year-old only child, was coming to the end of his holidays. He had been staying in a villa near the sea with his widowed mother and had been going to the beach with her every day. He had made friends with some older boys at a separate beach, and had been observing them dive through an underground tunnel and come out the other side. He had been practising diving and holding his breath so that he, too, would be able to go through the tunnel. He was on the verge of fulfilling his ambition when one day his mother suddenly announced that in four days' time they would be leaving the villa and going home.

3 🔊 **1.19–1.21** Close your book. As you listen to the story, think about the following questions.

1 What emotions did Jerry experience?
2 What difficulties did he encounter during the dive?
3 What was the outcome of his attempt to go through the tunnel?

4 Work with a partner. Discuss your answers. What images remain with you from the story?

5 Read some extracts from the story. Decide whether they occur before, during or after the dive and explain why.

1 He drifted to the surface, his face turned up to the air. He was gasping like a fish.
2 He was being continually pressed against the sharp roof, which felt slimy as well as sharp.
3 Supposing he turned dizzy in the tunnel? Supposing he died there, trapped?
4 Next summer, perhaps, when he had another year's growth in him – then he would go through the hole.
5 He could see the local boys diving and playing half a mile away. He did not want them.
6 He struggled on in the darkness between lapses into unconsciousness. An immense, swelling pain filled his head, and then the darkness cracked with an explosion of green light.
7 He must go on into the blackness ahead, or he would drown. His head was swelling, his lungs cracking.

6 The story ends with the words 'It was no longer of the least importance to go to the bay'. Why do you think that was? What does the tunnel represent, in your view?

Extend your vocabulary – ways of describing fear

Which of the sentences refer to …
- moderate fear?
- extreme fear?
a I'm *scared / frightened / afraid* of the dark.
b I'm feeling *apprehensive / nervous / anxious* about the interview tomorrow.
c I'm *petrified / terrified / scared stiff* of heights.
d I'm feeling *somewhat daunted / intimidated* by the amount of work that needs doing.
e Loud noises *startle me / make me jump*.
f I have a *horror of / phobia about* snakes.

Grammar

1 Look again at sentences which refer to events taking place before, during and after the story, and answer the questions.

> **Before the story**
> *Jerry **had been staying** in a villa near the sea with his widowed mother and **had been going** to the beach with her every day. He **had made** friends with some older boys at a separate beach.*

Which of the verbs in bold refer to …
1 a finished action?
2 a temporary situation?
3 a repeated action?

> **During the story**
> *He **put on** his goggles, **fitted** them tight, **tested** the vacuum. His hands **were shaking**. His lungs **were beginning** to hurt.*

Which of the verbs in bold refer to …
4 a continuous unfinished past action or state?
5 a finished action?

6 Which of the verbs below refer to 'future in the past'?

> **After the story**
> *He **had been practising** diving and holding his breath so that he, too, **would be able** to go through the tunnel. He **was on the verge** of fulfilling his ambition when one day his mother suddenly announced that in four days' time they **were leaving** the villa. He realised that he **would shortly be going** home.*

2 Find more examples of these verb forms in Speaking and Listening exercise 5.

Doris Lessing (born 1919) is a British author who was born in Iran and spent her early life in Zimbabwe. She is famous for novels such as *The Grass is Singing* and *The Golden Notebook* and a series of science fiction novels. In 2007, Lessing won the Nobel Prize in Literature; she was the 11th woman, and the oldest person ever, to do so.

3 Read the following imaginary paragraph from the story and put the verbs in appropriate forms.

> Jerry's mother (1) _____ (*sit*) on the terrace of the holiday house that she (2) _____ (*rent*) for the past few weeks. She (3) _____ (*think*) about the fact that their holiday (4) _____ (*soon / be*) over, and (5) _____ (*worry*) about Jerry. He (6) _____ (*behave*) so strangely in the past few days, she (7) _____ (*reflect*). He (8) _____ (*suddenly / become*) so cool and distant. Something (9) _____ (*change*) in their relationship.
>
> She (10) _____ (*get up*) and (11) _____ (*walk*) towards the balcony, and (12) _____ (*look*) out towards the beach, hoping to catch a glimpse of Jerry. He (13) _____ (*leave*) the house earlier that day to go swimming. She (14) _____ (*hope*) he (15) _____ (*not / do*) anything foolish. School (16) _____ (*start*) in a few days' time and she (17) _____ (*not / want*) him to begin the term in a state of agitation. She (18) _____ (*go down*) to the beach to look for Jerry when she suddenly (19) _____ (*catch*) sight of him slowly climbing the hill towards the house.

4 Work in pairs. Write a few lines about the story from the perspective of one of the local boys. Try to use a range of verb forms.

G **Grammar focus** – explanation & more practice of narrative tenses on page 134

Speaking

1 You are going to talk about a time when you did something that was difficult, scary or dangerous. Make notes on the following points:

- where and when the experience took place
- what you had done, had been doing before it took place
- what you were doing when the story started
- what happened and how you felt

2 Work in pairs. Tell each other your stories, and ask questions.

3 Retell your story to a different partner incorporating the additional information.

Function globally agreeing and disagreeing

Warm up

1 Read the statements and mark each sentence 1–5 (1= agree strongly, 5= disagree strongly).

1 The main reason for doing a degree is to get a job.
2 Governments should not fund the arts.
3 Children should not be made to study literature.
4 Most modern art isn't 'art' at all.
5 There's no point in studying an arts subject at university.
6 People who only study sciences have a narrow education.

2 Choose two statements and compare your ideas with a partner, giving reasons for your views.

Listening

1 🔘 **1.22–1.24** Listen to three conversations. Which of the opinions in Warm up exercise 1 do the speakers discuss in each case?

2 Listen again and answer the questions.

Conversation 1
1 How many people like the exhibit, and how many people dislike it?
2 In what way(s) could it be considered 'art'?
3 In what way(s) could it be considered 'not art'?
4 Note two instances of impoliteness in the conversation.

Conversation 2
1 Why do we need scientists?
2 Why will there always be artists?
3 Who should be funded, and why?

Conversation 3
1 What did the first speaker study at university?
2 Why does she regret it?
3 What is the value of studying the humanities?

Language focus

1 Match the sentence halves.

1	I can see both sides	a	that all modern art is rubbish?
2	Yes, but don't you think that	b	on subsidies for arts projects?
3	What are your views	c	views on that, actually.
4	Surely you're not saying	d	it's just that science is more useful.
5	It's not that art is unnecessary,	e	that doesn't mean it's art.
6	Just because it's original,	f	of their latest album?
7	What do you think	g	art is a leisure activity really?
8	I have mixed	h	of the argument.

2 Which of the sentences …

1 clarify the speaker's argument?
2 ask for an opinion?
3 question someone's viewpoint?
4 express ambivalence?

3 Categorise the expressions.

1 Absolutely! 5 Seriously? 9 I couldn't disagree more.
2 Come on! 6 Me too. 10 I totally agree.
3 Exactly! 7 Precisely. 11 Do you think so?
4 Me neither. 8 That's true. 12 Right.

Strong agreement: *Absolutely!*
Agreement:
Disagreement:
Strong disagreement:

Pronunciation

1 🔘 **1.25** Listen to someone reading the expressions below. What is the intonation pattern on the words in italics, and what does it express?

1 I see what you *mean*, but …
2 That's true *in a way*, but …
3 I take your *point*, but …
4 I hear what you're *saying*, but …

2 Listen again and repeat.

Speaking

1 Complete the sentences below in your own words.

1 In my view, the aim of university education …
2 My own view is that freedom of speech …
3 I personally feel that modern science …
4 Quite frankly, there's no point in studying …

2 Work in small groups. Take it in turns to read out some of the statements, and discuss them.

Global voices

Warm up

1 Do you know any of these phobias? Try to match them with their meaning. Use your dictionary to help.

1	acrophobia		small spaces
2	hydrophobia		heights
3	bibliophobia		water
4	claustrophobia	is the fear of	spiders
5	arachnophobia		books
6	agrophobia		people from other countries
7	xenophobia		public spaces

2 Do you know anybody who suffers from one of these fears? Do you know any other common phobias? What are their technical names?

Listening

1 🔊 **1.26** Listen to Giacomo from Italy and Caroline from France talk about the fear of the dark. Listen and answer the questions.

1 What do people base their decisions on, according to Giacomo?
2 Caroline believes sometimes people are attracted to the dark. What example does she give of this?
3 Who likes horror movies more?

2 Listen again. Which of the reasons below do the speakers give for a fear of the dark?

Because …
- you can't see
- it's evolutionary
- you imagine things
- sight is so important
- you don't know what is happening
- of scary movies

Giacomo, Italy   Caroline, France

3 You are going to hear Caroline tell Giacomo a story about being afraid of the dark. Make phrases with the words in A and the words in B.

A	B
a muffled	scratches
laughing	sound
hear	a shape
distinguish	out loud

4 🔊 **1.27** Listen to the story and check your answers to exercise 3. Then use the phrases to retell the story in your own words.

Language focus: *like*

1 *Like* is very common in spoken English. It can be used to give the speaker time to think. Look at the following examples from the listening. In which case is *like* being used as a verb?

1 It leaves you the door to like imagine much more things.
2 The tendency of most people is like to switch off the lights, don't you think?
3 Actually, I don't really like, personally, scary movies. Do you?
4 I can remember that I had seen like all the horror movies.

2 Read the other uses of *like* in spoken English. Then add an example of your own for each one.

To focus attention on something, by giving an example:
*I love old horror movies, **like** Dracula or Frankenstein.*
To ask for an example:
A: When I was a child I was afraid of so many things.
*B: Really? **Like what**?*
In informal reported speech, with the verb *to be*:
*So I ask her what's wrong and **she's like** 'Oh, I'm afraid of the dark.'*

Speaking

Work in pairs. Discuss one of the topics below.
- Choose one of the phobias from Warm up exercise 1, or another phobia and discuss why you think people are afraid of this.
- Describe an experience when you were afraid of the dark. Where and when was it? What happened? Did it affect you very much?

Writing a story

Reading

1 Read Taru's email to Alina.

1 What do you think is their relationship?
2 What sort of experience does Taru recount?

Hi Alina

Thanks for your email. It was great to hear from you. I'm so sorry to hear you haven't been well, but hopefully you're making a good recovery now.

I'm well, and enjoying my new job, though I quite often have to work late. In fact, I had a really scary experience as I was leaving work a couple of nights ago. I'd just finished my shift and I was making my way towards my car, which I'd parked in the main car park. It was pitch black and rather foggy, and on top of that there was no one else around, so I was feeling a bit nervous. I'd just got to my car when suddenly I heard footsteps behind me. Immediately, I turned round and to my horror saw a man running towards me and shouting something. I fumbled in my bag for my car keys, but I couldn't find them. I grabbed my mobile phone and was on the point of dialling the emergency number. But when I glanced over my shoulder I saw that the man was getting nearer and nearer, so I just started running for my life.

Anyway, I knew there was a pub just round the corner so I kept on running towards it. The man started chasing me, still yelling at the top of his voice. In the end I got to the pub and slipped inside, heaving a sigh of relief. Ten seconds later, the door opened and the man stepped in and came up to me, dangling my car keys in his hands!! It turns out I'd dropped them in the car park while I was getting my gloves out of my bag. As you can imagine I could have died with embarrassment. Luckily the man was quite amused when I explained why I'd been running away from him. But it was one of the scariest nights of my life!!

Anyway, I'll tell you all about my new job when you come to stay next week. I'm really looking forward to seeing you and I can't wait to hear all your news!

Lots of love

Taru

2 Close your book, and, with a partner, try to remember as much as you can about Taru's experience. Then open your books and check. Were there any details you had forgotten?

3 Which words or phrases does the writer use instead of these?

1	walking	7	entered quickly
2	looked for clumsily	8	sighing
3	took quickly	9	came inside
4	looked quickly	10	approached
5	running in panic	11	holding and swinging
6	shouting loudly	12	really want

Writing skills: an email to a friend

Delete the expression you would probably not use in an informal email to a friend.

1 *Hi Alina / Hello Alina / Hi / Hi there / Dear Alina / Hello friend*
2 *Sorry I haven't written for so long. / I apologise for the delay in replying.*
3 *I hope / I trust / Hope / Hopefully* you'll feel better soon.
4 *Can't wait / I'm dying / I am yearning / Longing* to see you.
5 *Write soon / Keep in touch / Drop me a line / I look forward to hearing from you.*
6 *Take care / With thanks in advance / All for now / Cheers*

Linking ideas: time expressions

1 In each of the sentences below, say whether the event in italics happens before, at about the same time as, or after the other event.

1 As *I was making my way* towards the car, I heard footsteps.
2 I was on the point of phoning the police when *I saw that the man was getting nearer.*
3 As soon as *I saw the man coming towards me*, I started running.
4 *I had no sooner arrived* at the pub than the man stepped in.

2 Rephrase the sentences in exercise 1 using the words or phrases below, as in the example. What grammatical changes (if any) would you need to make?

1 *when / while*

When / While I was making my way towards the car I heard footsteps.

I was making my way towards the car when I heard footsteps.

2 just about to
3 immediately / the moment
4 just / hardly

3 Match each of the words and phrases with one with a similar meaning.

1	meanwhile	a	before long
2	suddenly	b	straight away
3	soon	c	beforehand
4	in the end	d	initially
5	previously	e	in the meantime
6	immediately	f	eventually
7	at first	g	all of a sudden

4 Complete the text using one of the words or phrases from exercise 3. More than one answer may be possible.

I had a scary experience while I was driving to meet my sister in Scotland. My car was very old, but I had had it checked (1) _____ so I wasn't too worried. (2) _____, there were no problems, but (3) __ _____ clouds of steam started pouring from the bonnet. I came off the motorway at the next exit and (4) _____ phoned for emergency assistance. I ended up waiting for three hours in the blazing sun; (5) _____, my sister was waiting anxiously because she didn't have a mobile phone. (6) _____, the rescue service arrived to tow me and (7) _____ I arrived to meet my rather annoyed sister.

Preparing to write

Work with a partner and discuss ideas for a story using the prompts below, or your own ideas.

- What sort of experience was it? (scary / embarrassing ...)
- Where were you? (on a boat / in a jungle ...)
- When was it? (at night / during a thunderstorm ...)
- What were you doing? (trekking / celebrating ...)
- Who were you with? (your boss / a stranger / no one ...)
- What happened?

Useful phrases

- I'm *sorry* / *glad* to hear that ...
- You'll never guess what happened to me recently.
- As you can imagine, ...
- I can't wait to *hear your news* / *catch up* / *hear about* ...

Writing

1 Write your story in an email to a friend. Use link words, and briefly mention other news.

2 Exchange emails with your partner. How similar are your stories? Which parts do you like best in each email?

Exploring collocations

Collocation is 'the property of language whereby two or more words seem to appear frequently in each other's company' (Professor Michael Hoey). For example, it is normal to talk about *conducting* or *carrying out research*, but not *making research*. Using correct collocations makes your English sound natural, clear and fluent.

1 Work in pairs. Can you remember any nouns, adjectives, verbs or prepositions that collocate with the following words from Unit 2?

chance   light   rumble

2 Read extracts from the *Macmillan Collocations Dictionary* entry for *darkness*. Which of these collocation types are mentioned? What other information is given?

verb + noun   noun + verb   adjective + noun

adverb + verb   adverb + adjective

adj+N total absolute **complete, impenetrable, pitch, total, utter** *He rubbed his eyes, and soon became aware that he was alone in the church, and in utter darkness.*

v+N light up darkness **dispel, illuminate, light up, penetrate, pierce** *The only light that penetrates the darkness emits blurrily from the neon sign in the window.*

N+v **approach, close in, descend, engulf sth, envelop sb/sth, fall, shroud sb/sth in, surround sb/sth** *Darkness enveloped him again, but this time there seemed to be lights up ahead.*

3 Which of these strategies do you already use for developing your use of collocations? Compare with a partner, and decide what you will do in future.

- ★ Notice word combinations in texts.
- ★ When you record a word in your notebook, write it with words that it collocates with.
- ★ Use a learner's dictionary, eg *Macmillan English Dictionary*, or collocations dictionary to find the correct collocation to use.
- ★ Use an online corpus, eg the British National Corpus, to investigate common collocations.

Great & Small

Speaking

Read the quotation below about 'greatness' and answer the questions with a partner.

> 'Be not afraid of greatness: some are born great, some achieve greatness and some have greatness thrust upon them.'
> (William Shakespeare, *Twelfth Night*)

In your own words, explain what the quotation means. Can you think of examples of people who have become great in any of the ways?

Reading and Listening

1 You are going to read an excerpt from *Great Expectations*, a famous novel by the English writer Charles Dickens. Do you know anything about it?

2 🔵 **1.28** Read and listen to the extract. Answer the questions.

1 What is going to happen to Pip?
2 Look at the Shakespeare quotation again. In which of the three ways is Pip going to acquire greatness?

3 Mr Jaggers uses very old-fashioned language. Find the way he expresses these phrases in the text.

1 I have been asked to tell him. (line 8)
2 The current owner of the house wants him to leave. (lines 10–11)
3 You won't mind having to do this. (lines 21–22)
4 You mustn't try and find out about this. (line 29)
5 I have plenty of money for your education and costs of living. (lines 39–40)

4 Read the text again and answer the questions. Compare answers with a partner, and refer to the parts of the text that helped you with the answer.

1 What are the two conditions of the offer?
2 How does Pip feel about the situation?
3 How do you think the lawyer feels about Pip?

5 How might you react if you received a similar visit and offer?

Grammar

1 Look at the sentences about *Great Expectations* and underline the relative clauses. Then answer questions 1–5.

a *On Christmas Eve of 1812, seven-year-old Pip meets a man in the village churchyard whose manner and appearance terrify him.*
b *The man is a convict who has escaped from a prison ship.*
c *He wants Pip to steal food and a tool he can take off his leg shackles with.*
d *The next morning Pip takes some food and drink, which includes a Christmas pie, and gives it to the convict.*
e *He has to steal these things from his sister and her husband Joe, which makes him feel very guilty.*
f *This is an important event in the book because the convict will never forget the kindness Pip showed to him.*

1 What relative pronouns are used here?
2 Which relative pronouns could be replaced with the word *that*?
3 Why are there commas around the relative clause in sentence d?
4 What does the relative clause in sentence e refer to?
5 Which relative pronoun has been omitted in sentences c and f?

Great Expectations

The orphan Philip Pirrip, or Pip as he is known, lives with his older sister and works for his brother-in-law Joe the blacksmith. One day a lawyer, Mr Jaggers, comes to tell Pip some important news that will change his life …

5 'Now, I return to this young fellow. And the communication I have got to make is, that he has great expectations.'

Joe and I gasped, and looked at one another.

'I am instructed to communicate to him,' said Mr. Jaggers, throwing his finger at me sideways, 'that he will come into a 10 handsome property. Further, that it is the desire of the present possessor of that property, that he be immediately removed from his present sphere of life and from this place, and be brought up as a gentleman – in a word, as a young fellow of great expectations.'

15 My dream was out; my wild fancy was surpassed by sober reality.

'Now, Mr. Pip,' pursued the lawyer, 'I address the rest of what I have to say, to you. You are to understand, first, that it is the request of the person from whom I take my instructions, that 20 you always bear the name of Pip.

You will have no objection, I dare say, to your great expectations being encumbered with that easy condition. But if you have any objection, this is the time to mention it.' My heart was beating so fast, and there was such a singing in 25 my ears, that I could scarcely stammer I had no objection.

'I should think not! Now you are to understand, secondly, Mr. Pip, that the name of the person who is your liberal benefactor remains a profound secret, until the person chooses to reveal it. This is not for you to inquire into. The condition is laid down by 30 the person from whom I take my instructions. That person is the person from whom you derive your expectations, and the secret is solely held by that person and by me. Again, not a very difficult condition with which to encumber such a rise in fortune; but if you have any objection to it, this is the time to mention it. Speak out.'

35 Once more, I stammered with difficulty that I had no objection.

'I should think not! We come next, to mere details of arrangement. You must know that, although I have used the term 'expectations' more than once, you are not endowed with expectations only. There is already lodged in my hands, a sum of money amply 40 sufficient for your suitable education and maintenance. You will please consider me your guardian.'

I said I had always longed for it.

'Never mind what you have always longed for, Mr. Pip,' he retorted; 'keep to the record. If you long 45 for it now, that's enough.'

Glossary

come into *(verb)* – inherit (money or property)

handsome *(adjective)* – large

be encumbered with *(verb)* – have a difficult condition attached

derive *(verb)* – receive from

2 Look at the examples and do the tasks.

a *He wants Pip to steal food and a tool he can take off his leg shackles with.*

b *He wants Pip to steal food and a tool _____ he can take off his leg shackles.*

c *The name of the person who is your liberal benefactor remains a profound secret.*

d *That person is the person from whom you derive your expectations.*

In relative clauses with a preposition, there are two possible word orders.

1 Where is the preposition in sentence *a*?

2 Complete sentence *b* with the preposition directly after the noun.

3 Which word order is used in everyday speech and which is more formal?

4 Identify the relative clauses in sentences *c* and *d*. Why is *whom* used in sentence *d*? Rewrite the second sentence with the preposition at the end of the sentence.

Language note: *whom* is rarely used in spoken English. In more formal contexts and in written English, *whom* is used when it is the object of the relative clause.

3 Rewrite the sentences with a relative clause to make one sentence.

1 She was the one in my family. I thought she would go on to great things.

2 I let my parents down because they had high expectations for me. I just couldn't live up to them.

3 The exam was easier than we expected. That made for a nice change.

4 Their team showed great promise for the final. Their results were consistent all year.

5 I had a good feeling about the apartment. We were about to move into it.

6 I spoke to a lot of people. Many of them were disappointed about their career.

G **Grammar focus** – explanation & more practice of relative clauses on page 136

Speaking

1 Think of a time when you had high expectations or hopes about something or someone. Or a time when someone had high hopes for you.

2 Work in pairs. Tell each other about your hopes and expectations, using the sentences in Grammar exercise 3 to help you think of ideas.

Charles Dickens

(1812–1870) is considered one of the greatest English writers of the 19th century. He remains very popular today and is most remembered for creating vivid and memorable characters in his classic novels.

Great & Small

Reading and Speaking

1 Read *Great travel experiences*.

- Decide what sort of text this is and where you might find it.
- Would you like to experience either of these things? Why / Why not?

2 Work in pairs. Note which of the following topics the author mentions for each experience and what is written about them.

accommodation   activities   food
local people   scenery and surroundings
transport   travelling companions
weather

3 Work in pairs. Complete these sentences from the text.

1 I _____ myself in an entirely different world.
2 I _____ to see some of the most breathtaking scenery I have found to this _____.
3 I _____ to understand a little bit more of the incredible scope of … the United States.
4 This was my first _____ with wide bike lanes.
5 Switzerland also has … idyllic countryside _____ me thinking I'd stepped into a picture.
6 The best _____ was all that family bonding time.

4 Tell a partner about a great travel experience you have had and why it was so memorable.

Listening

1 Look at the names beginning with 'The Great'. Which one is not a place? What do you know about the others?

- The Great Lakes
- The Great Wall
- The Great Depression
- The Great Barrier Reef

2 🔊 1.29–1.31 Listen to three different people talking about the places in exercise 1. Decide which place each speaker talks about, and match them to one of the categories below. There is one you don't need.

- a description by a travel agent
- an account of a memorable trip
- a prepared talk by a tour guide
- a natural history TV programme

Great travel experiences
by Ricki

Which travel memories never fail to cheer you up? Put a smile on your face remembering some of the good times you've had out there. Here are two of my favourite travel experiences.

Working in White Sulphur Springs, Montana
I took a job on a guest ranch in Montana one summer. When I arrived in White Sulphur Springs from New York I found myself in an entirely different world. Instead of cabs I found cows, and instead of sky scrapers there was … sky. I myself was somewhat of an oddity, having never driven a pick up truck (or actually, any vehicle) or gone hunting. In any case, I got to see some of the most breathtaking scenery I have found to this day, and I came to understand a little bit more of the incredible scope of the people, landscapes, and lifestyles that makes up the United States.

Biking through Switzerland
This summer my mom, sister, and I joined a group biking through Switzerland. The weather was perfect – warm but not overwhelmingly hot, with occasional showers to cool us down (OK, maybe the showers were less than perfect). This was my first encounter with wide bike lanes and courteous – no, downright friendly – drivers in cities and towns. Switzerland also has mile upon mile of idyllic countryside that had me thinking I'd stepped into a picture. The best part was that all the biking freed me up to eat as much chocolate and cheese as I could. I mean, the best part was all that family bonding time.

3 Listen again and choose the correct answer.

Speaker 1

1 The Great Wall of China was built …
   a during the Ming Dynasty.
   b in the fifth century BC.
   c over hundreds of years.
2 Segments consisting of actual wall make up …
   a nearly 9,000 km.   b over 6,000 km.
   c nearly 3,000 km.

Speaker 2

3 What happened in the late 20th century to the Great Lakes?
   a They attracted people and industry as never before.
   b Research started into ways of stopping pollution.
   c They began to benefit from the development of previous decades.
4 Together, the Great Lakes cover an area of …
   a 245,660 square kilometres.
   b 260,450 square kilometres.
   c 246,560 square kilometres.

Speaker 3

5 Tours visit only a small part of the reef because …
   a it would take too long to see such a large area.
   b the entire reef area is still being mapped.
   c the majority is closed to tourists for conservation reasons.
6 How many individual reefs make up the Great Barrier Reef?
   a 2,900   b 2,600   c 344,000

4 Work in pairs. Ask and answer the questions below.

- Have you been to any of these places?
- Which of these places would you most like to visit, and why?
- What other places in the world would you most like to visit? Why?

Extend your vocabulary – great

Great is a very common word, and can have the following main meanings:
- important   • enjoyable
- enthusiastic   • bigger than usual

1 Match each sentence to the correct meaning of *great*.
   1 One of Junko Tabei's many great achievements was her solo ascent of Mount Everest.
   2 Many of the world's ancient forests are in great danger of disappearing.
   3 It's a great day out for both children and adults.
   4 My brother is a great fan of camping and the outdoors.

2 Write two true sentences, using the word *great* in a different way each time.

Vocabulary and Pronunciation

1 Look at Listening exercise 3, questions 2, 4 and 6. Answer the questions. Then listen and check your answers.

1 How do you say the numbers?
2 In which numbers is there a pause? Where is it?

2 1.32 Listen and write the numbers you hear. Compare answers with a partner – say the numbers.

3 Organise the numbers from exercise 2 into categories from the box below.

areas	decimals	fractions	percentages
ratios	round numbers	years	

4 1.33 How do you pronounce the words in bold below? Which sound do they all have in common? Say the words, then listen and check.

- two thousand eight hundred **and** forty
- sixty-two **per** cent   • two **to** one

5 Work in pairs. You are going to tell each other some facts about two historical events beginning with the word *Great*. Student A: turn to page 127. Student B: turn to page 130. Follow the instructions.

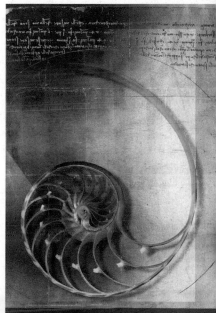

Mathematical patterns found in nature.

Great & Small

Writing

1 Write a short paragraph called *A small toy*. This could be about a toy you liked as a child, a toy your child or grandchild loves or a toy you like now.

2 Exchange your texts with a partner. Read your partner's text and write two questions about it. Give the text back to your partner with your questions.

3 Rewrite your paragraph, but answering your partner's questions. Then show your new text to your partner again.

4 In small groups, swap and read each other's texts. Did any of you choose the same toy?

Listening

1 Look at the photos of popular small toys of the past century from around the world. Do you know any of these? Did you play with any of them? Have you seen children playing with them?

2 🔊 1.34–1.37 Listen to four people talking about one of the toys in exercise 1. For each person, take notes on …
- the toy and any special characteristics it has.
- whether the speaker has good or bad memories of it, and why.

3 Listen again. Which speakers think this toy will be popular with future generations?

4 Do you agree with the opinions of the speakers in exercise 3?

Extend your vocabulary – *small* or *little*

1 Complete the sentences with *small* or *little*.
  1 Just a _____, please. That's great.
  2 Wow. It's a _____ world.
  3 Oh, it was late. The _____ hours, actually.
  4 That's because you didn't read the _____ print.
  5 Don't worry. We'll get there _____ by _____.
  6 Exactly. _____ do they know.
  7 It just makes me feel _____ when you do that.
  8 What a sweet _____ baby!
  9 I'm afraid these jeans are too _____.

2 For each of the above sentences, think of a context and write the question or sentence that comes **before** it. Use a dictionary to help you.

Grammar

1 Look at the following pairs of nouns. Work in pairs and decide which ones sound correct.

1 a board game / a board's game
2 a children's toy / a children toy
3 a pack cards / a pack of cards
4 a chess piece / a piece of chess
5 a doll house / a doll's house
6 the bathroom floor / the bathroom's floor
7 the house front / the front of the house
8 a lifetime's work / a lifetime work

2 Read the rules in the grammar box. Find other examples for each rule in the exercise above.

We use noun + noun for commonly accepted compound nouns which refer to familiar things, where
- the second noun shows the main class of noun (eg *shop, glass*)
- the first noun functions as an adjective (eg *music shop / clothes shop, water glass*)

We use noun + *of* + noun
- where no common compound noun exists (eg *centre of the Earth, colour of the sky*)
- for units and parts (eg *a glass of water, a piece of paper, a group of people, a slice of cake*)
- for certain fixed expressions (eg *the back of the room, the middle of the street, the side of the building*)

We use noun + *'s/s'* + noun
- to talk about possession (eg *my son's toys, the country's president*)
- to show the user or origin of the noun (eg *girls' magazines, cow's milk*)
- in general measurements of time (eg *a week's holiday, today's weather*)

G **Grammar focus** – explanation & more practice of compound nouns on page 136

3 Complete the sentences. Make noun phrases using the words in brackets.

1 I've got an old _____ (*box / picture books*) somewhere in my house from when I was a child.
2 The _____ (*girl / toy / section*) is over there, just on the right.
3 The government found _____ (*traces / lead*) in the toy soldiers and took them all off the shelves.
4 We gave all our old toys to a _____ (*shop / charity*).
5 This puzzle wasn't easy to solve. It took _____ (*work / three days*).
6 His hobby is making _____ (*model / planes*).

Speaking

1 Did you collect any of the following things as a child: toy soldiers or action figures, dolls, stamps, marbles, cards or coins? Tell a partner.

2 Read the quotation below about why people collect. Then choose three of the questions below and discuss.

- Do you know anyone who has a collection as an adult? What do they collect?
- Do you agree that collecting things is about love?
- Are collections a waste of time and money?
- If you had the money to indulge in a collection, what would you collect?
- Does gender play a role in collecting? Is collecting more of a man's thing or a woman's thing?

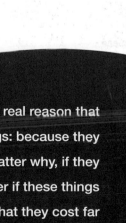

'This is the real reason that people collect things: because they love them. It doesn't matter why, if they even know why; it doesn't matter if these things are obsolete or ungainly or ugly, that they cost far too much and take up a ridiculous amount of space and serve absolutely no practical purpose whatsoever. In love, as in collecting, irrationality reigns supreme.'

Great & Small

Part 4

Reading & Listening
The God of Small Things

Pronunciation
Weak and strong forms

Vocabulary & Speaking
quiet and *silent*

Reading and Listening

1 There is a saying in English: 'Children should be seen and not heard.' What do you think? What would you think if someone said this in your culture? In what contexts is silence a good or bad thing in your opinion?

2 🔊 **1.38** You are going to read and listen to an extract from an Indian novel called *The God of Small Things* about a very quiet person. Read the extract quickly and answer the questions.

1 Do we know why Estha is quiet?
2 Is he surrounded by quiet people in his everyday life?

3 Read again. Are the sentences true (*T*) or false (*F*)? Explain why.

1 There wasn't an exact moment that Estha stopped talking.
2 Estha's silence was problematic.
3 People noticed immediately that Estha never spoke.
4 It seemed that Estha's silence was not just a passing phase.
5 His parents felt awkward at first about what he did at home.
6 Workers in the market were unkind to Estha.

4 Work in pairs. Discuss the questions. Give reasons for your answers.

• What does the text suggest about why Estha stopped talking?
• Do you feel comfortable or uncomfortable around very quiet people?
• Can you imagine not being able to speak? In what ways would it affect your life?

Pronunciation

1 🔊 **1.39** Listen to the first paragraph of the reading text again. How are the following words pronounced?

a/an	and	as	for	of	that	to

1 What sound do you hear?
2 Are they pronounced more slowly or more quickly than other words?
3 Are they said more quietly or more loudly?
4 What sort of words are they? What is their function in the sentence?

2 What is the 'strong' pronunciation of these words? When is it used?

3 These words follow the same pronunciation rule. What are their weak and strong forms?

at	but	from	than	them

4 Practise reading the final paragraph of the reading (until 'customers') to a partner. Listen to your partner and correct his/her pronunciation of these words if necessary.

The God of Small Things

Estha had always been a quiet child, so no one could pinpoint exactly with any degree of accuracy exactly when (the year, if not the month or day) he had stopped talking. Stopped talking altogether, that is. The fact is that there wasn't an 'exactly when'. It had been a gradual winding down and closing shop. A barely noticeable quietening. As though he had simply run out of conversation and had nothing left to say. Yet Estha's silence was never awkward. Never intrusive. Never noisy. It wasn't an accusing, protesting silence as much as a sort of evasion, a dormancy, the psychological equivalent of what lungfish do to get themselves through the dry season, except that in Estha's case the dry season looked as though it would last for ever.

Over time he had acquired the ability to blend into the background wherever he was – into bookshelves, gardens, curtains, doorways, streets – to appear inanimate, almost invisible to the untrained eye. It usually took strangers a while to notice him even when they were in the same room with him. It took them even longer to notice that he never spoke. Some never noticed at all.

Estha occupied very little space in the world. Estha finished school with mediocre results, but refused to go on to college. Instead, much to the initial embarrassment of his father and stepmother, he began to do the housework. As though in his own way he was trying to earn his keep. He did the sweeping, swabbing and all the laundry. He learned to cook and shop for vegetables. Vendors in the bazaar, sitting behind pyramids of oiled, shining vegetables, grew to recognise him and would attend to him amidst the clamouring of their other customers. They gave him rusted film cans in which to put the vegetables he picked. He never bargained. They never cheated him. When the vegetables had been weighed and paid for, they would transfer them to his red plastic shopping basket (onions at the bottom, brinjal and tomatoes at the top) and always a sprig of coriander and a fistful of green chillies for free. Estha carried them home in the crowded tram. A quiet bubble floating on a sea of noise.

Glossary

pinpoint *(verb)* – find out exactly

blend into *(verb)* – become part of

mediocre *(adjective)* – average

earn one's keep *(verb)* – work for food and accommodation

clamouring *(verb)* – shouting loudly for something

Vocabulary and Speaking

1 Without looking back at the text, can you remember how to complete the following phrases about Estha? How could you explain the phrases in italics in another way?

1 Estha had the ability to *blend into the b_____*.
2 It was as if he had *run out of c_____* and had *nothing l_____ to say*.
3 Estha's silence was never *an a_____ silence*.

2 Look at other sentences about quietness and silence. Choose the right word to complete the phrases and expressions. Use a dictionary to help you.

1 What's wrong with you? You've been giving me the *quiet / silent* **treatment** all day.
2 Everyone **fell** *quiet / silent* when the head teacher entered the room.
3 I'm looking forward to retiring and living a *quiet / silent* **life**.
4 Do you have a moment? I'd like to have a *quiet / silent* **word**.
5 You have the right to **remain** *quiet / silent*.
6 Can't we have a moment's **peace and** *quiet / silent* round here?
7 I'll tell you, but please **keep it** *quiet / silent*.
8 Just between you and me, he's been doing some other work **on the** *quiet / silent*.

3 Look at the sentences in exercise 2 again.

- Decide what the context is of each sentence: Who could be speaking? Who to? About what?
- Work in pairs. Choose one of the sentences and write a short dialogue containing this sentence. Act out your dialogue with another pair. Pay attention to the pronunciation of weak sounds.

Arundhati Roy (born 24 November 1961) is an Indian writer who writes in English, and an activist who focuses on issues related to social justice and economic inequality. She won the Booker Prize in 1997 for her novel *The God of Small Things* and has also written two screenplays and several collections of essays.

Function globally narrating and responding

Warm up

1 Work in pairs. Which of the sentences below are probably said by a small child, and which by an adult? What could they be talking about?

Because I say so!	Now, don't let go.
Can I have a go?	That's not fair!
It wasn't me!	We'll see.

2 Tell a partner about a situation when …

• your parents wouldn't let you do something when you were a child.

• you or a small child you know did something dangerous, naughty or amusing.

Listening

1 🔘 1.40–1.41 Listen to two people telling an anecdote related to a small child. For each one, make notes on …

1 what exactly the child did.
2 which other people were involved.
3 what happened in the end.
4 adjectives used to describe the experience.

2 Listen to conversation 1 again and say who …

1 had bought the kite.
2 was happily flying the kite.
3 had a naughty smile on his face.
4 had a tantrum.

3 Listen to conversation 2 again and choose the correct alternative.

1 Emily *let / didn't let* Alastair run up the hill.
2 He was lost for *about 15 minutes / more than 15 minutes*.
3 Alastair *had asked someone for help / had been looking for Emily*.

Language focus

1 Complete the story openings with a suitable word. Then compare ideas with a partner.

1 Have I ever told you about my first day at school? It was so _____ because I got locked in the classroom.
2 I had the most _____ experience when my parents took me to Disneyland for my fifth birthday.
3 You'll never guess what Zoe did the other day. She picked some flowers and gave me a big bouquet for my birthday. It was so _____.
4 I must have told you about the time I went ice-skating with Lucy? It was absolutely _____ because we kept falling over all the time and couldn't stop laughing.

2 Underline expressions in exercise 1 used to start an anecdote.

3 Put the listeners' responses into four categories: interest, sympathy, gladness and surprise.

Yeah.	What a nightmare!	I bet you were
You must have	Right.	worried.
been so annoyed.	What a relief!	Uhuh.
Fantastic!	It must have been	Poor little thing!
How incredible!	awful.	That was lucky.
You're joking!	Oh no!	

Pronunciation

1 🔘 1.42 Listen to someone say *Oh* four times. Which one expresses …

a interest? b sympathy? c surprise? d gladness?

2 🔘 1.43 Listen and repeat the expressions in *Language focus* exercise 3 using the correct intonation.

Speaking

1 You are going to tell a short anecdote on a situation from your childhood, eg your first day at school.

Make notes on what sort of incident it was (weird, amusing, etc), where and when it took place, what happened and how you felt.

2 Work in pairs. Take it in turns to tell your anecdote. As you listen, remember to use a range of responses.

Indian English
by David Crystal

Many factors influence the way a regional variety of English develops its character. Loanwords arrive from local languages – and the more contact languages there are in an area, the more loanwords there will be. The sounds and rhythms of these languages influence the way English is pronounced. Local cultural practices introduce new expressions, and the names of persons, places, and institutions provide fresh idiomatic references. The longer English is established in a country, the more we find the development of local dialects and the evolution of a literature that proudly articulates its culture in a distinctive voice in poetry, plays, stories, and novels. When this happens, a 'new English' has truly come of age, as most clearly seen in the mature literature of American (as distinct from British) English.

All these factors are present in India, which has had a longer exposure to English than any other country using it as a second language; and the words, idioms, rhythms, and grammatical constructions of Indian English have made it one of the most distinctive regional varieties. Dictionaries include thousands of words expressing local myths and legends, arts and culture, food and drink, and fauna and flora (such as *brinjal*, the fruit of the eggplant). To take just one domain: road travel. On the road between Pune and Mumbai there are signs that would not be found in other English-speaking countries, such as *Do not criss-cross on expressway, Road in curve ahead*, and *No 2-/3-wheelers* (*2-wheelers* are motorbikes and scooters; *3-wheelers* are auto-rickshaws). No dictionary yet includes all such usages or identifies the differences that have grown up around the country.

Regional variation is inevitable in a country with over a thousand languages and dialects and a population of over a billion. Some varieties are reflected in colloquial labels such as *Hinglish* (mixing English with Hindi), *Punglish* (Punjabi), and *Tamlish* (Tamil). But the stylistic range and regional diversity of Indian English is far greater than these labels suggest, as can be seen from the growing body of Indian literature which increasingly represents indigenous usage. Gone are the days when everyone in a novel, from sahib to servant, spoke standard British English, and the same linguistic diversity is apparent in Indian cinema.

Many in India still see British English as the only 'proper' English. At the same time, a fresh confidence is emerging among young people, and attitudes are beginning to change. We are still in an early chapter of the story of Indian English.

Glossary

loanword *(noun)* – a word from one language that is used in another language without being changed

contact language *(noun)* – language which is created through contact between two or more existing languages

Warm up

What do you think the words in italics mean? Choose the correct option.

1 He's wearing his new *opticals*.
  a trousers   b glasses   c rings
2 My brother is *out of station* this week.
  a out of town   b feeling unwell
  c out of the hospital
3 What is *your good name*?
  a your nickname   b your name
  c the name you like most
4 This is the perfect gift idea for your *near and dear* ones.
  a friends and family b neighbours   c co-workers

Reading

1 The above are all English expressions used in different parts of India. Read *Indian English* and find two more examples.

2 Decide if these sentences are true (*T*) or false (*F*). Give reasons for your answers. Read the text again and choose the correct answer.

1 Grammar, language laws and pronunciation are three factors that influence the development of a regional variety of English.
2 A new variety of English is fully developed when it produces a literature of its own.
3 India has a long history of English as a second language.
4 Indian English dictionaries still do not include all words relating to road travel.
5 All Indian films are in standard British English.
6 The author believes that Indian English will continue to develop.

Speaking

Choose three of the questions below and discuss in small groups.

- Are there different varieties of your own language?
- Are varieties or dialects of a language inferior to the standard version of a language? Why / Why not?
- What do you think will happen to English in the next 100 years?
- Do you think Indian English or other kinds of English will grow? Will people around the world learn them as well as British or American English?

Writing an essay

It is probably true to say that the last 50 years have seen the most remarkable scientific advances ever known to humankind. It is, however, difficult to single out just one of these as the greatest scientific breakthrough. One possible criterion for greatness is the range of potential benefits obtained by its discovery and development. On this basis, the laser must surely be one of the most important developments of the last few decades.

Lasers work by concentrating and focusing intense beams of light. Even though it was not developed until the late 60s, laser technology is now used in many different areas of modern society, ranging from science to commerce. Well-known applications include the field of surgery, where it has reduced the impact of major operations, as well as cosmetic interventions such as treatment for skin conditions. It is also used in industry to improve processes like the cutting and welding of metals, and in such disparate fields as archaeology and criminal detection. However, lasers are perhaps best known for their applications in daily life, not only in CD and DVD players, laser printers and bar code scanners, but also in fibre optic systems in computers and internet communications.

While most of the applications of laser technology are beneficial, it is undeniable that the laser has another 'dark side', namely, in the military industry, where it is currently used to target and detect weapons. Yet it has been the case throughout human history, that there has been a downside to many scientific breakthroughs. Indeed, it was Alfred Nobel's guilty conscience about having developed dynamite which led him to create Nobel Prizes in order to encourage helpful and harmless scientific achievements.

In conclusion, lasers have revolutionised many aspects of modern life and as the laser industry grows, scientists continue to discover new applications. Despite its potential for misuse, it is possible that in future lasers could be used for beneficial endeavours such as space exploration or the production of clean, powerful energy using nuclear fusion. It could even have other benefits of which we are still unaware. For this reason, I believe it merits consideration as the greatest scientific breakthrough of recent times.

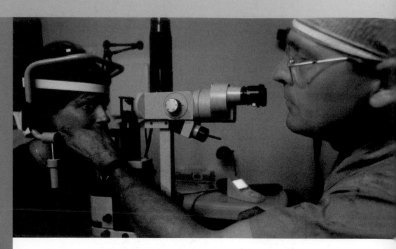

Reading

1 Read Marina's essay on the question 'What do you consider the greatest scientific breakthrough of the last 50 years?'.

1 What is her answer?

2 How does she justify it?

2 Answer the questions with a partner.

1 How does a laser work?

2 In which fields is laser technology used?

3 Which specific applications are mentioned? Which do you consider the greatest?

4 Do you think it is true that most scientific breakthroughs have 'a dark side'? Give examples.

Linking ideas: contrast

1 Where in the second sentence could you use the word *however*? What changes in punctuation are required? How does the position change the emphasis?

Lasers are used in a range of fields. They are best known for their applications in daily life.

2 Complete the sentences using one or more of the words and phrases in the box. What difference in emphasis, if any, is there between the alternatives?

although	but	despite	even so	even though
however	in spite of	nevertheless	while	yet

1 Laser technology is relatively new, _____ it is widely used in many areas of life.

2 _____ its recent development, laser technology is now widespread.

3 _____ nuclear fusion using lasers is not currently possible, it may be feasible in the future.

4 Laser technology has 'a dark side'. _____, its benefits outweigh its disadvantages.

5 Lasers have a range of beneficial applications. _____ they also have the potential for misuse.

Writing skills: gathering ideas

1 Read a list of possible strategies for planning an essay. Tick (✔) the ones you would use, and add any others that you might use.

1 Jot down random ideas on a piece of paper.

2 Discuss the topic with other people.

3 Research the topic in books.

4 Develop your ideas in your head.

5 Research the topic on the internet.

6 Use a 'mind map' (see page 41).

7 Make a list of paragraph headings.

8 Arrange your ideas under paragraph headings.

9 Write without planning.

10 Others _____

Example of a mind map

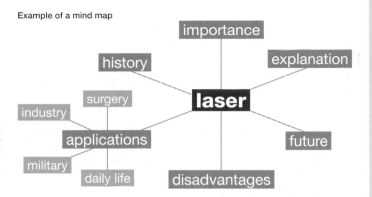

2 Compare your ideas in small groups. What are the advantages or disadvantages of each one? What procedure do you normally use?

Preparing to write

With a partner, choose one of the alternatives in italics and discuss the questions.

What is the greatest *scientific breakthrough / invention / political achievement / medical advancement / music phenomenon* of the last 50 years?

- How would you assess your category? What criteria would you use (eg impact, popularity)? What possible answers are there, and which would you choose?
- How could you define your chosen alternative? What are the applications and benefits?
- What problems or disadvantages are there?
- What are the possible future developments?

Giving a personal opinion

- It is *undeniable / undoubtedly the case / probably true to say / simply not true* that ...
- There is *no doubt / some truth* in the claim that ...
- It *could be argued / must be remembered* that ...
- *I personally believe / It is my view* that ...

Writing

Write your essay using each of the questions in *Preparing to write* as the topic for a paragraph.

Improving your reading efficiency

1 Read some strategies for improving your reading efficiency. Two of these can often be unhelpful. Which are they? Check your ideas on page 131.

- ⋆ Know why you are reading.
- ⋆ Ask yourself questions or predict the content of the text before you read.
- ⋆ Look up unknown words in a dictionary as you read.
- ⋆ Engage with the content of a text by questioning or summarising it as you read.
- ⋆ Read aloud to yourself as you read.
- ⋆ Try to guess the meaning of words from context.
- ⋆ If you want to find the gist of a text, try reading the first line of each paragraph.
- ⋆ Read selectively – do not feel you always have to read every part of a text.
- ⋆ Use the title, headings and visuals to predict and guess the gist of a passage.
- ⋆ Try to read to the end of a sentence without going back too often.
- ⋆ Move your finger from top to bottom to encourage your eye to move on.
- ⋆ Highlight or underline keywords, not unknown words.

2 Which three strategies do you think could help you personally the most? Discuss with a partner.

3 Read 'Improve your reading speed'. Follow the instructions and calculate your speed.

Improve your reading speed

Take a text that is typical of the kind you normally read, and read it for exactly five minutes. Then count the number of words you have read, and divide the total by five. This will tell you your average reading speed in words per minute. An average native speaker can read at 200–250 words per minute with 70% comprehension. Keep repeating the process as you try to improve your reading strategies to monitor your speed. Remember that you should be able to understand most of what you read as well.

Speaking and Reading

1 Work in pairs. Read the titles of some best-selling self-help books about differences between men and women, and discuss what they could be about.

- *Men are from Mars, Women are from Venus*
- *You Just Don't Understand*
- *Why Men Don't Listen and Women Can't Read Maps*

2 Read extract A from a book called *The Myth of Mars and Venus* by Deborah Cameron on page 43 in which she summarises some of the theories in the books in exercise 1. How true are these theories, in your experience?

3 Now read extracts B–D from the book. What is the myth of Mars and Venus, according to Cameron? Does she generally agree or disagree with the claims of the self-help books?

4 Look again at the words and phrases highlighted in the texts. Which suggest that …

1 this is the writer's personal belief?
2 the writer disbelieves or disapproves of this?
3 the writer has an open-minded attitude?

5 Find places in the texts where Cameron expresses these views. For which does she refer to evidence?

1 There are no significant differences in the way men and women use language.
2 It is not true that misunderstandings between the sexes are very common.
3 People tend to describe genuine conflicts as communication problems.
4 Communication can break down because of the limitations of language.
5 Most conflicts between men and women are not due to language differences.

Vocabulary and Writing

1 Read a summary of the texts. Two of the three options in italics are correct in each case. Delete the incorrect alternative.

In *The Myth of Mars and Venus*, Cameron (1) *debunks / expounds / refutes* the theory that men and women communicate differently. Her basic (2) *dogma / premise / proposition* is that there are more similarities than differences between the two sexes. She (3) *challenges / takes issue with / verifies* the received wisdom that men and women are from different planets. According to Cameron, this claim (4) *does not stand up to scrutiny / is not a sweeping generalisation / does not hold water*. She argues that research (5) *shows / indicates / questions* that, (6) *in practice / in fact / in theory*, men and women are very similar.

2 Write a few sentences either to support or debunk one of these theories.

- Men have better spatial awareness than women.
- Women are more emotional than men.
- Women are better at looking after children than men.

3 Read your ideas to a partner. How far do they agree / disagree, and why?

Listening

1 🔘 2.01 Listen to another extract in which Cameron describes how John Gray (the writer of *Men are from Mars, Women are from Venus*), suggests how women avoid communication problems. Make notes on the questions.

1 What advice does Gray give?
2 What is Cameron's response?
3 What point is illustrated by the examples of the trash and the ketchup?
4 What is different about her parents' generation and couples today?

2 Who do you agree with more – Cameron or Gray? Why?

The Myth of Mars and Venus

A At its most basic, what I am calling 'the myth of Mars and Venus' is simply the proposition that men and women differ fundamentally in the way they use language to communicate. All versions of the myth share this basic premise; most versions, in addition, make some or all of the following claims.

1 Language and communication matter more to women than to men; women talk more than men.

2 Women are more verbally skilled than men.

3 Men's goals in using language tend to be about getting things done, whereas women's tend to be about making connections to other people. Men talk more about things and facts, whereas women talk more about people, relationships and feelings.

4 Men's way of using language is competitive, reflecting their general interest in acquiring and maintaining status; women's use of language is cooperative, reflecting their preference for equality and harmony.

5 These differences routinely lead to 'miscommunication' between the sexes, with each sex misinterpreting the other's intentions.

B The idea that men and women 'speak different languages' has become a dogma, treated not as a hypothesis to be investigated, but as an unquestioned article of faith. It is a myth in the sense of being a story people tell in order to explain who they are, where they have come from and why they live as they do. But it is also a myth in the everyday sense: a widespread but false belief. Research debunks the various smaller myths that contribute to it: for instance, that women talk more than men (research suggests the opposite); that women's talk is cooperative and men's competitive (research shows that both sexes engage in both kinds of talk); that men and women systematically misunderstand one another (research has produced no good evidence that they do).

C The misuse of the word 'communication' has become increasingly common in our culture. Conflicts which are really caused by people wanting different things are persistently described as 'misunderstandings' or 'communication problems'. No doubt some conflicts between individual men and women are caused by misunderstanding: there is potential for communication to go awry in every exchange between humans, simply because language is not telepathy. But the idea that communication problems are the major source of conflict between them does not stand up to scrutiny.

D The reality is that there is a great deal of similarity between men and women, and the differences within each gender group are typically as great as or greater than the difference between the two. If these points were acknowledged, the science soundbites would be headed 'Men and women pretty similar, research finds', and popular psychology books would bear titles like *There's No Great Mystery About the Opposite Sex* or *We Understand Each Other Well Enough Most of the Time*. If we want real understanding to take the place of mythology, we need to reject trite formulas and sweeping claims about male and female language use. The evidence is more in line with what it says on a postcard someone once sent me: 'Men are from Earth. Women are from Earth. Deal with it.'

Glossary

debunk *(verb)* – prove that something such as an idea is false

go awry *(verb)* – not happen in the way that was planned

Grammar

1 Choose the correct function to describe each of the sentences below.

> complaint about an annoying habit
> making a suggestion   offer   promise
> recommendation   request
> request for permission
> suggestion of moral obligation
> unenthusiastic suggestion

1 *Can / Shall I get you a glass of lemonade?*
2 *You really **should / must** see that film.*
3 ***Can / Will / Could / Would** you empty the dustbin?*
4 ***Shall / Should** we go out for a pizza?*
5 ***Can / Could / May / Might** I use your phone?*
6 *You **will** keep interrupting me, and you **won't** listen.*
7 *You **should / ought to / could / might** apologise!*
8 *We **may as well / might as well** go to the cinema.*
9 *I **shall / I'll** give you a ring tonight.*

2 Work in pairs. Discuss the differences in meaning and register (directness, formality) among the verbs in bold.

3 With your partner, think of different ways to express the ideas below in a more direct way using a modal verb.

This room is very untidy – can you tidy it, please?

You might clear up this mess!

1 It's cold in here.
2 I don't feel like staying in tonight.
3 I'm fed up with doing the washing-up all the time.
4 You look busy.
5 I wish someone would answer the phone.

4 Choose two or three of the lines and improvise conversations around the sentences in exercise 3, using a range of modal verbs.

G **Grammar focus** – explanation & more practice of modals: language functions on page 138

Deborah Cameron
is a British linguist who is currently Professor of Language and Communication in the English Faculty at Oxford University. She has written several books, including *The Myth of Mars and Venus*.

Theory & Practice

Part 2

Vocabulary & Speaking
Cinema

Reading
Dogme 95

Grammar
Modals of obligation

Past modal forms

Writing
A manifesto

Vocabulary and Speaking

1 Write three questions about the cinema and films. Work in pairs and ask and answer your questions.

2 Read the following film descriptions below, ignoring the gaps. What genre is each one? Guess the films' names.

3 Complete each gap in the text with the appropriate words from the box.

adaptation	box office	budget	cast
digitally	nominated	props	score
screenplay	sequel	set	sets	shot
stars			

4 Tell a partner about a favourite film, using some of the vocabulary from exercise 3.

Film firsts include *The Toll of the Sea* (1922): first in colour; *The Jazz Singer* (1927): first with sound; and *Star Wars IV* (1977): first with 3D computer-generated images.

1 Filmed in black and white in Pinewood Studios, this classic thriller was directed by Alfred Hitchcock and _____ the Oscar®-_____ actors Trevor Howard and Jean Simmons.

2 All of the _____, _____ and costumes for this epic blockbuster were manufactured by crew members, and the scenes of Ancient Rome were _____ over a period of 19 weeks in Malta. A 15.8 m replica of part of Rome's Colosseum was used, but images of most of the building were added _____.

3 _____ in the South Pacific during the period of the Second World War, and filmed in Ibiza, the film includes the use of coloured filters during many of the song sequences. Many of the songs in the original _____ have now become classics.

4 This popular children's animation was completed on a $30 million _____, and with 27 animators using 400 computer models to animate the toy characters. A huge _____ hit, the film was so successful it prompted a _____, released in 1999.

5 Fans of costume drama will love this _____ of Jane Austen's 1813 novel, with a _____ written by Andrew Davis. The _____ includes Colin Firth and Jennifer Ehle.

Reading

1 Read the two opinions below. Do you agree with either of them? Why / Why not?

- Films today are so full of special effects and technical wizardry that nothing can surprise or amaze us anymore.
- Special effects today allow film-makers to create new and exciting experiences for the audience.

2 Read the text about Dogme 95. How could you summarise this theory of film-making, and what is their view of special effects?

3 Which rules did the films in Vocabulary and Speaking exercise 2 break, and how?

4 Read a quotation about the manifesto from Thomas Vinterberg, a Dogme 95 director, and answer the questions.

> Strangely, the strict set of rules we set ourselves have turned out to be a release, a relief and emancipation almost. The strictness of the rules have not hindered, but on the contrary, have encouraged my imagination. When adding a musical score was suddenly prohibited, this resulted in my film *Festen – The Celebration* – being filled with people singing. It came alive.

- Does the statement surprise you? What do you think would be the merits and downsides of making a film according to the guidelines?
- Do you generally prefer Hollywood or independent films? Why?
- Do you agree that, in general, rules can provide a sense of freedom and relief?

5 You are going to read and discuss two reviews of a Dogme film. Work in pairs. Student A: turn to page 128. Student B: turn to page 130.

Grammar

1 Delete the incorrect alternative in each statement about Dogme 95.

> a *Filming **mustn't** / **can't** / **doesn't have to** take place in a studio.*
>
> b *Films **needn't** / **don't need to** / **mustn't** / **don't have to** be filmed on Academy 35 mm film.*
>
> c *Music **can** / **must** / **may** be used in the films.*
>
> d *Films **must** / **should** / **have to** be shot in colour.*
>
> e *Films **shouldn't** / **can't** be filmed in widescreen.*

2 Which sentences suggest that something is …

1 forbidden?   4 necessary?
2 allowed?   5 unnecessary?
3 desirable?

3 Which of the sentences below would be said by the producer of the manifesto, and which by someone reporting the manifesto? Why?

1 The films must be made on location.
2 The films have to be made on location.

4 Look at these sentences using past modals. Which of these sentences imply that the person …

1 did something unnecessary?
2 regrets not doing something?
3 was obliged to do something?
4 managed to do something?
5 escaped an unnecessary task?
6 missed an opportunity?

> a *I **had to***   ***book** tickets in advance.*
> b *I **didn't have to***
> c *I **was able to***
> d *I **needn't have***   ***booked** tickets in advance.*
> e *I **could have***
> f *I **should have***

5 Complete the sentence openers in the grammar box in exercise 4 to write true sentences about recent activities, eg *I had to write a report last night.*

Read your sentences to a partner. Your partner should ask questions.

(G) **Grammar focus** – explanation & more practice of modals of obligation and past modal forms on page 138

Writing

1 Work in pairs. Design a manifesto with rules and guidelines for English lessons. Use a range of modal verbs, and adjectives including *forbidden*, *prohibited*, *allowed*, *permitted* and *(un)acceptable*.

Students should ideally talk in English during the whole lesson. / Use of the mother tongue is forbidden.

2 Read your manifesto to another pair. They should say how far they agree, and why.

Dogme 95   The Theory of a Back to Basics Film Movement

What is Dogme 95?

In 1995, frustrated with the technical wizardry of modern cinema, a group of independent Danish directors set out a manifesto, called Dogme 95, which included a set of rules about how films should be made. Their aim was to provide a blueprint for film-makers working on a low budget that would allow them to compete with Hollywood films. Some of the most famous films made according to these rules were *Festen* (*The Celebration*) (1998, directed by Thomas Vinterberg) and *Italian for Beginners* (2000, directed by Lone Scherfig).

What were the rules?

The following rules outlined Dogme 95's return to a more pure form of film. They were called the Vow of Chastity.

1 Filming must be done on location. Props and sets must not be brought in. If a particular prop is necessary for the story, a location must be chosen where this prop is to be found.

2 The sound must never be produced apart from the images or vice versa. Music must not be used unless it occurs within the scene being filmed.

3 The camera must be a hand-held camera. Any movement or immobility attainable in the hand is permitted. The film must not take place where the camera is standing; filming must take place where the action takes place.

4 The film must be in colour. Special lighting is not acceptable (if there is too little light for exposure the scene must be cut or a single lamp be attached to the camera).

5 Optical work and filters are forbidden.

6 The film must not contain superficial action (murders, weapons, etc must not occur).

7 Temporal and geographical alienation are forbidden (that is to say that the film takes place here and now).

8 Genre movies are not acceptable.

9 The final picture must be transferred to Academy 35 mm film, that is, not widescreen. Originally, the requirement was that the film had to be filmed on Academy 35 mm film, but the rule was relaxed to allow low-budget productions.

10 The director must not be credited.

Part 3

Speaking
Skills

Reading
El Sistema

Grammar
Determiners

Speaking

Work in pairs. Discuss the questions about the different skills below.

> cooking   driving   learning a language
> playing an instrument   reading
> riding a bike   swimming
> using a computer

- What do you think is the best age to learn each of the skills, and why?
- Which skill would you (or did you) personally find most rewarding or frustrating to learn, and why?
- What are the benefits of collective and individual practice, in your opinion? How have you personally benefitted from each?

Reading

1 Look at the photos below, and the quotation about *El Sistema*. What do you know, or can you guess, about what *El Sistema* is?

> An orchestra is a community where the essential and exclusive feature is that it is the only community that comes together with the fundamental objective of agreeing with itself.
>
> (José Abreu, the founder of *El Sistema*)

2 Read *What exactly is El Sistema?* on page 47 and check your predictions. Which of its aims and achievements are mentioned, and which do you consider the most important?

3 Read *Music Practice in El Sistema* by the musician Jonathan Govias, and choose the correct alternative. Find evidence for your choice in the text.

1 Training at *El Sistema* is offered *regardless of / on the basis of* musical ability.
2 Students normally practise *every day of the week / in mixed ability groups*.
3 *El Sistema* is innovative because of its emphasis on *individual attention / teamwork*.
4 Compared with traditional music training, practice is carried out *more frequently / less frequently*.
5 The practice schedule allows students to *progress more rapidly / eliminate errors*.
6 Private lessons are given to *certain students / everyone equally*.

4 Find words or phrases in both texts with the following meanings.

1 innovative (text 1)
2 extremely poor (text 1)
3 skilled (text 1)
4 publicly praised (text 1)
5 totally fascinated (text 1)
6 model or system (text 2)
7 from the start (text 2)
8 temporary failures (text 2)

1 What exactly is El Sistema?

Hailed as 'ground-breaking', 'a music miracle', 'the future of classical music' and 'the most extraordinary social phenomenon of our times', *El Sistema* is a unique programme of musical education founded in Venezuela in 1975 by the visionary former economist José Abreu. It has been subsidised by ten politically divergent governments and has offered free musical training to over 800,000 children and young people, 90% of them from impoverished backgrounds and some as young as two or three years old. Its aim is not primarily to produce accomplished musicians, but rather to make a positive social impact through the pursuit of musical excellence. And not only has it produced internationally renowned performers and conductors, but it has also been linked with a marked reduction in drug addiction and juvenile delinquency, and improved school attendance. The life-affirming vitality of its orchestral performances, which has so mesmerised audiences around the world, can be traced to one of the principles at the heart of its training: Passion first, refinement second. Music is meant to be fun.

2 Music Practice in El Sistema

As a matter of principle, no one is ever turned away because of lack of financial resources or proficiency. When students enrol in one of the 180 *núcleos* (community-based centres) based around Venezuela, they are assigned to groups from day one, whatever their level of ability, and are expected to contribute as best they can. The larger *núcleos* generally boast multiple orchestras of varying levels of ability but the practice is maintained consistently even at the smallest *núcleos*, which have only one orchestra. In these, the students can benefit from the ongoing support and guidance of the more experienced players.

This emphasis on collective music-making represents a complete inversion of the established music training paradigm, in which private lessons constitute the primary learning experience. Each method has its value, but the Venezuelan model would have little or no effect were it not paired with a level of frequency virtually unheard of outside the country. Children arrive at the *núcleos* after school and proceed to spend four to six hours a day, five to six days a week in rehearsals, and group or private lessons, thus acquiring habits of discipline and perseverance from the outset. The immediate advantage of this intensity is that instructors can oversee much more effectively their students' activity and progress, which means that lapses one day can be corrected before they become ingrained bad habits in the days after. Private lessons are then introduced much more strategically and resource-efficiently for those most able to benefit.

5 From what you have read, do you think *El Sistema* deserves the descriptions in lines 1–4 of text 1? Why / Why not?

Grammar

1 Read about determiners. Then choose the better alternative to complete the sentences.

- determiners include *a(n), the, this, that, each, every, some, no, any, either, neither, one, another* and possessive adjectives (eg *my, his*)
- *each, every, either* and *neither* are followed by a singular verb
- *every* means '*all, used for three or more*'; *each* means '*two or more, when seen as individuals*'
- uncountable and plural nouns can be used without a determiner, but singular nouns must always be preceded by a determiner

1 *Any / No* student is turned away because of lack of resources.
2 *Any / No* student can attend, regardless of their ability.
3 *Every / Each* student in Venezuela has the opportunity to join.
4 *Every / Each* student is assigned to one of the *núcleos*.
5 Students can start with *either / neither* a wind instrument or a string instrument.
6 *Either / Neither* instrument is better than the other.

2 Read the sentences and answer the questions.

a There isn't any time. / There is no time.
b He doesn't have a tutor. / He has no tutor.
c I don't like either piece of music. / I like neither piece of music.
d Have you got *any books / books / some books*?
e If you have *any time / time / some time*, come to the concert.

1 Which alternative in a–c is slightly more formal and emphatic?
2 Which alternative in d–e expresses a more negative idea?

3 Read some statements about practising music and add determiners where appropriate (more than one alternative may be possible).

1 With training and time, student can learn to play instrument.
2 It is good idea to find regular time day to practise.
3 Student can make progress without instructor.
4 Practice nor effort can compensate for lack of talent.
5 Individual has different learning curve.
6 You need discipline or perseverance, and preferably both, to succeed.
7 It is good idea to practise with student so you can encourage each, and correct one.

4 Work in pairs. Discuss how far you agree or disagree with the statements in exercise 3.

José Abreu: founder of *El Sistema*

G **Grammar focus** – explanation & more practice of determiners on page 138

Theory & Practice

Speaking

1 When you meet someone for the first time in your country, which of the topics of conversation below do you normally talk about? Are any of them taboo in your culture, and if so, why?

politics	religion	the news
the weather	your age	your family
your health	your job	your salary

2 What other topics might you discuss at a party with people you do not know well? In what other sorts of situations do you normally engage in 'small talk'?

3 Read the exchanges below. How do the 'a' responses break the 'rules' of polite conversation?

1 Lovely weather, isn't it?
 a I disagree actually.
 b Yes, beautiful. Let's hope it stays like this.
2 Do you come here often?
 a No.
 b No, only about once a month. And yourself?
3 How are you doing?
 a I've got a terrible headache.
 b Not too bad. How about you?

4 2.02 Work in pairs and think of polite ways to respond to these conversation openers. Then listen to the exchanges to compare your ideas.

- Great party!
- Have we met before?
- Hi, I'm Marina.
- May I join you?
- Do you mind if I open the window?

Pronunciation

1 2.03 Listen to the sentences and say whether the intonation on each question tag goes up or down.

1 Lovely weather, *isn't it*?
2 We've met before, *haven't we*?
3 You're from Mexico, *aren't you*?

2 Which of the tags in exercise 1 means:

a I'm almost certain.
b I'm not sure this is true.
c I know this is true, but I want to engage you in conversation.

Listen again and repeat the sentences.

3 Work in pairs. Make questions and comments using some of these tags and the topics in Speaking exercise 1. Your partner should respond.

aren't you?	don't you?	haven't we?
isn't it?	isn't (s)he?	wasn't it?

4 Choose two or three exchanges from exercise 3 and improvise conversations with a partner.

Listening

1 2.04 Read the information about George Bernard Shaw and his play *Pygmalion*. Then listen to the first part of a scene from the play in which Henry Higgins and his mother are discussing her 'at-home' party. Mark the statements true (*T*) or false (*F*).

1 Mrs Higgins is pleased that Henry is coming to her party.
2 Henry confesses that he has fallen in love with Eliza.
3 Eliza comes from a different social class from Henry and his mother.
4 Henry has ordered Eliza to talk only about the weather.
5 Henry is trying to teach Eliza to talk and act like a duchess.
6 Eliza is making good progress with her practice.

George Bernard Shaw

(1856–1950) was an Irish author who is the only person to have been awarded both a Nobel Prize for Literature (1925) and an Oscar® (1938), for his contributions to literature and for his work on the film *Pygmalion* respectively. *Pygmalion* was adapted into the successful musical film and play *My Fair Lady*. The story concerns Eliza Doolittle, a Cockney flower girl who takes speech lessons from Professor Henry Higgins, a phoneticist.

2 🔊 **2.05** Now listen to a later part of the scene, in which guests (Mrs Eynsford Hill, her daughter Clara and her son Freddy) arrive for the party. Answer the questions below.

1 How does Eliza manage the conversation?
2 Does she stick to the two topics of conversation?
3 What happens right at the end of the scene?

3 Complete the sentences with the correct preposition. Who said each one, and in what context?

1 Besides, I've picked _____ a girl.
2 I've a sort of bet on that I'll pass her _____ as a duchess in six months. I started on her some months ago; and she's getting _____ like a house on fire.
3 She's to keep _____ two subjects: the weather and everybody's health.
4 If I was doing it proper, what was you laughing _____?

4 🔊 **2.06** Listen to some short extracts to check your answers.

5 Which of the following endings to the play do you think is a) more likely, b) more satisfying, c) more realistic? Why?

- Higgins wins his bet and marries Eliza.
- Higgins wins his bet and Eliza decides to marry Freddy.
- Higgins loses his bet and Eliza returns to her family.

Speaking

In the play, Eliza was trying to lose her regional Cockney accent and learn standard British English pronunciation (also known as RP, or received pronunciation) so that she could sound more 'upper class'. Discuss these questions with a partner.

- How acceptable are regional accents in your country? Do you have an equivalent of RP?
- Does the pronunciation of young people differ from that of older people? In what ways?
- Which form of English pronunciation have you learnt? Which form would you like to use when you speak, and why?

Extend your vocabulary – similes

'She's getting on like a house on fire.'

1 Circle the correct alternative to make familiar comparative expressions (similes) with *like*.

1 I felt like *a fish out of water / a lemon in a bowl of apples* on my first day at school.
2 I'm like *a bear with a sore head / a lion with a broken paw* if I don't get enough sleep.
3 I have a memory like *a broken computer / a sieve* when it comes to remembering dates.
4 I always sleep like *a log / a stone* after I've been working out at the gym.
5 I was shaking like *a plate of jelly / a leaf* when I took my driving test.
6 My boss smokes like *a bonfire / a chimney*.
7 He takes no notice if you tell him off – it's like *water off a duck's back / talking to a sleeping elephant*.

2 Which of the alternatives do you prefer? Can you think of better alternatives? Do you have similar expressions in your own language?

3 Tell a partner about personal experiences using some of the similes.

Function globally asking for clarification

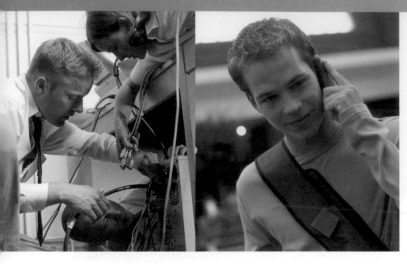

Warm up

1 Work in pairs. Have you ever been in any of these situations where communication broke down? Tell your partner about it.

- Someone was trying to explain a complicated idea or process, and you couldn't understand.
- You were speaking on the phone and the line was bad.
- Someone was explaining something important and you needed to ask questions to clarify their meaning.
- Someone was speaking English fast or with a strong accent.

2 How would you ask for clarification in each of the above situations?

Listening

1 🔊 2.07–2.10 Listen to four conversations. Match them to the situations in Warm up exercise 1, and answer the questions.

1 Where are the people and what is their relationship?
2 What does the person need to clarify in each case?

2 Listen again and complete the sentences about the conversations.

Conversation 1
1 You have to plug the cable into _____.
2 To get a picture, _____ on the remote.

Conversation 2
1 Football practice was going to be at _____.
2 The new time is _____.

Conversation 3
1 It's cheaper to join the gym _____.
2 To join the gym, you have to _____.

Conversation 4
1 Michael needs help with his _____.
2 Ellie is _____ than Michael.

Language focus

1 Which of these ways of asking for repetition is not usually considered polite? Which have you heard most frequently?

> Excuse me?   I beg your pardon?   Pardon?
> Say again?   Sorry?
> Sorry, could you repeat that, please?   What?

2 Which of the following expressions indicate that the speaker …

a did not hear?   b did not understand?

1 Sorry, you've *lost* me.
2 Sorry, can you speak up a *bit*, please?
3 Sorry, can you speak a *bit* more slowly, please?
4 Sorry, *what* does *'motor skills'* mean?
5 Sorry, I *didn't* catch that.
6 Sorry, I *don't quite* follow.
7 Sorry, what *exactly* do you mean by 'disruptive'?
8 *What*, you mean he *can't* write?

Pronunciation

1 What happens to the pronunciation of the /t/ sound in the words in italics in *Language focus* exercise 2?

2 🔊 2.11 Listen and check your ideas. Then practise repeating the sentences.

Speaking

Choose two or three of the situations to roleplay with a partner, and practise asking for and giving clarification.

1 One of you has just joined the class and you are explaining about the way the class and the school works.
2 You are on the phone making arrangements to meet a colleague. The line is bad.
3 You don't want to go on holiday with a friend, as arranged. Try to explain why.
4 Give directions on how to get to your house.

Useful phrases

- Yes, exactly.
- Yes, in a way.
- No, I'm not saying that exactly.
- No, what I'm saying is …

Global voices

Warm up

Read the following sayings about practice. Do you have any similar sayings or proverbs in your language? Do you think these are true?

- Practice makes perfect.
- If at first you don't succeed, try, try, try again.
- Practice is the best of all instructors.
- Practice is the best teacher.

Listening

1 🔊 **2.12–2.15** Listen to four people talking about how they learnt English to a high level. Who …

1 learns words from television?
2 repeats phrases?
3 speaks English to professional colleagues?
4 speaks to the teacher in English?
5 watches movies without subtitles?
6 practises English in the shower?
7 has studied abroad?
8 reads books in English?

2 🔊 **2.16–2.17** Listen to Rod and Carolina give their tips on how to improve your English. Write a short summary of what each speaker says, using the words in the box to help you. Do you agree?

conversation	embarrassed	experiment	mistakes
native	perfect	possible	relax	speak

Language focus: *I mean*

I mean is a very frequent discourse marker in spoken English. You can use it to expand on what you are saying.

Carolina: … *you will never speak English. I **mean**, you will never dare to speak English …*

You can also use it to correct yourself.

Rod: … *which is French, **I mean**, which was French.*

Continue these sentences with *I mean* and your own ideas.

1 My first English teacher was at university … (correct yourself)
2 It's so much easier to practise English these days … (expand)
3 I have studied English last year, … (correct yourself)
4 English is more popular now than when I was a child … (expand)

Speaking

1 Think of five ways that you can practise to improve your English. Make notes.

2 Work in pairs. Compare your list of ways. Decide on the top six ways and list these.

3 Work with another pair. Compare your lists from exercise 2. Now decide on the top four ways out of these and rank them from 1–4.

4 Compare your final top four ways to practise English with other groups in the class. Did you agree?

Miguel, Portugal   Katsuya, Japan   Carolina, Argentina   Rod, Gabon

Writing a review

The King's Speech, which won four Oscars® in 2011 (Best Picture, Best Director for Tom Hooper, Best Actor for Colin Firth and Best Original Screenplay), is a moving and thought-provoking portrayal of the struggle of King George VI, nicknamed Bertie, to overcome a speech defect and find his voice. A historical drama based on true events, the film is part of a wave of movies (such as *The Queen* and *Mrs Brown*) that depict the recent history of the British monarchy, and reflect the public's fascination with it.

The film is set in the 1920s and 1930s, when Germany and Russia were gaining power in Europe, and Britain was suffering from economic recession and on the brink of war. The film tells the story of Bertie's efforts to overcome his stammer – probably brought about by childhood experiences – with the help of an unorthodox speech therapist, Doctor Lionel Logue. Bertie struggled to pronounce consonants, and given that English words usually have more than one syllable (and hence, a number of consonants) he had huge problems. In the end, however, his efforts bore fruit and he succeeded in giving a bold and powerful speech to his nation.

The success of the film lies first of all in its vivid description of Bertie's psychological struggle, as well as in its exploration of the true friendship between him and Doctor Lionel Logue, and the unconditional support he received from his wife and children. Colin Firth gives an outstanding and subtle performance as Bertie, who comes across as a complex and multifaceted figure: a son who feels inferior to his father, a kind father to his own children, a somewhat childish husband to his wife, a true friend, and a great King to the country. The point was made at the end that King George VI's brave performance had in fact greatly encouraged the British during the Second World War. It suggests that, very often, we have to conquer ourselves first before marching forward. This is a brilliant and memorable film that should not be missed.

Reading

1 Read Wenchao's review of the British film *The King's Speech*. How many points out of ten do you think she gave it?

2 Have you seen this film? If so, do you agree with the review? If not, would you like to see it? Why / Why not?

Writing skills: writing a plan

1 Complete the plan for the review using the words from the box.

acting	~~awards~~	context	genre	message	plot
recommendation		~~setting~~	~~strengths~~	theme	

Paragraph 1
a _____awards_____
b _____
c _____
d _____

Paragraph 2
a _____setting_____
b _____

Paragraph 3
a _____strengths_____
b _____
c _____
d _____

2 Make brief notes for each category.

Linking ideas: extra information

1 Find these phrases and clauses in the text. What does each one give extra information about? How is each one punctuated in the text?

1 which won four Oscars®: *The King's Speech* (followed by a comma)
2 Best Picture, Best Director for Tom Hooper, Best Actor for Colin Firth and Best Original Screenplay
3 nicknamed Bertie
4 A historical drama based on true events
5 when Germany and Russia were gaining power in Europe
6 probably brought about by childhood experiences
7 Doctor Lionel Logue
8 who comes across as a complex and multifaceted figure
9 a son who feels inferior to his father

2 Which of the phrases and clauses in exercise 1 are ...

a relative clauses?

b nouns or noun phrases?

c participle clauses?

3 Link the ideas below into a single sentence (more than one way is possible).

1 The writer of the screenplay is David Seidler. He had a stammer as a child.

2 The film was released in January 2011. It was widely praised by critics.

3 *The King's Speech* received numerous awards. It received Oscars®, BAFTAs and Golden Globes®.

4 King George was crowned in 1936. His brother abdicated then. His brother was King Edward VIII.

5 King George was a shy man. His daughter was Queen Elizabeth II.

6 The film stars Colin Firth, Geoffrey Rush and Helena Bonham Carter. It is set in the period before World War II.

7 Bertie was a complex figure. Bertie was played by Colin Firth.

Preparing to write

Tell a partner about a film you would recommend. Give information using the categories in *Writing skills*. Your partner should ask questions to get further information.

Describing a film

- The film *depicts / portrays / tells the story of / recounts / explores* ...
- It *is set in ... / stars ... / is directed by ... / was shot in ...*
- Firth gives a *moving / brilliant / subtle / memorable / powerful* performance as ...
- This is a(n) *hilarious / compelling / entertaining / insightful / thought-provoking* film.
- The success of the film lies in its *vivid description of ... / moving portrayal of ...*
- This film *is well worth seeing / should not be missed*.

Writing

Write your review, based on information from *Preparing to write*.

Working on pronunciation

1 How would you describe your pronunciation? Choose one alternative.

- My pronunciation is almost like a native speaker's.
- I have a slight accent, but am mostly clear and intelligible.
- I have quite a strong accent, but am usually clear and intelligible.
- I have a strong accent and people sometimes do not understand me.

2 Place an arrow next to the sentence that represents your target pronunciation. Then discuss your ideas with a partner.

3 Tick (✔) the areas of your pronunciation that you feel need more work. If you are unsure, ask a teacher or fellow student.

- [ ] individual sounds (vowels and consonants)
- [ ] sound changes in combination with other sounds
- [ ] word stress
- [ ] phrase and sentence stress
- [ ] sentence rhythm
- [ ] intonation patterns

4 Compare your answers with a partner and discuss these questions.

- What resources do you know of that can help you, eg books, CDs, websites?
- What do you do, or intend to do, to work on these?

5 Study the phonemic chart of standard British English and answer the questions with a partner.

- Which areas of the chart represent a) vowels, b) diphthongs, c) consonants?
- How many of the sounds do you recognise?
- What is the value of studying these symbols?

iː	ɪ	ʊ	uː	ɪə	eɪ
e	ə	ɜː	ɔː	ʊə	ɔɪ	əʊ
æ	ʌ	ɑː	ɒ	eə	aɪ	aʊ
p	b	t	d	tʃ	dʒ	k	g
f	v	θ	ð	s	z	ʃ	ʒ
m	n	ŋ	h	l	r	w	j

6 After the class you can download the chart and listen to the sounds that you want to improve at www.soundspronapp.com.

Heroes & Villains

Part 1

Speaking & Vocabulary
Heroism and personal qualities

Reading & Listening
Gilgamesh

Vocabulary
Expressions with *stand* and *give*

Speaking and Vocabulary

1 Work in pairs. Can you think of any historical or contemporary figures (male or female) who are commonly regarded as heroes or heroines in your culture?

2 Read some possible characteristics of a hero. Which are true of the people you suggested in exercise 1? Compare your ideas with a partner.

A hero is someone who …
1 faces dangers and trials without fear.
2 is concerned about the welfare of others rather than about himself/herself.
3 has complete faith in his/her abilities.
4 follows strong moral principles.
5 if necessary, will die for the sake of another person or group.
6 never betrays friends, family or nation.
7 is not distracted from his/her goals.
8 keeps going regardless of obstacles or discouragement.
9 has strong beliefs and a sense of mission.
10 is not arrogant, and is modest about his/her qualities and achievements.

3 Match the qualities in the box to the statements in exercise 2.

conviction   courage   humility
integrity   loyalty   perseverance
self-confidence   selflessness
self-sacrifice   single-mindedness

4 Work in pairs. Write the adjectives for as many of the nouns in exercise 3 as you can, eg courageous. What other qualities can also be considered heroic?

5 'Our age has celebrities and role models, but no heroes.' Do you agree?

Reading and Listening

1 What is an 'epic'? Can you think of any examples of epics in literature or movies?

2 Read *Gilgamesh: the epic* and answer the questions.
1 Why is the poem historically significant?
2 Is it fact or fiction?
3 Which two senses of the word 'hero' are referred to?

3 🔴 **2.18** Read and listen to the extract from the poem on page 55, which starts when Gilgamesh and Enkidu are about to confront the monster Humbaba. Who experiences fear, and who offers encouragement?

4 Answer the questions with a partner.
1 Which heroic qualities are described in the extracts?
2 Underline words and phrases that describe:
   • the physical experience of fear
   • the emotion of fear

5 In the poem, find places that suggest that …
1 heroism leads to fame and glory.
2 fighting together is more effective than fighting alone.
3 heroes should not show fear.

6 Do you agree with the statements in exercise 5? How far do you think the poem depicts a male view of heroism?

Gilgamesh: the epic

Written in about 2000 BC, *Gilgamesh* is one of the oldest literary works in the world, and is set in the cradle of Western civilisation, between the Tigris and the Euphrates (where present day Iraq is situated). This epic poem was lost for centuries, and then discovered in 1844 written on stone tablets in the ancient language Akkadian. In the introduction to his modern version, Stephen Mitchell writes: 'Its hero, Gilgamesh, was a historical king who reigned in the Mesopotamian city of Uruk in about 2750 BC. In the epic, he battles monsters with his good friend, Enkidu.'

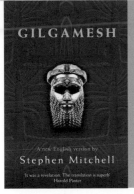

GILGAMESH

A new English version by
Stephen Mitchell

'It was a revelation. The translation is superb'
Harold Pinter

Stephen Mitchell

is a writer of poetry and fiction who
is widely known for his original
and definitive versions of spiritual
writings and poetry. His many books
include the best-selling *Tao Te
Ching*, *Gilgamesh*, *The Book of Job*,
Bhagavad Gita and *The Selected
Poetry of Rainer Maria Rilke*.

Gilgamesh

Gilgamesh said, 'Courage, dear brother,
this is no time to give in to fear.
We have come so far, across so many mountains,
and our journey is about to reach its goal.
Though your arms feel weak now and your legs tremble,
you are a warrior, you know what to do.
If we help each other and fight side by side
we will make a lasting name for ourselves,
we will stamp our fame on men's minds forever.'
They came within sight of the monster's den.
He was waiting inside it. Their blood ran cold.
He saw the two friends, he grimaced, he bared
his teeth, he let out a deafening roar.
He glared at Gilgamesh. 'Young man,' he said,
'you will never go home. Prepare to die.'
Dread surged through Gilgamesh, terror flooded
his muscles, his heart froze, his mouth went dry,
his legs shook, his feet were rooted to the ground.
Gilgamesh backed away. He said,
'How dreadful Humbaba's face has become!
It is changing into a thousand nightmare
faces, more horrible than I can bear.
I feel haunted. I am too afraid to go on.'
Enkidu answered, 'Why, dear friend,
do you speak like a coward? What you just said
is unworthy of you. It grieves my heart.
We must not hesitate or retreat.
Two intimate friends cannot be defeated.
Be courageous. Remember how strong you are.
I will stand by you. Now let us attack.'

From *Gilgamesh: A New English Version*,
Stephen Mitchell, Profile Books 2004

Vocabulary

1 Read the following opinions and match the phrases in
italics with the synonyms in the box.

abandon	be loyal to	compromise	confront
defend	make concessions	obstruct	remain firm

1 You should always *stand up to* bullies, no matter how
much they may threaten you.
2 Never *give up* hope, however bleak a situation
may appear.
3 It is best to *stand your ground* in an argument, however
convincing your opponent's arguments may be.
4 Governments should never *give in* to terrorists,
regardless of the danger they may pose.
5 You should never *give way* on your principles,
however tempted you may be.
6 Parents should not *stand in the way of* their
children's ambitions, irrespective of their views
and whether they are right or wrong.
7 You should *stand up for* the rights of all people,
regardless of their race, gender or political or
religious affiliation.
8 Always *stand by* your friends and family,
whatever they may have done.

2 Underline the words and expressions in the sentences
in exercise 1 that express a contrast. Then complete the
rules with the phrases below.

however / wherever, etc	irrespective of
no matter how / what / where, etc	regardless of

1 Use _____ or _____ followed by a noun or
noun phrase.
2 Use _____ or _____ followed by a verb phrase.

3 Read the statements in exercise 1 again and for each
statement, write down how far you agree on a scale of 1–5
(1 = agree strongly, 5 = disagree strongly). Then choose some
of the statements to discuss in small groups.

Heroes & Villains

Listening and Speaking

1 Read the newspaper headline below. What do you think it might refer to? In what way could local volunteers be 'unsung heroes'?

> **'Local volunteers unsung heroes of flood relief,' says international development charity**

2 Delete the word which does not usually collocate with the word in bold. How could each of the collocations relate to the work of an international development charity?

1 humanitarian natural timely **disaster**
2 emergency help immediate **relief**
3 aid community staff **workers**
4 preventable life-threatening humanitarian **diseases**
5 emergency long-term sustainable **development**

3 🔊 **2.19** You are going to listen to an interview with Justin Byworth, a director of the international charity World Vision. As you listen, make notes on the following topics.

1 the sort of work he does
2 specific emergencies mentioned
3 the role of local volunteers
4 two examples of heroism

4 Work in pairs. Compare your notes and try to summarise the work of World Vision.

5 Work in pairs to answer the following questions:

• Do you think that if you had a job like Justin Byworth's you would be an optimistic or a pessimistic person? Why?
• Can you think of any other examples of 'unsung heroes' that you have heard of, or from your own experience? Why do you think some people behave altruistically even when they are in danger or difficulties themselves?

Vocabulary

1 Complete the sentences with some of the words and phrases from the box.

> corruption   debt   displacement
> drought   epidemic   famine   flooding
> genocide   health care   hurricanes
> illiteracy   inequality   legal representation
> malnutrition   sanitation   tsunamis
> volcanic eruptions

1 Experts fear the recent outbreak of TB could develop into a major _____.
2 Due to the recent lack of rainfall, there is a severe _____.
3 The livelihoods of people in the world's poorest regions are continually threatened by natural disasters such as _____, _____ and _____.
4 The quality of life of millions of people in developing countries would be improved by increased access to adequate housing, _____, _____ and _____.
5 Protesters are demonstrating against the _____ of senior government figures, who have pocketed millions of dollars in aid donations and left the country in severe _____.
6 Tribal conflict is rife in the area, and the recent brutal _____ has resulted in widespread migration, and _____ of whole populations on a massive scale.

2 Discuss the questions in small groups.

• Have any of the issues in exercise 1 been in the news recently? What do you know about them?
• Are any of them a problem in your country?
• What other problems are currently causing problems in developing countries?
• Whose responsibility is it to tackle these problems? Choose one or two of them, and brainstorm possible solutions.

ASEAN	BRIC	IMF	NATO
NGO	OPEC	UN	UNESCO
UNICEF	WB	WHO	WTO

1 What do the abbreviations and acronyms above stand for?

2 How do you pronounce them? Which are used with 'The'?

3 Choose four of the organisations and discuss with a partner what you know about their work.

Grammar

1 Work in pairs. Try to explain the reason for the choice of tenses in each pair.

a   *There **has been** an earthquake in Japan.*

b   *The earthquake **struck** at 4.00am.*

c   *$50,000 **was raised** last year.*

d   *$50,000 **has been raised** this year.*

e   *She **has won** many prizes for her work.*

f   *She **won** many prizes for her work.*

g   *He **has been working** in China for 15 years.*

h   *He **has worked** in six different countries.*

i   *They **have been building** a new hospital.*

j   *They **have built** a new hospital.*

k   *They **have been appealing** for money.*

l   *They **have appealed** for money.*

2 In each sentence, say whether only one or both alternatives are possible. If both are possible, explain the difference.

1 They *have lived / have been living* in the capital since they *have arrived / arrived*.

2 How long *have you known / have you been knowing* about the problem?

3 It *hasn't rained / hasn't been raining* in the region for several months.

4 *It's / It's been* 20 years since elections *have been held / were held* in the country.

3 Read *Good news*. Which of the issues in the Vocabulary section do they refer to? Say whether the verb forms in italics are correct or not. If they are incorrect, change them.

Good news

1 Following the failure of the harvest, five million people *have migrated* earlier in the year to refugee camps and since then *have been suffering* from severe malnutrition. We're happy to announce that thanks to the efforts of local volunteers, food aid *was distributed* to most of the camps.

2 Two years ago this region *suffered* from one of the world's highest mortality rates due to malaria. Since we *began* a programme of distribution of insecticide-treated bed nets, the incidence of malaria *decreased* dramatically, and we *have not been treating* any new cases in the last three months.

3 This year alone our organisation *has been digging* 12 wells and *installing* 30 hand pumps. Our team of volunteers *worked* very hard, and often under very difficult weather conditions.

4 It *was* five years since The Clean Hands education programme *has been launched* in the city's slum areas. Since then, infant mortality *has been reduced* by one third and we expect these numbers to get better.

5 Meena's daughter *graduated* from school in May. Ten years ago this *has simply not been* possible. Through the tireless work of the overseas volunteers and women in the community who *encouraged* parents like her, school enrolments *increased* by 10%.

G **Grammar focus** – explanation & more practice of present perfect simple and continuous on page 140

Writing

1 Work in pairs. Choose one of the topics below and write a short report similar to the ones in the *Good news* text.

- Homes have been found for over 500 children orphaned in the recent inter-tribal conflict.
- $1.3 billion of debt has been written off by the IMF.
- The gap between rich and poor has narrowed by 10%.
- $6 bn of aid has been sent to earthquake survivors.

2 Work with another pair. Read your reports. Then ask and answer questions about them.

Heroes & Villains

Vocabulary and Speaking

1 Read *Crimes and punishments*. Underline the punishments. Do they seem harsh, or lenient compared with nowadays?

2 Look at the crimes in the box and discuss the questions with a partner.

armed robbery	arson	assault
blackmail	blasphemy	bribery
burglary	fraud	libel	manslaughter
murder	piracy	theft	treason

1 Which of the crimes are described in *Crimes and punishments*?
2 Which are common and which less common in most of the world nowadays?
3 Can you think of more 'modern' crimes and punishments?
4 Do you know how a person convicted of some of these crimes would be punished in your country?

Crimes and punishments

a Thomas Briggs was sentenced to death for forging cheques in 1829, but his sentence was later overturned and he was acquitted.

b In 1815 Warren Kerr was found guilty of stealing boot-tops, and was jailed for six months. He was later flogged for stealing timber from a government yard.

c In 1788 ten-year-old Mary Wade hit another girl, pushed her into a ditch and robbed her of her clothes. She received the death penalty, but her sentence was commuted to transportation to Australia.

d In 1724, Benjamin Goddard and Samuel Axtell demanded money from Richard Wise in exchange for not revealing secrets about his private life. They were fined 20 pounds each and sentenced to six months' imprisonment.

e In 1878, the Australian outlaw Ned Kelly was convicted in his absence of the attempted murder of a policeman. After a series of killings and bank robberies, he was later arrested and tried for murder. He was finally hanged in 1880.

f Stede Bonnet, a rich landowner who captained a boat named the *Revenge*, raided ships off the Virginia coast. He was caught and hanged in 1718.

Reading

1 Can you think of any famous historical or fictional pirates? Do you think of them as heroes or villains? Why?

2 Read *Piracy* on page 59 and answer the questions.

1 Where do the pirates operate?
2 What sort of boats do they attack?
3 How do they conduct their operations?
4 Why is it hard to combat piracy?

3 If you were the captain of a ship that had to sail across the Gulf of Aden, what would you do to protect your crew and your cargo, and how would you react if you were hijacked?

Listening and Speaking

1 🔊 2.20 Listen to one captain's experiences of crossing the Gulf of Aden. Say whether the following statements are true (*T*) or false (*F*).

1 The pirates' operations are more complex than in the past.
2 The situation has made him and his family feel afraid.
3 He is grateful for the protection of the coalition warships.
4 The crew are powerless if the pirates board the boat.
5 Nowadays the pirates are starting to attack and shoot their hostages.

Piracy

Piracy is sometimes viewed as a purely historical phenomenon, but in fact it is alive and well in some parts of the world, notably around the Gulf of Aden on the Indian Ocean and off the coast of Somalia. In recent years, there has been a steady increase in attacks by Somali pirates on international fishing and merchant vessels and, increasingly, on pleasure craft. The pirates run highly sophisticated operations using high tech satellite phones, navigation systems and weapons. They board the vessels, take the crew hostage and demand ransom payments, often running to millions of dollars. Although ships from an international coalition force regularly patrol the area and provide convoys to escort ships across the seas, there is no international legal system for prosecuting people accused of piracy. It has been argued that the problem will continue to increase until there is an international court, backed by the UN, with power to send those convicted of piracy to an international prison.

2 ⬳ **2.21** Listen to a Somali pirate's account of his life as a pirate. Make notes on …

1 his reasons for becoming a pirate.
2 how the pirates board the ships.
3 what they do on board.
4 how he views piracy.

3 Discuss the questions in small groups.

1 What do you think the pirate means when he describes piracy as 'a road tax'? Do you have any sympathy with his point of view?
2 Which of the following suggestions do you think is the most effective or realistic way to combat piracy? Can you think of any other solutions?
   • increase security on ships passing through the area
   • establish an international court and prison for pirates
   • increase international aid to countries where pirates operate

Pronunciation

1 ⬳ **2.22** Read the sentences below. How are the words in italics pronounced? Listen and check your answers.

1 The problem will continue to *increase* until there is an international court.
2 Recently there has been a steady *increase* in attacks by Somali pirates.
3 Coalition ships provide convoys to *escort* ships across the seas.
4 Coalition ships provide an *escort* for ships in the area.

2 Choose the correct alternative to complete the rule.

In many two-syllable words beginning with the prefixes *con-*, *re-*, *in-*, *de-*, *pre-*, *ex-*, *de-*, *pro-*, *sub* and *ob* …
1 stress the *first* / *second* syllable if the word is a noun.
2 stress the *first* / *second* syllable if the word is a verb.

3 Work in pairs. Say each of the words below as either a noun or a verb, and your partner should identify which it is.

conflict	convert	convict	decrease
desert	insult	object	present
progress	protest	rebel	reject

4 Complete the sentences with the correct form of the words in the box above. Then read the sentences aloud.

1 Pirates are seen by many as rogues and criminals. However, others _____ to this view, and idealise them as heroes and _____ against authority.
2 The evidence _____ by the police _____ with some eyewitness reports.

5 Write two sentences using other words from the box, leaving a gap for the word you have chosen. Show them to a partner. Can they guess the word and pronounce it correctly?

Heroes & Villains

Part 4

Speaking
Stanford experiment

Reading
The nature of evil

Extend your vocabulary
Ways of describing bad people

Grammar
Participle clauses

Speaking

1 Read the introduction to a classic psychological experiment and look at the photo. Describe what is happening using these words:

> cell   handcuffs   inmate
> solitary confinement

> In 1971, the psychologist Dr Philip Zimbardo and his colleagues at Stanford University, California, conducted an experiment to find out how ordinary people behaved when cast in the roles of prisoners and guards in a simulated prison. They recruited student volunteers, and after a series of interviews and psychological tests randomly assigned 25 of them to act as either guards or prisoners in a mockup jail set up in the basement of Stanford's department of psychology.

2 Work in pairs. Answer the questions.

• Do you think the students took the roleplay seriously?

• What do you think they had to do during the experiment?

• Do you think it would be easier to pretend to be a prisoner or a guard? Why?

Reading

1 Read *The nature of evil*, an account of the experiment. Were your ideas right?

2 Put the stages in the experiment in the correct order 1–8.

a   Some prisoners rebelled.   ___
b   Prisoner 8612 began to break
    down emotionally.   ___
c   The experiment was ended early.   ___
d   The volunteers were given their roles. *1*
e   The first prisoner was released.   ___
f   The guards put an end to
    the rebellion.   ___
g   An external consultant spoke out
    against the experiment.   ___
h   The volunteers found it hard to
    adopt their new roles at first.   ___

3 Choose the best meaning of the words and phrases below as used in the text.

1	disorientating	fake / causing confusion
2	harassing	treating badly / comforting
3	toed the line	obeyed / disobeyed
4	ratted on	supported / betrayed
5	salutary	unpleasant but useful / pleasant but useless

4 Discuss these questions with a partner.

• Does anything surprise you about the way the experiment developed?

• The experiment has been criticised by some people for being unscientific and unethical. Do you agree?

5 Which of the following conclusions could be drawn from it, in your opinion?

• Anyone can behave cruelly if put in a position of power and authority.

• People will do anything to conform to group pressure and social roles.

• Dehumanising conditions can alter a person's personality.

6 Work in small groups. Choose one of the statements in exercise 5 to discuss. What evidence do you have for your opinions?

Extend your vocabulary – ways of describing bad people

> badly-behaved   brutal   corrupt
> evil   infamous   mischievous
> naughty   notorious   sinful
> wicked

1 Which of the adjectives in the box …
  1 are used mainly of children?
  2 mean extremely cruel, and are often used in fairy tales?
  3 describe famous bad people?
  4 has a connotation of dishonesty?
  5 has a connotation of violence?
  6 has a connotation of playfulness?
  7 has religious connotations?

2 Can you think of real or fictional examples of people with any of the above characteristics?

Grammar

1 Read the sentences from the text. Which of the clauses in bold contains …

1. a present participle referring to a previous action?
2. a past participle referring to a previous event in the passive?
3. a present participle showing the result of an action?
4. a present participle referring to events happening together?

a. *At the next roll-call he told fellow inmates that there really was no escape,* **triggering genuine fear among them**.

b. **Arriving at the 'jail' blindfolded**, *they underwent strip-searching and delousing.*

c. *Prisoner 8612 began showing clear signs of mental distress,* **crying uncontrollably**.

d. **The rebellion crushed**, *the guards then set up a 'privilege cell' system.*

2 Read more sentences about the text and match them to a rule below.

a. *They were given a number – the aim* **being** *to simulate the disorientating processes.*

b. **Having reviewed** *the experiment, they decided to call a halt to the process.*

c. *They underwent strip-searching and delousing before* **being dressed** *in a simple smock.*

d. **Not realising** *they were being sucked into the events, the psychologists continued with the experiment.*

e. *The psychologists* **observing** *him finally accepted that he wasn't faking.*

- use *not* before a participle to make a clause negative
- use a perfect participle to stress that one action is completed before another starts
- some participles have their own subject
- participle clauses can be used to replace relative clauses
- participle clauses can be used after certain conjunctions, eg *after, before, while*

The nature of evil:
can **good** people do **bad** things?

The experiment began one Sunday morning when real police officers arrived at the homes of the volunteer prisoners and arrested them. Arriving at the 'jail' blindfolded, they underwent strip-searching and delousing before being dressed in a simple smock, and given a heavy chain around their ankle, and a number – the aim being to simulate the disorientating processes used on real prisoners. The 'guards', meanwhile, were given a uniform, a truncheon, reflective sunglasses, and freedom to act pretty much as they liked.

At first, both sets of students found the role-playing rather awkward, with some struggling to take a roll-call at 2.30am seriously. The next morning, however, things turned very serious indeed. When the morning-shift guards arrived for duty, they found that some prisoners had already had enough of the experiment, and had staged a rebellion. Annoyed at what they saw as the leniency of their night-shift colleagues, the guards took action. Spraying the prisoners with fire extinguishers, they rounded up the ringleaders and put them in solitary confinement, while harassing the others. The rebellion crushed, the guards then set up a 'privilege cell' system, rewarding prisoners who toed the line. They also occasionally put troublemakers in the cell, creating the impression they had ratted on their friends – thus unwittingly reinventing a standard prison technique for breaking down solidarity between inmates.

As the psychologists eavesdropped on the unfolding drama, they realised that they were no longer watching mere role-playing. What they failed to notice was that they too were being sucked into the events taking place in the 'jail'. Barely 36 hours into the experiment, Prisoner 8612 began showing clear signs of mental distress, crying uncontrollably. Despite this, the reaction of the psychologists was to dismiss his symptoms as a feeble attempt to win early release, and send him back to the cells. At the next roll-call he told fellow inmates that there really was no escape, triggering genuine fear among them. When he began screaming uncontrollably, the psychologists observing him finally accepted that he wasn't faking, and brought him out.

At this stage the experiment was monitored by external consultants, including a young psychologist named Dr Christina Maslach. Called in to interview the participants, she was horrified to see what was being done to them. Her vehement protests broke the spell, and six days into what should have been a 14-day experiment, Dr Zimbardo and his colleagues finally realised that things had gone too far, and called a halt. Unthinkable in these litigious times, the Stanford Prison Experiment remains a salutary lesson in what can happen within institutions where one group is officially given total power over another far more vulnerable group.

3 Work in pairs. Practice using participle clauses.
A: turn to page 128.
B: turn to page 130.

Ⓖ **Grammar focus** – explanation & more practice of participle clauses on page 140

Glossary

blindfold *(verb)* – to cover someone's eyes with a cloth to prevent them from seeing

strip-search *(verb)* – to remove someone's clothes in order to look for anything hidden such as a weapon

delouse *(verb)* – to remove lice from someone's skin or hair

smock *(noun)* – long, loose shirt

eavesdrop *(verb)* – to listen to someone else's conversation

litigious *(adjective)* – keen to resolve disputes by going to law

Function globally managing conversations

Warm up

Work in pairs. Choose a different topic each from the list below, and prepare some ideas for a talk. Take it in turns to talk for one minute. Then ask your partner questions about what you heard.

- airports
- a kind deed
- neighbours
- luggage
- operations

Listening

1 🔵 **2.23–2.28** Listen to five people chatting around a table and exchanging stories. Number the topics 1–11 in the order your hear them (there is one topic you will not need).

5	a cutlery in a rucksack	___
8	b a hip operation	___
2	c a kind stranger	___
10	d a phone call	___
7	e a knee operation	___
9	f friendly neighbours	___
6	g a flick knife	___
1	h coffee and cookies	___
3	i stolen luggage	___
4	j cheap flights	___
11	k a request for a lift	___
	l a rude neighbour	___

2 Compare your answers with a partner. What can you remember about each topic?

3 🔵 **2.29–2.34** Can you remember how any of the topics were linked in the conversation? Listen to extracts from the conversation and note the links.

Language focus

1 Match the groups of expressions 1–6 to the functions a–f.

a Holding your turn
b Inviting someone to continue
c Interrupting
d Introducing a totally new topic
e Returning to the subject
f Changing the direction of the conversation

1 Sorry, can I just say something?
  Sorry to interrupt, but …

2 If I can just finish, please.

3 Sorry, do go on.

4 Anyway, going back to my neighbour …
  As I was saying …

5 By the way, talking of neighbours …
  Incidentally, on the subject of operations …
  That reminds me of a time when I missed a flight …

6 Changing the subject completely, …

2 Why do you think we use expressions like these to manage the conversation? What other forms of body language are sometimes used to interrupt or hold your turn?

Pronunciation

1 🔵 **2.35** Work in pairs. Listen and underline the word or words that carry the main stress in the expressions in *Language focus* exercise 1.

2 Listen again to check your ideas. Then practise by repeating the phrases.

Speaking

1 Work in small groups, and appoint a monitor. One person should choose a topic from the Warm up and start the conversation. Then continue the conversation, interrupting and changing the topic as appropriate. The monitor should tick (✔) the expressions used during the conversation, and at the end, give feedback to the group.

2 Repeat the process with a different topic, and without a monitor.

Global English

Linguistic **heroes** and **villains**
by David Crystal

People are very ready to speak of language users as heroes and villains. Among the heroes are **those** who have been prepared to go on hunger strike, fight, or even die to get their language officially recognised by their country. One
5 of the most famous events took place in Dhaka in former East Pakistan on 21 February 1952. A number of students demonstrating for recognition of Bangla as **one** of the country's two national languages were shot and killed by police. In 1999, the United Nations designated that
10 date as International Mother Language Day to promote linguistic and cultural diversity and multilingualism. We've been celebrating it ever since.

International languages are often described as linguistic villains because of the way they are perceived to be
15 unstoppable forces crushing the life out of minority languages. English, as the language with greatest global presence, attracts the label more than **most**, but any major language, eg Chinese, Spanish, Arabic, Russian, has been called a villain at some point or other by minority communities
20 who see language loss as a daily reality. Nor does **it** have to be one of the great international languages. Just as a small fish can be eaten by a bigger fish, so a language spoken by very few people can be threatened by another language spoken by not many more. It is all a question of power.

25 Any government can be a villain if it does not care for the linguistic diversity in **its** community.

How do governments show they care? By developing a language policy that recognises the two motivations for language use in the modern world. As soon as a country
30 finds itself interacting – politically, economically, and socially – with others who speak different languages, it needs to adopt a *lingua franca*. Intelligibility is then the prime consideration. At the same time, it needs to recognise the wishes of **those** within its borders who
35 wish to preserve their individuality, as expressed through local languages and dialects. Identity is then the prime consideration. The two motivations do not have to be in conflict: the need for intelligibility is outward-looking; the need for identity
40 is inward-looking. The optimal outcome is when a country sees a place for both and manages the process efficiently.
45 Where there is an intelligent and sensitive language policy, there are no villains.

Warm up

1 Work in pairs. Which of the following sentences are true for your language?

- My language is spoken in more than one country.
- My language is a minority language.
- My language threatens, or has threatened, other languages.
- My language is well known internationally.
- My language is or has been in danger of disappearing.

2 Which sentences could be true for English, in your opinion?

Reading

1 Read *Linguistic heroes and villains* and answer the questions.

1 Does the author think English is a hero or a villain or neither?

2 What is the author's conclusion about how to avoid *linguistic villains*?

2 Read the text again and choose the correct answer.

1 In 2000 Bangla was recognised as an official language in Pakistan.
   a true   b false   c the text doesn't say

2 Why are international languages described as villains?
   a because their national governments impose them
   b because people believe they destroy minority languages
   c because they are the biggest languages

3 What should be the prime consideration for a language policy?
   a intelligibility between nations
   b identity of the people who speak it
   c both a and b

3 What do the following words in bold in the text refer to?

1 those (line 2)   3 most (line 17)   5 its (line 26)
2 one (line 7)   4 it (line 20)   6 those (line 34)

Speaking

1 Look at the following ways that governments can impose or protect languages. How effective do you think they are? Give each one a mark from 1 (largely ineffective) to 4 (very effective).

- Establish an academy that 'protects' the purity of the language.
- Introduce language study at an early age for children.
- Ban or prohibit use of other languages in public spaces.
- Make a language obligatory in all public offices.
- Give money to artists, authors, film-makers, etc to produce works in the language.
- Change the language to make it simpler to learn.

2 Compare your answers with a partner.

Writing a report

Reading

1 Look at the charts below.

1 With a partner, discuss what they illustrate, and what main conclusions can be drawn from them.

2 Read Jose Manuel's report. Does it mention the same ideas that you discussed?

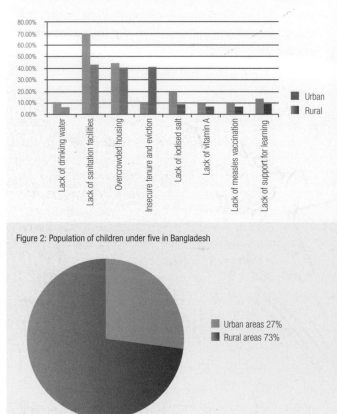

Figure 1: Deprivation among children under five in rural and urban areas of Bangladesh

Figure 2: Population of children under five in Bangladesh

Urban areas 27%
Rural areas 73%

1 Child poverty is one of the most serious issues in the world today. Indeed, given that an estimated one in two children worldwide live in poverty, it should be an urgent priority for the world's governments to tackle. Although there is no universal consensus on how to define poverty, a useful picture can be gained by using a definition agreed at the 1995 World Summit for Social Development. According to this formula, poverty can be measured by studying degrees of deprivation in eight key dimensions, namely: food, safe drinking water, sanitation facilities, health, shelter, education, information and access to services.

2 In Bangladesh, where children under 18 account for around 44% of the population, the problem of child poverty is particularly acute. Figure 1 shows the percentages of children under five years old in urban and rural areas of Bangladesh who suffer deprivation in specific situations related to the dimensions. It demonstrates that by far the most urgent problem affecting all children is lack of access to sanitation facilities, and that this is worse in rural than urban areas (71% and 46% of children respectively). Overcrowded housing is the second most severe deprivation overall, affecting around 40% of all children. In general, there is greater deprivation in rural areas, which is a matter of concern given that the majority of children in Bangladesh live in rural areas (see Figure 2). By contrast, lack of security in tenure and risk of eviction is higher in urban areas, where 41% of children are deprived, while the figure is closer to 11% in rural areas.

3 There are some signs of improvement, however. The growth rate of the Bangladeshi economy has increased steadily from 4% in the 1980s to an average of 5.5% since 2000, with a peak of 6.7% in 2006. Moreover, there has been a significant fall in population growth over the last few decades, from annual average of 3% in the 1970s to 1.5% in 2000. These trends need to be sustained if Bangladesh is to achieve the Millennium Development Goal of reducing poverty by half by 2015.

2 What do these phrases relate to?

1 one of the most serious issues in the world today
2 this formula
3 eight key dimensions
4 44% of the population
5 by far the most urgent problem
6 the second most severe deprivation overall
7 a matter of concern
8 some signs of improvement
9 these trends

3 Draw graphs to illustrate the trends mentioned in paragraph 3.

Writing skills: paragraph structure

1 Read the information about paragraph structure.

A paragraph normally expresses a single idea. This is usually stated in the *topic sentence* (often the first or second sentence), and the following *supporting sentences* then give more details. These should be linked together in a logical order.

2 Look at the supporting sentences in paragraphs 1 and 3 of the report. In which of the following ways does each one support or extend the topic sentence?

- elaboration
- a reason
- an example or evidence
- a consequence
- a definition
- a conclusion

3 Reorganise the following sentences into a logical paragraph. Which is the topic sentence, and which types of supporting sentence are included?

1 Nowhere is this phenomenon more clearly seen than in the Amazon rainforests.
2 As a result of this, many species of plants and animals are seriously endangered.
3 It is therefore vital to act now to save the rainforests before these are all lost.
4 Here, deforestation is due to a number of factors including logging, mining and the hunger for land.
5 The Earth's forests are disappearing fast.

Preparing to write

1 With a partner, choose one or two global issues that you would like to research and write about. How would you define the issue(s), and what do you already know about current and recent trends and developments?

2 Research your topic and make notes for your report.

Describing facts and figures

- *As illustrated in Figure 1, ... / The chart shows / demonstrates that ...*
- *In recent decades / Since 2010 / Over the last few years* poverty has declined.
- There has been a(n) *fall / drop / decrease / decline / rise / increase* in *the number of people visiting the country / tourism*.
- In 2010 the GDP *rose / increased / rocketed / peaked / fell / decreased / plummeted*.
- From 2005 to 2010, there was a *sharp / dramatic / marked / significant / slight* fall in the incidence of malaria.
- Between 2000 and 2010 unemployment *rose steadily / fluctuated / remained stable*.

Writing

Write your report, paying attention to paragraph structure.

Register awareness

1 Read the text. In what ways do you think an awareness of register can help you express yourself?

An important skill at advanced level is understanding the *style* or *register* of a word, expression or grammatical structure. These terms relate to features such as level of formality and the kind of situations, activities or social settings in which they are used. Most words and expressions are neutral in style or register, but some are marked in a particular way, eg *old-fashioned*, *spoken*, *slang*, *business*, *academic*, *scientific*.

2 Read some extracts from texts in Unit 5. How can you tell whether they are from written or spoken texts?

1 Lack of access to education has resulted in high levels of illiteracy.
2 We've got our work globally across the world at community level where we're actually seeing some good things.
3 I was like no, I haven't got anything in here, I haven't got scissors, I haven't got a knife, nothing.
4 The rebellion crushed, the guards then set up a 'privilege cell' system.

3 Try to guess the register of the words or expressions in italics, and match them to a word or words from the box. More than one may be applicable.

disapproving   formal   informal   legal   literary
old-fashioned

1 Don't be such a *goody-goody*! You're always trying to get in the teacher's good books.
2 So is he the good guy in the movie? No, he's the *baddy*.
3 Your words are unworthy of you. *My heart grieves*.
4 He was charged with *grievous bodily harm* and attempted murder.

4 Compare your ideas with a partner and discuss these questions.

- What clues did you use to make your decision?
- Can you think of any words you have learnt recently that have a special register?
- Which of the following have you used to check a word's register?
  - a the context
  - b other words in the text
  - c a dictionary
  - d asking someone

Trade & Commerce

Listening

1 Work in pairs. Discuss the questions.

• Which countries or areas are your country's main trading partners? What items or commodities do you import from them, and how are they transported to your country?

• What do you know about the trade route known as the 'Silk Road'? What images does it conjure up for you?

2 2.36–2.40 Listen to someone talking about different aspects of the Silk Road, and match each section 1–5 to one of the pictures.

3 Work in pairs. Look at the pictures and discuss what you can remember about each section. What were the most interesting facts that you learnt?

4 Work in pairs. Can you remember which items in the box were traded from East to West, and which from West to East? Listen to sections 3 and 4 again to check your ideas.

algebra	astronomy	compass	ginger
glass	gunpowder	linen	paper-making
porcelain	printing press	saddles	
shipbuilding	silk	spices	wool

5 2.41 Listen to the final part of the talk and answer the questions.

1 What else was exchanged on the Silk Road as well as goods?
2 What does the speaker say about the links between the Silk Road and globalisation?
3 How is the Silk Road being used today?

6 Would you be interested in going on a modern Silk Road tour? Why / Why not? What would be the highlights or downsides of such an experience?

Extend your vocabulary – *change* and *exchange*

1 Delete the noun that does not normally collocate with the verb.
1 **exchange** contracts / addresses / views / your hair style
2 **change** trains / house / gear / the subject
3 **swap** places / roles / currency / comics
4 **switch** lanes / sides / smiles / channels

2 Using some of the collocations, tell a partner about …
1 details of things that you have done in the last week, month or year.
2 things you have never done.

Pronunciation

1 Read the following sentences from the listening passage, and discuss with a partner whether your voice goes up or down on the words and phrases in italics.

1 Silk was ideal for overland travel as it was *light*, easy to *carry* and took up little *space*.
2 They also faced the ever present threat of *bandits*, not to mention *wars*, *plagues* and *natural disasters*.
3 Caravanserai were used not only by traders and *merchants*, but also by *pilgrims*, *missionaries*, *soldiers*, *nomads* and *urban dwellers*.

2 2.42 Listen to check your answers. Then practise reading the sentences with the audio.

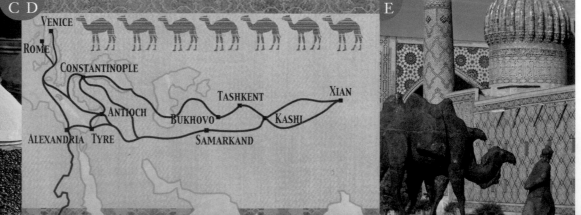

VENICE
ROME
CONSTANTINOPLE
ANTIOCH
ALEXANDRIA TYRE
BUKHOVO
SAMARKAND
TASHKENT
KASHI
XIAN

3 Work in pairs. Compile lists for two of the following categories:

- scarce commodities or resources
- items or commodities that are often illegally traded
- items that are currently in great demand in retail outlets
- things you can buy in your local street market

4 Read your lists and compare them with another pair.

Grammar

1 Read the sentences in the grammar box and do the tasks below.

> a *The Silk Road **consisted** of an extensive network of land and sea routes.*
> b *Many important scientific and technological innovations **were transported** to the West.*
> c *When the silk arrived in Europe it **was made into** luxury goods.*
> d *Caravanserai **were used** not only by traders and merchants, but also by pilgrims, missionaries, soldiers, nomads and urban dwellers.*
> e *By the end of the 14ᵗʰ century, its importance **had** greatly **diminished**.*
> f *Today the Silk Road **is again being used** by traders.*

1 Which sentences contain an active verb form and which a passive verb form?
2 Choose the correct alternative:
- use *an active / a passive* verb form when the main focus of the sentence is the *doer* of the action (or *agent*)
- use *an active / a passive* verb form when the main focus of the sentence is the *action* or the *object* of the action
3 Complete the rule:
- to form the passive, use the appropriate form of the verb _____ + the _____
- Which of the passive sentences mention an agent? Why is an agent not mentioned in the other passive sentences?

2 Complete the text with an appropriate active or passive form of the verb.

> Trade (1) _____ (*conduct*) between different groups or societies since prehistoric times. The earliest trade (2) _____ (*probably / consist*) of forms of barter, in which goods (3) _____ (*exchange*) without using a medium of exchange such as money. Later, currency (4) _____ (*introduce*) to facilitate a wider exchange of goods and services. The importance of international trade (5) _____ (*increase*) in recent decades, and trade organisations such as the EU and NAFTA (6) _____ (*establish*) to promote trade between member countries. Nowadays, trade (7) _____ (*increasingly / carry out*) with few restrictions within countries; however, trade blocs (8) _____ (*may / regulate*) international trade by means of quotas and restrictions. Tariffs (9) _____ (*usually / impose*) on imports, and some form of taxation (10) _____ (*may / also / impose*) on exports. However, it is unlikely that completely free trade (11) _____ (*ever / establish*) in the future or that forms of taxation (12) _____ (*completely / disappear*).

3 Work in pairs. Think of two or three commonly traded items or commodities (eg wheat, coffee, oil, cars, electronic goods). Write passive sentences about the past, present and future of the commodities using some of the words below and a range of verb forms.

> design   discover   export   grow   import
> introduce   invent   manufacture   trade   use

4 Read your sentences to another pair without mentioning the names of the items. Can they guess what you have written about?

5 Work in small groups. Tell your group about an important contribution that your country, or another country you know, has contributed to the world. This could be:

- an art form
- a commodity
- a custom
- an invention
- an institution
- a manufactured item
- a religion or philosophy
- a technique

Ask and answer questions about each contribution.

G **Grammar focus** – explanation & more practice of the passive on page 142

Trade & Commerce

Part 2

Speaking
Freedom and slavery

Reading
The Long Song

Vocabulary
Ways of looking

Speaking

1 Look at the pictures, and with a partner discuss their connection with trade.

2 ⊘ **2.43** Read some quotations about freedom and slavery, and complete each one with a suitable word, as in the example. Then listen to compare your ideas with the original quotations.

1 The moment the slave resolves that he will no longer be a slave, his fetters fall. Freedom and slavery are mental ___states___. (Gandhi)

2 The danger of the past was that men became slaves. The danger of the future is that men may become _____. (Erich Fromm)

3 The history of men's _____ to women's emancipation is more interesting perhaps than the story of that emancipation itself. (Virginia Woolf)

4 I disapprove of what you say, but I will defend to the death your _____ to say it. (Voltaire)

5 To be free is not merely to cast off one's chains, but to live in a way that respects and enhances the freedom of _____. (Nelson Mandela)

6 Freedom is never voluntarily given by the oppressor; it must be demanded by the _____. (Martin Luther King)

7 Governments need _____ to protect them against their enslaved and oppressed subjects. (Tolstoy)

8 Everything can be taken from a man but one thing; the last of the human freedoms – to choose one's _____ in any given set of circumstances. (Viktor Frankl)

3 Which quotation do you like best, and why? Choose two or three of the quotations to discuss with a partner.
- How far do you agree or disagree with the ideas, and why?
- Can you think of any real current or historical situations to which they could be applied?

Reading

1 Read extracts from *The Long Song* by Andrea Levy. What is the relationship between Caroline, Godfrey and July? Do you think the story takes place *before*, *during* or *after* the emancipation of the slaves? Why?

2 Which of the underlined words refer to …
- facial expression?
- sounds?
- movement?

3 Guess the meaning of each of the highlighted words.

4 Find evidence in the text for the following statements.

1 Caroline does not initially understand Godfrey's refusal to serve her.
2 July was surprised by Godfrey's reaction.
3 Godfrey starts behaving like the master.
4 Caroline resists Godfrey's refusal to help.
5 Caroline realises that their roles have been reversed.

5 Which of these words could describe the characters' attitudes, and why?

aggressive	arrogant	controlling
defiant	loyal	self-confident
submissive	timid	

1 In what way(s) could Caroline be 'like a fish newly landed from the water' (last paragraph)?
2 Which of the characters, if any, did you sympathise with? Why?

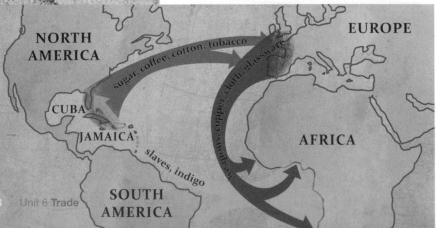

NORTH AMERICA

EUROPE

sugar, coffee, cotton, tobacco

weapons, copper, cloth, glassware

CUBA

JAMAICA

AFRICA

slaves, indigo

SOUTH AMERICA

The Long Song

'Hurry along, Godfrey. Pick up these things', Caroline said. Godfrey stared at the sack, the small trunk and the cloth **valise** that stood between him and the **missus**. His missus, with an exasperated sigh, indicated again the items she wished Godfrey to transport.

But Godfrey, still <u>scratching</u> his head, said, 'You wan' me put these on the cart and take you into town?'

'Of course, into the **gig**. And I am in a hurry to be gone'.

'So you wan' me lift them into the gig and then drive you into town?'

'Godfrey, do not play the fool with me. You know I must go to town for my own safety until all this trouble is past. Now, let us be gone'.

And Godfrey, looking down on the missus, sucked loudly on his teeth before saying, 'Then you must pay me, missus'.

July cupped her hands over her mouth so her <u>gasp</u> and <u>giggle</u> would not escape. While all Caroline managed to <u>utter</u> was, 'What did you say?'.

'Me said', Godfrey began, 'that me will need payment if me is to take you into town'.

'Payment?', the missus repeated. She <u>frowned</u> upon Godfrey, then looked quizzically to July for some explanation of his behaviour. But July was silent – her mouth fixed with a <u>grimace</u> of a child in the thrill of a game.

'Don't be ridiculous, Godfrey', Caroline said, 'Now, pick up the things or I will see you punished for this'.

Godfrey <u>sighed</u>. He then walked past the missus into the hall and sat himself down upon one of the **massa**'s wooden chairs. 'Then punish me, missus', he said as he lifted first one leg, and then the other, over the arms of the planter's seat and sat as if waiting for someone to remove his boots …

'Get up, get up!' Caroline jumped twice in her fury. 'Do as you are **bid**', then made to strike Godfrey with her closed fist. But Godfrey <u>seized</u> both her wrists with so tight a grip that the missus's face contorted into a <u>wince</u>. Her mouth fell in wordless agony as Godfrey raised himself from the chair. As he stood higher, he bore down upon the missus's wrists until the pressure of the pain impelled her to <u>kneel</u> in front of him. As the missus, overwhelmed by him, went limp upon the ground, Godfrey let go of her wrists.

July made a move towards the missus, but Godfrey shouted, 'Stop!'.

He sat once more and began playing with his fingernail, while Caroline Mortimer, quivering at his feet like a fish newly landed from the water, slowly lifted her head, wiped her snivelling nose upon the back of her hand, and quietly asked him, 'How much?'

Vocabulary

1 Read two sentences from the text. Which of the verbs in bold has a literal meaning, and which could have both a literal and a metaphorical meaning?

*Godfrey **stared at** the sack, the small trunk and the cloth valise …*

*And Godfrey, **looking down on** the missus, sucked loudly on his teeth …*

2 Work in pairs. Decide whether each of these multi-word verbs has a literal meaning, a metaphorical meaning or both.

> look after   look away   look back on
> look forward to   look into   look on
> look out for   look round   look up
> look up to

3 Work in pairs. Read texts 1 and 2 below. Guess the meaning of the underlined words. Then check your ideas with a dictionary.

1 Lucy opened the kitchen door and <u>peered</u> inside the room. In the darkness, she could just <u>make out</u> a figure standing next to the fridge. She switched on the light and <u>glimpsed</u> James just about to eat a slice of the chocolate cake she had baked earlier in the day. When James <u>caught sight of</u> her standing in the doorway, he refused to <u>look her in the eye</u>. She <u>glared</u> at him. 'What on earth were you doing?' she snapped.

2 David sat <u>gazing</u> at the bill in disbelief, and frowning. 'There must be some mistake', he gasped and tried to <u>catch the waiter's eye.</u> Charles <u>glanced</u> at his watch. 'I'd better be going,' he mumbled, and quickly made his way out of the restaurant.

4 Write a few sentences describing a scene in which two people meet and there is some conflict. Include …

- a description of the way they looked at each other.
- their facial expressions.
- what they said.

5 Read your scenes to other students, paying attention to the past tense endings. Which scene do you like best, and why?

Andrea Levy is a novelist who was born in London in 1956 after her parents immigrated there from Jamaica. She has written a number of widely acclaimed novels, including the prize-winning *Small Island*. *The Long Song*, published in 2010, is set in a Jamaican sugar plantation around the time of the abolition of slavery and tells the story of Godfrey and July who are slaves of Caroline Mortimer, the plantation owner.

Reading and Speaking

1 Work in pairs. Look at the industries in the box. Which are the main sources of income in your city or area? Are these industries growing or declining? Give reasons for your answers.

> agriculture   finance   fishing   forestry
> IT   manufacturing   mining
> service industries   tourism

2 Read three different descriptions of Bangalore on page 71, a modern industrial and commercial city in India. Decide what sort of text they are (factual, descriptive, narrative, literary or persuasive, etc) and where you might find them. What words and phrases in the texts tell you this?

3 Read again and answer the questions.

1 What is the main industry in Bangalore?
2 What are the positive points about the city that each author puts forward? What words does the author use to describe them?
3 In text A, how does the author describe the transition taking place in Bangalore?
4 Is the author optimistic about the city's future?
5 What basic problem is the city faced with? What is the cause of this?

4 Find words in the texts that mean:

1 develop into (text A)
2 very poor area of a city (text A)
3 waste substances (text A)
4 friendly (*formal*) (text B)
5 very interesting (text B)
6 pleasant and comfortable (*formal*) (text B)

5 Work in pairs. Discuss the questions.

• What overall impression of Bangalore do you get from these texts?
• If you were going to Bangalore (on business or as a tourist), what aspects of the city would you be interested to learn more about?

Listening

1 Read the definition of the word *outsourcing*. Can you think of any examples of outsourcing in your country? What are the advantages and disadvantages of this type of arrangement?

> **outsourcing BUSINESS:** an arrangement in which work is done by people from outside your company, usually by a company that is expert in that type of work.

2 🔊 **2.44** Listen to an Indian entrepreneur talking about India's IT (information technology) and BPO (Business Process Outsourcing) industries. How has increased demand ultimately affected India's outsourcing business?

3 Listen again and answer the questions.

1 What do companies typically outsource?
2 Why did India's IT-BPO sector become a world-leading industry in the 1990s?
3 What has the increased demand for outsourcing in India led to?
4 What have some British and American companies begun to do?
5 How have Indian companies begun to adapt to changes in the outsourcing destination?

4 The growth of the IT-BPO sector in India was very much linked to English. What role does English or other foreign languages play in the main industries in your country?

Bangalore

A When I drive down Hosur Main Road, when I turn into Electronics City Phase 1 and see the companies go past, I can't tell you how exciting it is to me. General Electric, Dell, Siemens – they're all here in Bangalore. And so many more are on their way. There is construction everywhere. Piles of mud everywhere. Piles of stones. Piles of bricks. The entire city is masked in smoke, smog, powder, cement dust. It is under a veil. When the veil is lifted, what will Bangalore be like?

Maybe it will be a disaster: slums, sewage, shopping malls, traffic jams, policemen. But you never know. It may turn out to be a decent city, where humans can live like humans. A new Bangalore for a new India. And then I can say that, in my own way, I helped to make New Bangalore.

B What do you call a congenial, captivating, cosmopolitan confluence of software and shopping malls, electronics and environment friendliness, salubrious climate and cleanliness, modern outlook and old worldliness, precision engineering and pubs? You call it India's best city for business. It is also called Bangalore.

C City and capital (since 1830) of Karnataka (formerly Mysore) state, southern India. One of India's largest cities, Bangalore lies on an east-west ridge in the Karnataka Plateau in the south-eastern part of the state. Pleasant winters and tolerable summers make it a popular place of residence, but water supply for its increasing industrial and domestic needs is a problem, because its 914 mm of annual rainfall is inadequate and there are no rivers nearby.

From the late 20th century the city became a centre of high-technology industry, and a number of large multinational technology corporations opened offices there. In addition, major domestic firms such as Infosys and Wipro established headquarters in the city.

Vocabulary

1 Choose the correct word to complete the phrases from the listening. Which of the phrases refer to a problem? Which refer to dealing with a problem?

1 For companies, **becoming / getting rid of** these tasks means lower costs.
2 This has kept **pushing / pulling** up the cost of salaries.
3 Infrastructure in these areas has not been able to keep **speed / pace with** growth.
4 There have been some attempts to find a **way / path** round these issues.
5 India has become a **sacrifice / victim** of its own success.

2 Look at the adjectives (1–3) that can collocate with *problem*. Match them with the correct meaning (a–c). Do the same with the verbs (4–8) and meanings (d–h).

1	major	a	urgent
2	pressing	b	very difficult
3	intractable	c	very big
4	pose	d	lessen
5	tackle	e	find a solution to
6	alleviate	f	make worse
7	exacerbate	g	deal with
8	solve	h	present

3 Complete the dialogues with the correct form of phrases from exercises 1 and 2.

A: It's a(n) (1) _____ problem. It's at the root of the nation's troubles. It's why we're not (2) _____ with other countries.
B: But it's difficult to see how it can be (3) _____ or even (4) _____ in some way. Unfortunately, I can't see any (5) _____ it.
A: The fact that child poverty still (6) _____ a huge problem in some European countries is a scandal. The EU need to (7) _____ this now.
B: Absolutely. I think what is vital is recognition that it's a(n) (8) _____ problem. More has to be done immediately to make sure it isn't (9) _____ any further.

Speaking

1 Look at these issues and decide which three are the most problematic in your country. Make notes on the problems in these areas.

- employment and job creation
- benefits, social security and health care
- pre-school childcare
- education
- higher education
- infrastructure
- cities / urban policy
- rural areas
- environment

2 Work in small groups. Discuss the problems you have noted down. How are they being tackled? How successful are these measures? How else could the problems be tackled?

Trade & Commerce

Part 4

Speaking
Investments

Reading
The new golden age

Extend your vocabulary
gold and *golden*

Grammar
Cleft sentences

Speaking

1 Look at the following eight things that people invest in. Which do you think are the safest investments? Rank them in order from 1 (safest investment) to 8 (riskiest investment).

art	bank accounts	collectables
gold	government bonds	land
property	stocks	

2 Compare your answers with a partner, giving reasons for your opinions. Try and agree on the three safest investments.

Useful phrases

- can be *risky / tricky / high-risk*
- *isn't going to hold its value / will depreciate*
- is dependent on *supply and demand / the state of the economy / fashion and trends*
- is *a safe bet / low-risk / guaranteed to*
- will *hold its value / appreciate in value / show a profit / give a good return of interest*
- *offers protection against inflation / can provide income*

Reading

1 Read *The new golden age* and choose the best summary of the article.

- After a long absence, gold is popular again now.
- Gold is popular now, but it always has been for many reasons.
- The popularity of gold is misguided.

2 Match the words in bold in the text to the definitions below.

1 apparently unimportant (though actually important)
2 easy to press into different shapes
3 things that can be bought and sold
4 increasing quickly by a large amount
5 existing now as a modern example of something or someone from the past
6 laughing at
7 uncontrolled activity or excitement
8 passion

3 Read again. Decide if the statements are true (*T*), false (*F*) or the text doesn't say (*DS*).

1 The price of gold always rises in moments of crisis.
2 It is important to distinguish real gold from imitations.
3 Gold contains small quantities of toxic material.
4 Gold represents much more than a simple metal.
5 Transmutation is the process by which gold is converted into base lead.
6 The author views bankers as modern alchemists.
7 Gold will be worth less in the future.

4 Answer the questions, giving reasons for your answers.

- The reading text was written in 2010. Do you think gold is still as important now?
- Do you agree with the author that gold is more than just a valuable metal?

Extend your vocabulary – *gold* and *golden*

The adjective *gold* means 'made of gold':
People are investing in gold jewellery.
The adjective *golden* can mean 'gold in colour':
He has lovely golden hair.
Golden can also mean 'successful':
We're living in a new golden age.

1 Is *gold* or *golden* the correct word in these sentences?

1 She's the company's _____ girl at the moment.
2 He just missed out on the _____ medal.
3 They were the _____ years of jazz.
4 There are miles and miles of _____ beaches.

2 *Golden* can also be used in fixed phrases with different meanings. Cross out the words below which do not collocate with *golden*. Use a dictionary to help you. What do the other phrases mean?

address	anniversary	dream
handshake	oldie	opportunity
remark	rule	

3 Use two of the collocations and make sentences to show their meaning.

The new golden age

Gold is more valuable than ever. But what inspires our **lust** is more than mere money – gold speaks to something elemental in all of us.

The price of gold is rising, both **mocking** and relieving the gloom and **turmoil** of a worldwide recession. The world market price of this valuable metal is **shooting up** faster and more than most other **commodities**. This always happens. It did when the world turned fearful of terrorist attacks and when the dotcom bubble burst. In uncertain times it is gold that the hard-headed and stony-hearted financial gamblers invest in.

Gold has been used as currency for more than 5,000 years.

Through the centuries efforts have been made to ensure its genuineness – using official stamps and symbols. It is soft and **malleable**. When alloyed with other elements its density changes and you can get a whole range from reddish orange to white. Talented artisans and craftsmen have been inspired by it and worked it to make objects of eternal beauty, treasured and desired by humans through the world, through the ages.

'Gold is just a metal.' Yes and no. What this **mere** metal represents is meanings far beyond high price tags – emblematic, metaphorical, literary and emotional meanings.

It is in the heads of old alchemists that the most important symbolic aspect of gold is to be found. The idea of turning base lead into noble gold, a transmutation, took many into the clouds of fantasy. In their pursuit of gold, what they were also pursuing was the 'elixir of life'. They didn't find it. High-flying financial gamblers and investment bankers were **latter-day** alchemists, making fantastical promises. They couldn't turn paper into gold. So the people only trust the real stuff now, an act of faith. Its value depends on how much people believe in it. Millions clearly do. What will be fascinating is to see what comes next in this new golden age and whether the shining yellow hope people are clutching will turn to straw.

Glossary

the dotcom bubble *(noun)* – the rapid increase in value of the shares of internet (.com) companies and their subsequent crash at the end of the 1990s

alloy *(verb)* – combine two or more metals

Grammar

1 Look at the two sentences. Decide which phrase in bold is being emphasised in the second sentence. Then read the grammar box.

More than mere money inspires our lust.
*What inspires **our lust** is **more than mere money**.*

> To emphasise information in a sentence we can use sentences beginning with:
> - *It is / was* … (+ relative clause)
>   *It is gold that financial gamblers invest in.*
> - *What* + clause + *is / was* (+ clause / noun phrase)
>   *What will be fascinating is to see what comes next.*
>   *What they were also pursuing was the 'elixir of life'.*
> - in a *What* clause, the auxiliary *do / did* can also be used to emphasise actions
>   *What the bankers did was make fantastical promises.*

2 Rewrite the sentences to emphasise the words in italics. Use the word in bold.

1 The most precious of all metals is *gold.*   **it**
_____ is the most precious of all metals.

2 I really hate *how gold makes people greedy.*   **what**
_____ how gold makes people greedy.

3 He could never resist *the sight of gold.*   **was**
_____ the sight of gold.

4 *The price of gold* went up.   **that**
_____ went up.

5 The alchemists experimented *with turning base lead into gold.*   **did**
_____ with turning base lead into gold.

3 Complete three of these sentences with your own ideas.

- All I really want is …
- What annoys me most …
- The first time I saw … was …
- What the world needs now is …
- It is … that causes most problems.

G Grammar focus – explanation & more practice of cleft sentences on page 142

Yasmin Alibhai-Brown is a well-known journalist originally from Uganda. She has worked for many major English newspapers and writes on issues relating to race, immigration and multiculturalism.

Function globally negotiating

Warm up

1 Work in pairs. What would you do and say in the following situations?

- You have a ticket for a plane, and at the check-in desk you are told that the flight is fully booked.
- You open your bank statement and find that you have been charged for going overdrawn for a few hours.
- You are the manager of a wholesale business and you want to persuade a retailer to switch their custom to you.
- You are interested in buying a second-hand car, but the price is too high.

2 Have you ever been in a similar situation? What happened?

Listening

1 🔘 **2.45–2.48** Listen to four conversations and match each one to a situation from the Warm up section.

1 What is the outcome in each case?
2 How similar were the people's reactions to your own ideas?

2 In which of the conversations did you hear the following, and what is the speaker referring to?

1 It didn't clear in time.
2 This is the one I've got my eye on.
3 45 is pushing it.
4 Surely those few hours shouldn't have incurred such a hefty fine?
5 You won't budge on that at all?
6 We could do 50.
7 We can throw in some cover.
8 There is availability.

Language focus

1 Read some sentences in which people are making an offer or concession, and complete each one with a word or phrase from the box.

| absolutely the best | acceptable | could | if you can |
| if you like | prepared to | then I can | what I can do |

1 _____ is upgrade you. Would that be _____?
2 Tell you what. _____ bring the price down, _____ place a firm order.
3 OK, I'm _____ throw in this radio, and I'll knock ten euros off.
4 We _____ offer you a credit note _____.
5 I'm afraid that's _____ we can do.

2 Read the responses below. Which express …

a acceptance? b refusal?
c indecision or a desire for further concessions?

1 Is that your final offer?
2 That sounds like a good compromise. I'll take it.
3 I'll leave it, thanks.
4 Fantastic, it's a deal.
5 I'm going to have to think about it and get back to you.
6 It will have to do I suppose.
7 Is there anything else you can do for me?
8 I'm afraid that wouldn't be viable for me.

Pronunciation

1 🔘 **2.49** Listen and complete the sentences. What is the function of the missing word(s)? Say the sentences.

1 But you _____ it's not my fault?
2 You _____ into overdraft.
3 Well, that _____ good.

2 🔘 **2.50** Listen and repeat the sentences you hear, adding an auxiliary verb.
You said you'd deliver them today.
You did say you'd deliver them today.

Speaking

Choose two opening lines, and improvise a conversation with a partner. What concessions did you obtain?

- I just wanted to talk to you about my overdraft limit.
- I bought this scarf here last month, and I was wondering if I could have a refund?
- I really like it, but I'm afraid it's beyond my price range.
- I'm sorry, but I asked for a non-smoking room.

Global voices

Warm up

Do you think customer service in shops and restaurants is good where you live? Think of a recent example to support your opinion. Then discuss in pairs.

Listening

1 🔊 **2.51** Listen to Marion from The Netherlands and Scott from England discuss customer service in different countries. Decide if these statements are true (*T*) or false (*F*) according to the speakers.

1 Marion thinks there are great differences between The Netherlands and England.
2 Marion thought it was unusual for the shop assistant to ask her if she needed help.
3 Scott felt that he was ignored in the mobile phone shop.
4 Both Scott and Marion think that some customer service is too much.

Marion, The Netherlands   Scott, England

2 🔊 **2.52** Now listen to Lillian from Kenya and Dominika from Poland talk about their experiences in shops in England. Answer the questions.

1 What does Lillian say about customer service in Kenya?
2 What did Lillian want to buy? Did she get it in the end?
3 Who has the better experience?
4 What difference did Dominika see between customer service in England and in Poland?

Lillian, Kenya   Dominika, Poland

Language focus: stance markers

1 Stance markers are words or phrases that mark a speaker's attitude or point of view. Look at the examples below. What is the stance marker in each one? How does it affect the meaning of the sentence?

… but sadly this is not extended to the, to the low-class citizens. You literally walk inside the door and then you get five people come up to you …

2 Match the phrases in A to phrases with similar meanings in B.

A	B
frankly	obviously
basically	in fact
actually	luckily
thankfully	to be honest
clearly	fundamentally

3 Work in pairs. Prepare a two line dialogue between a customer and a shop assistant. Try to incorporate one of the words from exercises 1 or 2 into your dialogue.

Speaking

1 Look at the following example of an English customer service questionnaire. Do you have similar things in your country? Evaluate the customer service in a shop you know by giving each statement below one of the following ratings: excellent, good, average, poor.

- Staff greeted you and offered to help you.
- Staff were friendly and cheerful.
- Staff answered your questions.
- Staff showed knowledge of the products / services.
- Staff were polite throughout.

2 Compare with a partner. Do you think these questionnaires …

- are a good idea?
- are useful?
- have any effect on customer service?

Writing emails

a Dear Anne

Thank you for your interest in our apartment. Yes, it is possible to snorkel off the local beaches, not to mention many other beautiful beaches nearby. You can see pictures of **all these** on our website. I am not an expert on snorkelling or water sports, but my husband Goran knows a lot about **such matters** and will be happy to give you advice!

Kind regards

Ivana

b Dear Anne

Thank you for your enquiry. In fact, we have two apartments, namely Villa Gemma and Villa Maria. **The former** is unfortunately not available for **the period you mention**, but we have availability for Villa Maria **at that time**. The weekly rate is 645 euros (in other words, slightly higher than for Villa Gemma, but it is a larger apartment and has recently been completely refurbished). Please visit our website for more details about **the accommodation**. We require a 15% deposit in advance (ie 96 euros) and the balance is due on arrival.

Kind regards

Ivana

c Dear Ms Petrovic

I have seen your apartment (Villa Gemma) on the Holiday Croatia website and am writing to enquire whether it is available for the period 19–26 July. We are four adults (two married couples, to be precise), and non-smokers. Also, could you please confirm the price, and your payment arrangements?

Best wishes

Anne Le Tissier

d Hi Ivana

Just a quick mail to say a big thank you to you and Goran for your kindness and hospitality during our stay in Croatia. It was great meeting you and we had a brilliant time. We'll certainly recommend Villa Maria to all our friends and hope to be back again very soon!

All the best

Anne

e Dear Anne

Further to our phone call, I can confirm that Villa Maria is reserved for you from 19–26 July. I would be grateful if you could now complete the booking by making a deposit **as discussed**, either by cheque, through the Cashbookers website or via a bank transaction. I look forward to hearing from you soon.

Kind regards

Ivana

f Dear Ivana

Thanks for your mail regarding Villa Maria. We are very interested in **this apartment**. Just one query – we are all keen on water sports (snorkelling in particular) and are ideally looking for a place near a good snorkelling beach. Is it possible to go snorkelling near the apartment?

Best wishes

Anne

Reading

1 Read a series of emails and put them in the correct chronological order. What was the outcome of the correspondence?

2 Without looking at the emails, what can you remember about …

1 Anne and her friends?
2 Villa Maria?
3 payment?
4 the local area?
5 Ivana and her family?

Writing skills: cohesion

1 Look at the phrases highlighted in the text. What does each one refer back to (in the same email or a previous email)?

2 Choose the correct or more natural alternative to complete the sentences.

1 There are two courses, namely Spanish A and Spanish B. The former is for complete beginners, while *the latter / the next* is at elementary level.

2 *As I promised / As promised*, I attach a visa application form for you to complete. Could you please return *this / that* at your earliest convenience?

3 Unfortunately, we have still not received the form. *This / That* means that we cannot process your application, so could you please forward it to me asap?

4 *Further / Farther* to our conversation, I have decided to cancel my order.

Linking ideas: clarification and emphasis

1 Read the emails on page 76 again and find expressions used to give clarification and emphasis.

2 Read the email below and delete the incorrect alternative.

My flight arrives in the early hours, at 2.25am (1) *to be precise / in particular*. I'd therefore be grateful if someone could meet me at the airport, or (2) *ideally / in other words / preferably* book me a taxi. There is no transport available at that time (3) *or rather / not to mention / to say nothing of* the fact that I will be exhausted. I'd like to request a ground floor room for my mother. She finds it difficult to walk far (4) *let alone / ie* climb stairs. I'd (5) *particularly / especially / precisely* like a quiet room, as during our last visit we were kept awake by noise – traffic (6) *for the most part / ideally / in particular*.

Preparing to write

With a partner, decide on one or more transactions that you would like to correspond about, eg enrolling on a course, booking a ticket or renting a flat or room.

A semi-formal email

- *I am writing / Just a quick email* to *enquire about / whether ... / thank you for ...*
- *Thank you / Thanks* for your *email / reply / enquiry*
- *I would be grateful if you could / Can you please* send me details of ... / *let me know ...*
- *I am attaching / Please find attached* a booking form
- *(Kind / Warm) Regards / Best wishes / (All the) Best / Many thanks / All for now*

Writing

Work in pairs. Using email conventions, you should each write an initial enquiry about the transaction you chose in *Preparing to write*, and pass the sheet of paper to your partner. Your partner should then write a reply to the enquiry. Continue the correspondence until the transaction is complete.

Learning language in context

1 Read a suggestion on how to extend your knowledge of English. With a partner, discuss which of the suggestions, if any, you already follow.

A good way to extend your knowledge of English at advanced level *is to* study language as it occurs naturally in real (spoken or written) texts. Here is a useful *procedure to follow*:

* Choose a text that interests you or that is *relevant to* your work or study, or one that you have already studied in class.

* Read or listen to the text until you understand it fully.

* Underline (or note down) any words, phrases, collocations and parts of sentences that you find interesting or useful, and that you would not normally use.

* Record the new language in your vocabulary notebook, including the original sentence.

* *Extend your knowledge* of the new items by looking them up in a learners dictionary or collocations dictionary. Add any useful information to your notebook.

* Use the new language in a sentence to help you remember it.

* Read through your vocabulary notebook *on a regular basis*; *the more often* you study something, *the better* it goes in.

2 Look again at the above section and notice the words and expressions in italics. The first two of these could be recorded as follows:

A good way to ... is to ...: A good way to make friends is to join an English class.

follow a procedure: adhere to, comply with, follow, go through, use a procedure (Macmillan Collocations Dictionary) If you follow the safety procedures when you dive, you are unlikely to suffer a serious accident.

3 Write a record for the other words and phrases. Then compare ideas with a partner.

Hearts & Minds

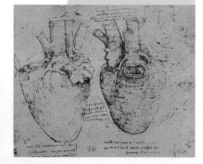

Reading

1 Discuss the questions in pairs.

1 Can you locate your heart? your pulse?

2 How is a person's heart rate calculated? Do you know what your own heart rate is?

2 Look at the photos of the animals. Which one do you think has …

1 the most heartbeats in its natural lifetime?

2 the fastest heart rate?

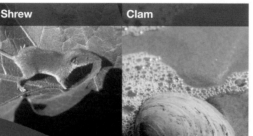

Shrew   Clam

3 Read *The Beating Heart* by the scientist, Ted Bianco and find answers to the questions in exercise 2. Then complete the chart with facts from the text, where possible.

	Whale	**Shrew**	**Clam**
weight			
heart rate			
lifespan (years)			

4 Match the explanations with the highlighted words in the text.

allowed number   be careful
extreme laziness
one animal eating another   relaxed
right   speed   wasteful

5 Work in pairs and discuss the questions.

1 Why may animals have the same number of heartbeats, yet their lifespans vary so much?

2 Make a list of five things that could speed up your heartbeats and five that could slow them down. In your view, is it better to use your quota of heartbeats by living 'fast and furious' or by having a slow and calm pace of life?

THE BEATING HEART

1 *Life on this planet beats out a tune; but while the notes are the same, the* tempo *varies both within the life of an individual and amongst individuals across the animal kingdom.* Whether you are incarnated as a shrew or a whale, you have a quota of around one billion heartbeats. Use them fast, or use them slow; that is the prerogative of each genus or species. But mind how you use them, because it is likely to govern your fundamental experience of life.

2 Weighing in at 2 grams, the Etruscan pygmy shrew is one of the lightest among mammals, while the blue whale tips the scales at an alarming 100,000 kilograms. A whale's heart is ten million times the size of that of a shrew, which is the difference between a drop of engine oil and a Volkswagen Beetle. Before its working life is over, each heart will have fed 38 litres of oxygen to each gram of tissue in the body. *Such remarkable consistency across the animal kingdom underlines the fact that, due to their underlying biochemical and biophysical processes, our bodies all wear out at roughly the same rate. We all have built-in obsolescence, rather like the automobiles constructed for the mass market during the boom years of the 1960s.*

3 But while the shrew and the whale may share some surprising characteristics, they depart from one another dramatically when one considers the tempo of their lives. The heart of the shrew beats at an exhausting 835 beats per minute, while that of the whale pumps away at just 20 per minute. Their lifespans also differ dramatically. The shrew is dead within a year, having been profligate with its lifetime ration of heartbeats. The whale chugs along for the best part of a century. There may have been some laid-back shrews out there once, but when you're that low in the food chain, living fast and furious is clearly the strategy of choice to ensure that you leave your mark, before succumbing to the pressures of predation.

4 The record for lethargy, however, goes to an altogether different class of organism; this accolade belongs to the clam. *At rest, a clam's heart beats just twice per minute.* And even when excited, it only makes it up to a frequency of 20. At the other end of the spectrum, the heart of the Etruscan shrew has been clocked at a record-breaking high of 1,511 beats per minute. It's hard to envisage a pump with so many moving parts working at such a rate. This is not a record that one should aim to emulate.

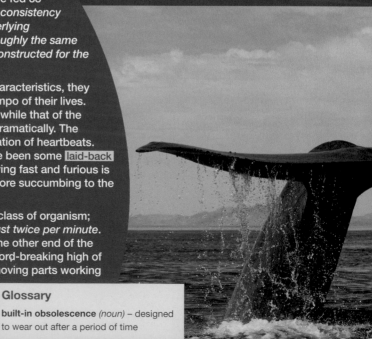

Whale

Glossary

built-in obsolescence *(noun)* – designed to wear out after a period of time

Grammar

1 Read some generalisations and delete the incorrect alternative(s) to complete the rules.

> *Exercise is good for the body.*
> *Humans have built-in obsolescence.*
> *The whale lives for over 100 years.*
> *An adult heart beats at around 72 beats per minute.*
>
> 1 use the zero article (–) to make a generalisation about a *singular / plural / uncountable* noun
> 2 use *the* to make an abstract, formal generalisation about a *singular / plural / uncountable* noun, seen as a representative of its class
> 3 use *a / an* to make a generalisation about an individual *singular / plural / uncountable* noun

2 Work in pairs. Write generalisations about one of the alternatives in each pair.

- doctors or hospitals
- heart surgery or medication
- a check-up or a cure
- the brain or the heart

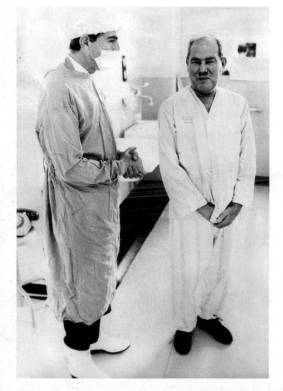

3 Read more rules about article use below. Then look again at the sentences in italics in the reading text and match each use of *the*, *a / an* or – to one of the rules below.

> 4 use *a / an* (with a singular noun), or – (with a plural or uncountable noun), to mention something for the first time, eg *I've joined **a** gym.* ***Exercise*** *is good for you.*
> 5 use *the* when a noun, or a characteristic or property of the noun, has already been mentioned ***The*** *gym is great, but **the** monthly rate is expensive.*
> 6 use *the* when a noun is defined to distinguish it from other nouns, for example with a defining relative clause or adverbial phrase, eg ***The** gym **I joined** is very expensive.* ***The** lifespan **of a clam** is very short.*
> 7 use *the* to refer to something seen as unique in our experience, eg ***the** sun*, ***the** food chain*
> 8 use *the* with superlatives (eg ***the** quickest*), ordinals (eg ***the** first / **the** tenth*) and words like ***the** same / **the** maximum / **the** main*

(G) Grammar focus – explanation & more practice of articles on page 144

Pronunciation

1 Where is the tongue when you pronounce the sounds /ð/ in *the* and /θ/ in *mouth*? What is the difference between the two sounds?

2 🔊 **3.01** How is *the* pronounced in these expressions? What is the pronunciation rule? Listen and repeat.

> the arm   the eye   the heart
> the mouth   the teeth   the tongue

3 Match the two halves of the proverbs and practise reading them aloud.

- Do you understand all the proverbs? Do you have similar ones in your language?
- Which is your favourite, and why?

1 In the eyes of the mouse
2 Never tickle the nose
3 The dog that is going to bite
4 When the stomach is full
5 The tongue is more to be feared

a the heart is glad (The Netherlands)
b the cat is a lion (Albania)
c than the sword (Japan)
d of a sleeping bear (Germany)
e does not show its teeth (Turkey)

Part 2

Reading & Listening
Romeo and Juliet: The balcony scene

Extend your vocabulary
Collocations with *heart*

Grammar
Unreal conditionals 1

Writing
Advice

Reading and Listening

1 Work in pairs and answer the questions.

- What do you know about Shakespeare's play *Romeo and Juliet*? Have you ever seen it?
- Read *Tragic Love*, and check your ideas.

2 Read a graphic novel version of the famous 'balcony scene' from the play, and answer the questions.

1 What does Romeo compare Juliet to?
2 What does Juliet say about Romeo's name, and her own name?
3 Why does Juliet compare Romeo to a rose?
4 What is the essential problem in their relationship?

Tragic Love

Shakespeare's *Romeo and Juliet* is one of the most iconic love stories of all time. It tells the tale of two teenagers from warring families (the Montagues and Capulets) who fell in love at first sight and married without their parents' knowledge or consent. Soon afterwards, Juliet feigned death in order to avoid an arranged marriage with a relative. Romeo, mistakenly believing that she was really dead, killed himself, and Juliet, broken-hearted at Romeo's death, also took her own life.

But what's that light coming from the window? It must be Juliet! She's so beautiful – bright like the sun, so much lovelier than the pale sickly moon. Oh, if only she knew how much I love her!

Ah …

She's speaking! Oh, speak again, bright angel! Because you are like an angel to me, looking down on me from above.

Oh Romeo, Romeo! Why does your name have to be Romeo? Tell me that you're not a Montague! Change your name! Or if you can't do that, just swear that you love me, and I'll stop being a Capulet.

It's only your name that's my enemy. You'd still be the same person after all, even if you had a different name. What is a name, anyway? It has nothing to do with who a person really is. A rose would still smell as sweet even if it wasn't called a rose. And Romeo would be just as perfect, even if he had a different name.

Juliet:
O Romeo, Romeo! wherefore art thou Romeo?
Deny thy father and refuse thy name;
Or, if thou wilt not, be but sworn my love,
And I'll no longer be a Capulet.
'Tis but thy name that is my enemy:
Thou art thyself, though not a Montague.
What's Montague? It is nor hand, nor foot,
Nor arm, nor face, nor any other part
Belonging to a man. O, be some other name.
What's in a name? That which we call a rose
By any other name would smell as sweet;
So Romeo would, were he not Romeo call'd,
Retain that dear perfection which he owes
Without that title.

Glossary

wherefore *(adverb)* – why

art *(verb)* – are

thou, thee *(pronoun)* – you

but *(conjunction)* – only

thyself *(pronoun)* – yourself

though *(conjunction)* – whether or not

owes *(verb)* – owns

3 🔊 **3.02** Read and listen to an extract from the original balcony scene from *Romeo and Juliet*. Then work in pairs and discuss the questions.

- Have you heard or read this scene before? How easy did you find it to understand?
- Do you think that the graphic novel version makes Shakespeare more accessible to a modern reader, or does it destroy the beauty of the original text?
- How far are the themes of the play still relevant today? Do you know any similar stories of tragic love?

Extend your vocabulary – collocations with *heart*

1 Which of the adjectives below does not collocate with *hearted* to make a compound adjective?

broken	cold	down	half
hard	kind	light	up
warm	whole		

2 Which refer to …
- character?
- sadness?
- enthusiasm?
- lack of enthusiasm?
- lack of seriousness?

3 Use three of the compound adjectives to describe a personal experience to a partner.

Grammar

1 Read the sentences and answer the questions.

If a rose **were** called If a rose **was** called If a rose **were to be** called **Were** a rose **to be** called	*something else, it would* *still smell as sweet.*
If they were from different families, they	**might** **would** *get married.* **could**

1 Are the situations real or imaginary?
2 What is the difference in meaning or register between the alternatives in bold?

2 Complete the sentences. Then compare your ideas with a partner.

- If Romeo and Juliet were from the same family, …
- Were Juliet / Romeo to ask for my advice, I …
- If Romeo and Juliet were to fall in love nowadays, …
- If I were in a similar situation, …

Ⓖ Grammar focus – explanation & more practice of unreal conditionals on page 144

Writing

1 Choose one of the situations below. Write a few lines of advice to a teenage niece or nephew who …

- has fallen madly in love with an unsuitable person.
- wants to get married, but is still very young.
- is suffering from unrequited love.
- wants to meet someone they have contacted on the internet.
- is broken-hearted after the end of a relationship.

Useful phrases

- If I were you, *I'd / I wouldn't* …
- It might be *an idea / advisable to* …
- You might regret it if you …

2 In small groups, read aloud what you have written. Do you agree with the advice given?

William Shakespeare
(1564–1616) was an English poet and playwright, widely regarded as the greatest writer in the English language.

Hearts & Minds

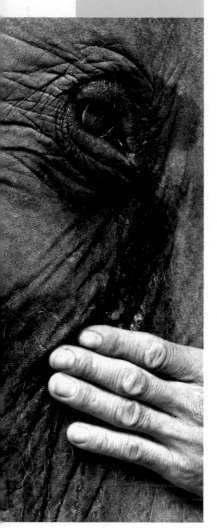

Speaking

1 How important is it to concentrate in each of these situations, and why? Which requires the most concentration, and which can be done while your mind is on other things?

- climbing a mountain
- cooking
- doing a grammar exercise
- driving along a motorway
- having a deep conversation
- listening to music
- playing a musical instrument
- playing tennis

2 Can you think of any other activities that require deep concentration?

3 Complete the sentences so that they are true for you. Then compare with other people.

- My mind often starts wandering when …
- I find it relatively easy to stay focused on …
- When I get distracted I sometimes daydream about …

Reading

1 Have you heard of *mindfulness*? Which of the following definitions do you think it could be?

1 the ability to pay attention to more than one thing at the same time
2 a clear awareness and acceptance of present experience
3 the ability to think clearly and make rational decisions

2 Read three short texts about mindfulness and see if you were right.

3 Do these words and phrases from the text relate to mindfulness or to its opposite?

alert	aware	brooding	critical thinking
monkey mind	non-judgementally		
the present moment	tunnel vision		

4 Choose the best explanation for the following words underlined in the texts.

1 slumber *sleep / wakefulness*
2 stalking *trying to catch / trying to escape from*
3 nip it in the bud *worry about it / stop it before it grows too large*
4 halt *increase / stop*
5 elusive *fascinating / difficult to achieve*
6 transience *temporary existence / importance*

5 Find answers to the questions in the texts.

1 What two examples of mindfulness in everyday life are mentioned?
2 In what way were stone age hunters practising mindfulness?
3 What sometimes happens if a person's mood is low?
4 How can mindfulness help in this situation?
5 What is the best way to learn to practise mindfulness?
6 What difficulties do beginners often experience and how can they overcome them?

6 Work in pairs. Choose two or three questions to discuss.

- Have you ever had experiences similar to the ones mentioned in the texts?
- How easy do you find it to sit in silence and completely empty your mind?
- Would you consider learning to practise mindfulness? Why / Why not?
- At what times of day are you most and least alert? What helps increase your alertness?

Mindfulness

A Have you ever suddenly become aware of a background noise that had been going on for some time unnoticed? Or have you ever woken up just moments before your alarm clock went off, as if an inner force had lifted you from <u>slumber</u>? That was mindfulness. Mindfulness is a mental faculty, like intuition or musical ability. It reminds you of what you didn't know you had forgotten, and wakes you when you didn't realise you were sleeping – or daydreaming. Think of stone age hunters stealthily <u>stalking</u> their quarry while on guard for predators that might be stalking them. Their minds are quiet but alert, empty but present, sharply focused on the immediacy of the situation, knowing that anything can happen. That is also mindfulness.

B Sometimes we do not notice the moment when a spiral of low mood is starting. It is a sort of tunnel vision; we can only see part of the landscape. Mindfulness practice helps us to see more clearly the patterns of the mind; and to learn how to recognise when our mood is beginning to go down. This means we can '<u>nip it in the bud</u>' much earlier than before. Mindfulness helps to <u>halt</u> the escalation of negative thoughts and teaches us to focus on the present moment, rather than reliving the past or pre-living the future. When we start to feel low, we tend to react as if our emotions were a problem to be solved. We end up over-thinking, brooding, ruminating, living in our heads. Mindfulness teaches us to shift mental gears, from the mode of mind dominated by critical thinking (likely to provoke and accelerate downward mood spirals) to another mode of mind in which we experience the world directly, non-conceptually, and non-judgementally.

C Just to sit and 'be' is not that easy. It takes practice and a good teacher simply to learn how to sit up straight without strain for periods of 40 minutes at a time and to breathe evenly and well. But it is this attentiveness and quietness that can lead to the deeper and transformational quality of the process. Learning to tame what the Buddhists call our 'monkey mind' – the internal chaos that keeps us flitting back and forwards, obsessing about the minutiae of life – can be frustrating and <u>elusive</u>. Beginners to meditation will notice their mind regularly wandering back to the past and forward to the future: 'I'll never be able to do this'; 'My hips are killing me'; 'How much longer?'; 'What am I going to cook for dinner?' and so on. 'You must allow for the <u>transience</u> of each thought like bubbles forming in a pot of water or weather patterns in the sky. It's an important part of the learning process' says Dr Jon Kabat-Zinn, who has developed a technique called mindfulness based stress reduction (MBSR).

Vocabulary

1 Match each sentence 1–7 with a follow-on sentence a–g.

1 Now, what was I going to say?
2 Sorry, your birthday completely slipped my mind.
3 Where on earth have you been?
4 I've been racking my brains for a good present for Stephanie.
5 Yes, I'd love to go out tonight, thanks.
6 I'm sorry, I didn't think to bring an umbrella.
7 That song is so catchy.

a It never crossed my mind that it might rain.
b Can I take you out for a meal to make up for it?
c My mind's gone blank.
d It's driving me mad – I just can't get it out of my mind.
e Where did you have in mind?
f I've been out of my mind with worry.
g I'm afraid nothing comes to mind, though.

Glossary

quarry *(noun)* – an animal or person being hunted

tunnel vision *(noun)* – concentrating on one thing without considering anything else

brooding *(adjective)* – worrying

minutiae *(noun)* – small or unimportant details

2 With a partner, choose some of the exchanges and continue the conversation.

3 Work in pairs. Write what the speaker might say before two of these sentences. Then read your sentences to another pair. Can they guess which ones you have chosen?

1 You can do it if you set your mind to it.
2 Great minds think alike!
3 I must have been out of my mind!
4 But that was yesterday – I've changed my mind!
5 You should do something to take your mind off him.
6 I don't mind, it's up to you.
7 Mind your head!
8 He should mind his own business.

Hearts & Minds

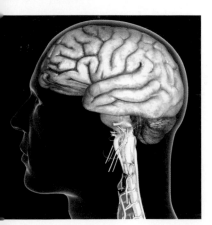

Speaking and Vocabulary

1 Read about the Nature vs Nurture debate. Which of the opinions and statements below refer to nature and which to nurture?

> *Nature or Nurture?* What determines our behaviour more – our genetic make-up or the environment around us?

1 People say I'm *the spitting image of* my brother. Red hair *runs in the family*.
2 My mother is quite reserved and cautious. I *put it down to* her strict *upbringing*.
3 I *take after* my father – neither of us is any good at sports. It must be *in the genes*.
4 I *look nothing like* my sister. She's *inherited* my mother's fair skin, whereas I tan easily.
5 I *was brought up* to believe that telling lies is wrong.
6 My sister seems to have *an innate ability* to get on with other people.

2 How much do you have in common with members of your family, and what do you put it down to? Explain your ideas to a partner using words and phrases from exercise 1.

3 Work in pairs. Choose one of the statements and take opposing views, giving examples.

- We are *conditioned* by the media *to* believe that our country's way of life is the best.
- Personality differences are *down to nature*, not *nurture*.
- Criminal behaviour is *culturally*, rather than *genetically determined*.

4 Work with another pair and discuss your real opinions about the nature vs nurture debate.

Useful phrases

- Yes, but *don't you think / surely* …?
- That may well be true, but …
- Yes, but on the other hand …

Listening and Pronunciation

1 Look at the picture of the human brain below and discuss the questions with a partner.

- What do you know about the functioning of different parts of the brain?
- What are the best ways to help a baby's brain develop?

2 3.03 Listen to the first part of an interview with Sue Gerhardt, an expert on child development. Make notes on the following topics.

1 in what sense the brain is *a social organ*
2 why the first two years of life are important
3 the three main emotion systems
4 how the body responds to stress
5 why stress can be *toxic*
6 what parents can do to regulate a baby's stress

3 3.04 Listen to another extract from the interview. What does Sue Gerhardt say about the nature vs nurture debate, and how do her own two children illustrate this?

4 3.05 On the basis of what you have heard, what advice do you think she will give on how to bring up babies? Listen to a further extract, and check your predictions.

5 3.06 Listen to someone reading the pairs of words below.

1 What is the difference between the two sounds? Practise making them.

/tʃ/	/ʃ/
cheap	sheep
catch	cash

2 3.07 Find examples of both sounds in the words below. Then listen and repeat.

- attachment
- crucial
- nurture
- attention
- culture
- predisposition
- children
- emotion
- relationship
- conditioned
- nature
- social

3 Use some of the words to tell a partner what you can remember about the interview, and your reactions.

Attachment theory

Attachment theory is a widely-accepted theory of human development, initially formulated by John Bowlby. Its main tenet is that, in order to develop emotionally, a baby needs to be securely attached to a reliable care-giver (usually, but not necessarily, a parent), who acts as a 'secure base'. In fact, relationships are as essential to healthy functioning as air, or food or water, since the baby's ability to regulate his own emotions is dependent on his having an attentive care-giver to help him deal with his distress. As he grows older, a child needs to learn how to explore the world so as to attain independence. The care-giver allows him to move away when he feels able, and return when he needs to be protected or comforted. Such positive experiences lead to the setting up of 'internal working models' (or characteristic patterns) in the mind, which continue to operate in adulthood. Learning to cope with loss is another important developmental milestone, and a baby who can do this without being overwhelmed by anxiety will be better able to manage losses in later life. Attachment theorists maintain that an adult's capacity to form healthy relationships is largely a result of having had at least one secure attachment as a baby. It is, however, possible to compensate for a lack of secure attachments by going on to develop positive relationships in later life.

Reading and Grammar

1 Read *Attachment theory*. According to the theory, which of these does a baby need, and why?

1 a secure base
2 parents
3 relationship
4 exploration
5 boundaries
6 comforting
7 an experience of loss
8 discipline
9 secure attachment

2 Read the text again and underline uses of verbs, nouns or adjectives followed by …

1 an infinitive with *to*.
2 a gerund.
3 an infinitive without *to*.

3 Find examples in the text to illustrate the rules below.

1 if a verb is the subject of a sentence, use the gerund
2 if a verb comes after a preposition, it is always a gerund
3 form a past gerund with *having* + past participle – this use is often more formal
4 form a passive gerund with *being* + past participle (present) or *having been* + past participle (past)
5 form a passive infinitive with *to be* + past participle (present) or *to have been* + past participle (past)
6 use *my / your / his* (formal), or *me / you / him* before a gerund to refer to another person
7 in formal discourse, use *the* + gerund + *of* + noun to make a noun phrase
8 to express purpose, use *to* + infinitive, *so as (not) to* + infinitive, or *in order (not) to* + infinitive

4 Read part of a letter from a teacher to a parent and delete any incorrect alternatives.

Please forgive (1) *my writing / me to write / me for writing* to you like this, but I am extremely concerned about Amelia's progress. I regret (2) *to tell / telling / tell* you that as a result of (3) *missing / having missed / her miss* the first month of this term, she has fallen significantly behind her peers in her coursework. She also appears (4) *to not complete / not to have completed / to not have completed* any of her homework. Clearly, (5) *having missed / missing / miss* such a huge chunk of term will impact on her final grades at the end of this year. I have tried (6) *to explain / explain / explaining* this to her, but she seems to object to (7) *being told / be told / having told* what to do. (8) *So as not to / Not to / In order not to* fall behind any further, she needs to make a concerted effort (9) *to catch up / for catching up / for catch up* with her classmates by (10) *complete / completing / having completed* all her project work.

5 Work in pairs.

1 Discuss whether the verbs below are followed by an infinitive (with or without *to*), gerund or either. Check your ideas in a dictionary.

| advise | appreciate | avoid | encourage | enjoy |
| get used | let | make | prefer | suggest | would rather |

2 Use some of the verbs to write a reply to the teacher. Read your letter to another pair.

6 Complete the sentences so they are true for you. Read them to a partner, and ask each other questions about your experiences.

• At school, I sometimes had difficulty …
• I used to think there was no point …
• At my school there was no opportunity …
• If I have children / grandchildren, I have no intention …

G **Grammar focus** – explanation & more practice of gerund and infinitive on page 144

Function globally dealing with difficult situations

Warm up

1 Work in pairs. Roleplay two of the situations below.

- Telephone a colleague to say that you can't meet him/her as arranged. Explain why.
- Ask a friend to lend you his/her car. Explain why.
- Apologise to a friend for losing a book he/she lent to you. Offer to replace it.
- Tell a child that he/she can't have a pet. Explain why.
- Ask a landlord for a reduction in your rent.
- You have already asked your boss for one day off. Now you need another one. Ask him/her, and say why.

2 Work in pairs and discuss the questions.

- What is 'difficult' about each of the situations? Which is the most difficult, in your view?
- Have you been in any similar situations recently, or in the past? What happened?

Listening

1 🔊 3.08–3.11 Listen to four conversations and answer the questions.

1 What is the relationship between the two speakers?
2 What is difficult about each situation?
3 What is the outcome?

2 Listen again and note down expressions used to …

1 make a request.
2 turn down a request.
3 agree to a request.
4 make an apology.

Language focus

1 Complete the conversation openers with a word from the box. What do you think comes next?

about	apology	ask	do	know	make	slight
thing	trouble	word				

1 I've got a(n) _____ to make.
2 You _____ that book you lent me?
3 Sorry to _____ you, but …
4 I'm afraid there's a(n) _____ problem.
5 Could I _____ you a favour?
6 Could you _____ me a big favour?
7 Right, _____ the holiday. The _____ is, …
8 I've got a request to _____.
9 Could I have a(n) _____?

2 Change the sentences using the word(s) in brackets to make a more polite request.

1 Could I change the appointment? (*possible*)
2 Could I have a second opinion? (*wondering*)
3 Could you give me a lift to the hospital? (*suppose*)
4 Could you possibly pick up my prescription? (*any way*)
5 Can I use your phone? (*mind*)
6 Can I park outside? (*all right*)

Pronunciation

1 Which of the following expressions can answer …

a a request?   b an apology?   c either?

1 Sure.	5 I wish I could, but …	9 Don't worry.
2 Actually, that's a bit difficult, because …	6 That should be OK.	10 That's fine.
3 No worries.	7 Oh no!	11 I'd like to help you out, but …
4 No problem.	8 I'm afraid that's out of the question.	12 I'm afraid it's not allowed.

2 🔊 3.12 Listen and repeat the expressions. What do you notice about the intonation patterns?

Speaking

Look again at the situations in the Warm up, and roleplay different ones with a partner using the phrases from *Language focus* and Pronunciation.

Global English

Shakespeare: the best English teacher? by David Crystal

What does Shakespeare offer the English language learner – apart from the aesthetic, theatrical, and literary experience awaiting anyone who hears or reads his poems and sees or reads his plays? A great deal. Shakespeare is in many ways the ideal advanced teacher, because he shows us how to exploit the resources of a language to maximum effect.

He has of course been an important general influence on the development of English, because many of his words and idioms have become part of everyday modern use. You are quoting Shakespeare when you say that *truth will out*, *the game is up*, and you *haven't slept a wink*, or if you've *knitted your brows*, *made a virtue out of necessity*, and *laughed yourself into stitches*. If you look in the unabridged *Oxford English Dictionary*, you'll find over 2,000 words which have their first recorded use in Shakespeare, such as *assassination*, *outswear*, and *weather-bitten*. Some he coined himself; others he simply helped to popularise.

Far more important, though, is the way his linguistic strategies provide guidelines for modern users. He adds *un-* to make new words, such as *unbuild* and *unmusical*; today we do the same thing with *uncool* and *unfunny*. He adds *-less* to make *airless* and *languageless*; today we say such things as *computerless* and *iPadless*. He was one of the great manipulators of parts of speech. In particular, he readily turned nouns into verbs: his characters *nose* things as well as *smell* them; they *ear* things as well as *hear* them; they are *windowed* (displayed in a window) and *mudded* (covered by mud). Today, the internet provides many examples of people

texting, *spamming*, *googling*, and *tweeting*, and doing many things that were originally nouns. This is well within the spirit of Shakespeare.

It's impossible to interpret many headlines in modern English newspapers if you don't know Shakespeare. What would a Shakespeareless reader make of an article on population control headed *To breed or not to breed*, or one on nutrition headed *To diet or not to diet*, or one on a possible army invasion headed *To fight or not to fight*? All derive from Hamlet's *To be or not to be*.

Shakespeare teaches learners how to be daring in their use of English. It is a sign of real fluency when learners can take a rule and adapt it to suit their purposes. Perhaps we should start using the acronym *ESP* (English for Special Purposes) in a new way: English for Shakespearean Purposes.

Glossary

make a virtue out of necessity *(phrase)* – pretend you are doing something because it will bring you benefits, when in fact it is something that you must do

outswear *(verb)* – swear more than someone

Warm up

1 Can you match the two halves of the following famous quotes from Shakespeare?

1	To be or	a	all men and women merely players. (*As you like it*)
2	But love is blind,	b	not to be (*Hamlet*)
3	Now is the winter	c	of our discontent (*Richard III*)
4	Out damned spot!	d	and lovers cannot see (*The Merchant of Venice*)
5	All the world's a stage and	e	that wears the crown (*King Henry IV*)
6	Uneasy lies the head	f	Out I say! (*Macbeth*)

2 Have you heard any of these quotations before? Have you ever seen a Shakespeare play or film of a play?

Reading

1 Read *Shakespeare: the best English teacher?* and put the paragraph titles in order.

a   Inventor of new language   ___
b   The world's best Advanced English teacher   ___
c   Shakespeare as a cultural reference   ___
d   Word building strategies   ___
e   Behaving like Shakespeare   ___

2 Read the text again and decide if the sentences are true (*T*) or false (*F*) according to the author.

1   Shakespeare is a good teacher because he was creative with language.
2   Shakespeare invented at least 2,000 words in the *Oxford English Dictionary*.
3   Much of the language arising from the internet is developed in a similar way to how Shakespeare used language.
4   Shakespeare did not use verbs like *smell* or *hear*, preferring to use nouns instead.
5   Some knowledge of Shakespeare helps make sense of many contemporary news headlines.
6   Learners should be careful of changing language – not everyone can be Shakespeare.

Speaking

The author says learners should be daring in their use of language. Work in pairs. Look at the examples of how Shakespeare experimented with English vocabulary. Can you invent similar words or expressions?

Writing an argument

Reading

1 With a partner, make a list of five ways to achieve good health. Then read Alex's essay. How many of your ideas does he mention? Does he suggest other ways?

It is often argued that the best way to achieve good health is through practising sports or following a regular fitness routine. Conversely, it is also commonly suggested that special diets or preventive medicine are the key to staying healthy. In my view, a healthy lifestyle includes all of these elements, but I also believe that it is also essential to have a regular routine and a balanced lifestyle in order to maintain an optimum level of health and fitness.

It is undeniable that the sedentary lifestyle of most people nowadays is a major cause of ill health. People sit at their desks staring at their computers from 9 to 5, then kill time after work by watching television. Consequently, the metabolism of these couch potatoes slows down little by little, leading to obesity and other health problems. Engaging in physical activity on a regular basis would result in not only increased fitness, but also improved self-confidence.

Special diets and preventive medicine also have a role to play in maintaining good health. For example, some people adopt a vegetarian diet or eat only organic food so as to avoid consuming toxic additives. Moreover, recent advances in nutrition have allowed people to combat illness by taking vitamins or other nutritional supplements. Take the case of my parents, for example. Their bone density had gradually deteriorated due to age but, thanks to taking glucosamine tablets over a three-month period, it has now returned to normal.

It is my opinion, however, that the single most important factor in remaining healthy is having a regular routine and a balanced lifestyle. Even if people eat carefully, work out regularly at the gym and take supplements, they can still become ill as a result of excessive work or anxiety. Given that a large number of illnesses are related to stress, lack of sleep and erratic eating patterns, trying to reduce stress can be the first step towards leading a healthy life for many people.

2 Discuss the questions with a partner.

- Which of the suggestions in the essay do you already follow?
- Are there any suggestions that you disagree with? Why?
- What is the single most important step you could take to improve your health?

Writing skills: structuring an argument

1 Look at two ways of structuring an argument. Which has Alex used?

A	B
Introduction and personal opinion Your views and reasons for holding them Conclusion	Introduction and presentation of problem Opposing arguments and why you disagree Your views and reasons for holding them Conclusion

2 In your view, which of the following ideas could be included in …

- an introduction?
- a conclusion?
- either?

1 your own view
2 a historical or geographical view of the topic
3 a question
4 an overview of the current situation
5 a recommendation
6 a summary of the arguments

Linking ideas: cause and consequence

1 Complete the expressions with a suitable preposition. Then check your answers in the text. Is each one followed by a cause or a consequence?

1 are the key _____
2 is a major cause _____
3 leading _____
4 result _____
5 have a role to play _____
6 are due _____
7 thanks _____
8 is the most important factor _____
9 as a result _____
10 the first step _____

2 Complete the sentences (1–6) with one of the groups of words (a–f) below. There may be more than one possible answer.

a Because of / Thanks to / As a result of
b are due to / are related to / can be attributed to
c can lead to / can result in / can produce
d is a key factor in / is at the root of / is a major cause of
e Given that / Since / In view of the fact that
f have a part to play in / are the key to / are the first steps towards

1 _____ a healthy diet is vital to health, children should be educated to know what constitutes healthy eating.
2 _____ improved hygiene, many illnesses have been eliminated.
3 Overwork and anxiety _____ high levels of stress.
4 Regular exercise and a healthy diet _____ staying fit.
5 Smoking _____ heart disease.
6 Many relationship difficulties _____ stress.

Preparing to write

With a partner, discuss one of the alternatives, and answer the questions together.

What is the best way to find *happiness / success / wealth / wisdom / love*?

- In what ways do people sometimes try to achieve this goal?
- What are the reasons for, and consequences of, each way?
- In your view, what is the best way, and why?

Useful language

- It is *commonly / widely / generally acknowledged / believed / agreed* that ...
- It is often *claimed / suggested / argued* that ...
- Some people claim that ..., *while / whereas* others argue that ...
- *All the evidence suggests / There is little evidence* that ...

Writing

Write your essay, following one of the structures in *Writing skills*.

Improving your speaking skills

1 Mark these statements true (*T*) or false (*F*) about spoken English. Then check your ideas on page 131.

1 It is very unusual for native speakers to make errors when speaking.
2 It is best to avoid hesitations and fillers, eg *um, I mean*.
3 It is not a good idea to use too many fixed expressions.
4 Speakers should always try to use a wide range of language.
5 You should express your ideas using precise vocabulary and avoiding general words like *thing*.
6 Preparing for speaking can improve the accuracy, fluency and range of the language used.
7 Repeating a spoken task can improve accuracy, fluency or range.

2 Which of these aspects of speaking would you like to improve the most? Choose the five most important, and add others if appropriate. Then compare your ideas with a partner.

- fewer hesitations
- better pronunciation
- less self-correction
- better interaction skills
- more fixed expressions
- fewer errors
- more confidence
- ability to speak at length
- strategies for when you don't know the right word

3 Try the following procedure to help you work on your speaking skills.

- ★ Decide which aspect of speaking you need to improve.
- ★ Prepare to do a speaking task that is relevant to your aim (alone or with a partner). Make notes on the content and keywords.
- ★ Record yourself speaking.
- ★ Listen to analyse your performance, focusing on your key aim. It can be helpful to transcribe word for word, or get help from a teacher or fellow student. Decide how you could improve it.
- ★ Re-record the task, then listen again to note any improvements.

Chance & Design

Reading

1 Have you ever been in a queue at the bank or the supermarket and the other queue is moving faster? Or have you experienced a similar situation in traffic? Work in pairs.

- Compare your experiences, giving details.
- Can you think of any other examples of minor good or bad luck?
- Do you think you are a lucky or unlucky person?

2 Read *What are the chances?* What is the author's conclusion? Does luck play a role in this situation?

3 Read the text again more carefully. Then work in pairs and summarise the findings of the text. Take turns, using the following words and phrases to help you.

A queue / traffic lane … faster
B coincidence … non-coincidence
A slow lanes and queues … more people
B on average … not always
A consequences … analysis of data
B bias … conclusion

4 Work in pairs and discuss these questions.

- Did the author's conclusion surprise you, disappoint you or confirm your own ideas?
- How trusting or sceptical are you about the results of scientific data in articles or on websites?

Extend your vocabulary – *chance*

How certain is the speaker that something will or won't happen?

1 The chances are that you'll be wrong. (*spoken*)
2 You stand a good chance of winning.
3 You have a fifty-fifty / an even chance.
4 You could phone, on the off-chance.
5 Any chance of some help? (*spoken*)
6 Could you lend me ten euros by any chance? (*spoken*)

What are the chances?
Everyday odds explained

You will have noticed that when you join a queue at the airport or post office, the other queues always seem to move faster. When the traffic is heavy on the motorway, the other lanes always seem to move faster than the one you chose. Even if you change to one of the others, it still goes slower. This situation is often known as 'Sod's Law' and appears to be a manifestation of a deeply antagonistic principle at the heart of reality. Or, perhaps it is merely another manifestation of human paranoia or a selective recording of evidence. We are impressed by coincidences without pausing to recall all the far more numerous non-coincidences we never bothered to keep a note of. In fact, the reason you so often seem to be in the slow queue may not be an illusion. It is a consequence of the fact that on average you *are* usually in the slow queue!

The reason is simple. On average, the slow lines and lanes are the ones that have more people and vehicles in them. So, you are more likely to be in those, rather than in the fast moving ones where fewer people are.

The proviso 'on average' is important here. Any particular queue will possess odd features – people who forgot their wallet, have a car that won't go faster than 30 mph and so on. You won't invariably be in the slowest line, but *on average*, when you consider all the lines that you join, you are more likely to be in the more crowded lines where most people are.

This type of self-selection is a type of bias that can have far reaching consequences in science and for the analysis of data, especially if it is unnoticed.

When we do science or are confronted with data the most important question to ask about the results is always whether some bias is present that leads preferentially to draw one conclusion rather than another from the evidence.

John D Barrow is a British physicist and mathematician. In *100 Essential Things You Didn't Know You Didn't Know* he examines how maths informs everyday situations.

Glossary

manifestation (*noun*) – evidence that something exists

antagonistic (*adjective*) – hostile

paranoia (*noun*) – a worried feeling that people or things are against you

proviso (*noun*) – condition

invariably (*adverb*) – always

bias (*noun*) – unfair tendency

Grammar

1 Look at the examples. Match them to the category of real conditionals in the box. Underline the verbs used in the *if* clause and in the result clause.

> general truths and scientific facts
> instructions, requests and suggestions
> predictions

a When you consider all the lines that you join, you are more likely to be in the more crowded lines.

b Unless you check the data, you won't know whether it's correct.

c Supposing that we get in that queue, will it be quicker?

d If you get in that queue, you're going to be behind that man with the huge trolley.

e If you only have two items, get in that queue there.

f Providing that we stay in this queue, we might be OK.

g Assuming we ever get out of here, let's go straight home.

h This type of self-selection can have far reaching consequences if it is unnoticed.

- in real conditions for predictions, we usually use the present simple in the *if* clause. However, *will* and *should* can also be used in the *if* clause

- *will* expresses politeness or emphasis
  *If **you'll go** over to that checkout there, I'll open the till.* (polite form)
  *If they **will** only have one checkout open, of course there'll be a long queue!* (emphasis)

- *should* implies that the action is unlikely, and is often used for suggestions or advice in more formal contexts
  *If you **should** go by car, allow a little more time. / **Should** you go by car, allow a little more time.*

2 Work in pairs and answer the questions.

1 Which words in exercise 1 replace *if*?
2 In what type of conditional can *if* and *when* be used with the same meaning?
3 Which word means *if not*?
4 Which word means *if and only if* or *as long as*?
5 Which two words mean *just imagine that*?

> **Language note:** *provided* can be used instead of *providing* and *suppose* instead of *supposing* with the same meaning.

3 Complete the text about the use of probability in weather forecasting. Sometimes there is more than one possibility.

> You've planned a picnic tomorrow, but don't want to go (1) _____ the weather is fine. If you check the weather forecast, it (2) _____ say the chance of rain is 80%. Where does this figure come from? If you'll bear with me, I (3) _____ explain. (4) _____ that there is data for 100 similar days and that on 80 of these days it rained, the probability of rain on the next similar day (5) _____ be 80/100. And if the probability of rain is 80%, the probability that it (6) _____ rain is only 20%. So (7) _____ you still want to go on your picnic, you'll need to take an umbrella.

G **Grammar focus** – explanation & more practice of real conditionals on page 146

Speaking

Read the following probability puzzles. Work in pairs and discuss what you think the answers could be. Then check your answers on page 131.

1 The chance of a coin flip coming up heads or tails is invariably fifty-fifty. But if you flip a coin five times and get heads each time, do you stand a higher chance of getting tails than before?

2 Suppose you're on a game show, and you're given the choice of three doors: Behind one door is a car; behind the others, goats. You pick door No. 1, and the host opens No. 3, which has a goat. He then says, 'Do you want to pick door No. 2?' Are the chances of you winning higher if you switch your choice?

Chance & Design

Speaking and Listening

1 What do you think *people watching* means? Do you ever do it? If so, where and when?

2 Work in pairs. Look at the photos on page 93 and describe the appearance of the man and the woman.

- What do you think the man might be doing?
- Can you guess anything about their ages, occupations, characters and lives?

3 3.13 Listen to an extract from the beginning of a novel by Kate Grenville called *The Idea of Perfection* and answer the questions.

1 Where exactly are the man (Douglas) and the woman (Harley)? What are they doing?
2 Take notes on what Douglas notices about Harley's appearance and what he imagines about her character and life.
3 How similar were his observations and thoughts to your ideas about the photos?

4 3.14 Listen to another extract, which describes a chance encounter between Douglas and Harley a few moments later, and answer the questions.

1 Where do they meet?
2 What exactly happens?
3 How does each of them react?
4 In what way is the encounter 'awkward'?

5 Arrange the lines of the conversation in order. Then listen again to check your answers.

a Well.   ____
b No, no.   ____
c So clumsy. Me, I mean.   ____
d My fault. Completely my fault. Stupid.
  Totally stupid. Not thinking at all.   *1*
e Hurt me?   ____
f Well.   ____
g I hit you. There.   ____
h Did I hurt you? Hitting you?   ____

6 Work in pairs.
- Practise saying the conversation first awkwardly, then apologetically.
- Imagine the characters were both angry, and act out a different conversation.

7 What would you do in this situation? Discuss your reactions with a partner.

Vocabulary and Speaking

1 Read sentences about minor accidents. Complete the sentences with the correct form of one of the verbs below. Which other two verbs could be used and which one could **not** be used in the gap?

1 If I happened to _____ and spill coffee over someone, I'd apologise profusely.

| slip | stumble | tread | trip |

2 If I were to reverse into a car while I was parking, and _____ the bonnet, I might leave a note.

| dent | rip | scrape | scratch |

3 If I accidentally knocked over a vase in a shop and it _____, I definitely wouldn't pay for it.

| bump | crack | shatter | smash |

4 Were I to sit on someone's hat by mistake, and _____ it, I'd probably feel acutely embarrassed.

| bang | crush | flatten | squash |

2 What do the different verbs mean, and what other nouns could they be used with?

3 Work in pairs. Ask and answer about what you would do in the situations in exercise 1. Then ask and answer about other minor accidents using some of the verbs from exercise 1.

The **of** Idea **of** Perfection

Reading

Read a synopsis of *The Idea of Perfection*.

1 What examples of 'chance encounters' and fortuitous observations are mentioned?

2 What transformations take place at the end of the novel?

Grammar and Pronunciation

1 Delete the incorrect alternative in the sentences below. Then answer the questions.

a If Douglas **hadn't / hadn't been / wasn't** looking out of the window, he would have missed Harley.

b If Harley had stayed in Sydney, she **wouldn't / shouldn't / might not / couldn't** have met Douglas.

c **If Douglas had taken / If Douglas would have taken / Had Douglas taken** a different room, he might not have been looking out on the street.

d **If it hadn't been for / But for / What for** her interest in quilts, Harley would never have gone to Karakarook.

e Had it not been for meeting Harley, Douglas **would still have suffered / would still suffer / would still be suffering** from vertigo.

1 Which sentences refer to a hypothetical situation …
 • in the past?
 • in the past with present consequences?

2 Which verb forms are used in the *if* clause, and which modals in the result clause?

3 What kind of word or phrase comes after *But for* or *If it hadn't been for* in sentences d and e?

4 Are the inverted forms in sentences c and e *more* or *less* formal?

Because of her interest in antique quilts, and her need to earn more money for medical bills, Harley Savage, an assistant museum curator from Sydney, accepts an invitation to set up a heritage museum in Karakarook, a sleepy town in the Australian outback. Douglas Cheeseman also arrives from Sydney to demolish a bridge damaged when the local river flooded. Douglas is an engineer whose fear of heights means he can only work on small jobs that are close to the ground. Harley and Douglas bump into each other at the beginning of the novel, and then meet again when walking in the countryside, when Harley helps him escape from a herd of cows that is about to attack him. Douglas notices Harley leaving a precious quilt in a first-floor room opposite his hotel room. Later, he notices smoke coming from the room and, overcoming his vertigo, he climbs in to rescue the quilt. Harley and Douglas, who had both given up on the idea of love due to bad experiences, start to change their minds, and Douglas sees a way of preserving the bridge without knocking it down.

Glossary

quilt *(noun)* – bed cover, often made of different pieces of cloth

2 🔊 **3.15** What is the pronunciation of *have* in sentences a–d? Listen and check.

3 Complete the sentences about the story in a suitable way. Then compare your ideas with a partner.

If Harley had had more money, …

But for the floods, …

Harley might have stayed in Sydney if …

Had Douglas not been looking at the building opposite, …

Harley might still be suspicious of men if …

4 Write the first part of three more sentences about the story and pass them to a partner to finish. Read the completed sentences to each other. Do you agree with what your partner has written?

5 Think of some chance events or encounters in your own life, or the lives of family members. Tell a partner how things might have been different, or might be different now, if they hadn't happened.

G Grammar focus – explanation & more practice of unreal conditionals on page 146

Kate Grenville (born 1950) is one of Australia's best-known authors and has written several award-winning novels. Her novel *The Idea of Perfection* won the UK Orange Prize for Fiction in 2001.

Chance & Design

The High Court, Chandigarh, India

Pompidou Cultural Centre, Paris

The Beehive, Wellington, NZ

Listening and Speaking

1 Look at the photos of the four buildings below. What do you think they have in common?

2 🔊 **3.16–3.17** Listen to two people talking about two of the buildings. Identify the buildings and write down if the speaker's reaction is positive or negative.

3 Listen again. Note down what the speakers say about these characteristics:

Building 1
The look of the building
Materials and colour
Building 2
Features of the building
Style and colour

4 Work in pairs. Do you agree with the opinions of the speakers? Why / Why not? Compare the other photos and say why you think they might be controversial.

5 Have you seen any of these places? Which of them would you most like to see, and why?

Reading

1 Read *Four highly controversial designs*. To which building or buildings do the following phrases refer? Find at least one (the same phrase may refer to more than one building).

1 praised by critics
2 controversial because of its surroundings
3 extremely expensive to build
4 got mixed reactions
5 inspired by a physical object
6 a popular tourist attraction

2 Read again. Choose the word or phrase with a similar meaning.

1 abstract (paragraph 2) *conceptual / realistic*
2 proximity (paragraph 3) *closeness / likeness*
3 accentuate (paragraph 3) *minimise / emphasise*
4 a stone's throw from (paragraph 5) *very near / quite far from*
5 out of keeping with (paragraph 5) *not in competition / harmony with*

3 Work in pairs. Choose three of the questions and answer them.

- Are there any famous buildings in your country which are or were controversial? What do you think of them?
- Describe some examples of attractive or interesting buildings near where you live.
- What building in your country would you describe as a national treasure? Explain why it is important.
- Is beauty really in the eye of the beholder? Explain why or why not.
- Which is more important to you: form or function? Why? Give examples.

National Centre for the Performing Arts, Beijing

Four highly controversial designs

Even with top architects, the best of intentions and a huge budget it's still possible to get a building's design horribly wrong. Or is it? Beauty is in the eye of the beholder, and what may be horrendous to one is a symbol of style and modernism to another. The following four buildings all provoked strong reactions when they were first built, and yet have their fair share of fervent admirers. In some cases they have even become national treasures.

The High Court, Chandigarh (Chandigarh, India)

The High Court in Chandigarh, part of a whole city designed by the French architect Le Corbusier, attracted praise from critics all over the world for its clean sculptural lines. But the building proved decidedly less popular with the high court judges, both in terms of design and functionality. They took down the abstract wall hangings in the courtrooms and parked their cars defiantly on the pedestrian walkways under the parasol roof – causing Corbusier to remark that they were judges of law and not judges of art.

The Beehive (Wellington, New Zealand)

A slide projector that fell on a wedding cake that fell on a waterwheel is one description of this impressive building known as 'The Beehive'. One of the New Zealand government buildings, The Beehive was built during the 1970s. Part of its problem was its proximity to the neighbouring Edwardian neo-classical Parliament House, which only accentuates the architectural aspects of The Beehive that many disliked.

Pompidou Cultural Centre (Paris, France)

Once referred to as 'the back of a refrigerator', the Pompidou Cultural Centre has also been called grotesque, monstrous or just plain ugly. Its distinguishing feature is that all of its piping, elevators, and so on, are on the exterior freeing up space inside for displays of artworks. The centre is in one of the oldest neighbourhoods in Paris, which added to many local residents' outrage. However, it gained instant critical acclaim on its opening in 1977 and remains one of the most visited places in the city.

National Centre for the Performing Arts (NCPA) (Beijing, China)

Nicknamed 'the egg', the NCPA divided opinion even before its opening concert in 2007. The titanium and glass dome set in an artificial lake is just a stone's throw from the ancient Forbidden City and was felt by many to be out of keeping with the latter's imperial architecture – although others applauded its futuristic design. At ¥2.69 billion ($336 million dollars), the cost of the building – like many other major architectural projects – also sparked debate.

Vocabulary

1 Look at the descriptive adjectives below. Put them into three groups: neutral, positive and negative. Which would you use, if any, to describe the buildings featured in this lesson?

awe-inspiring	classic	dreary
grotesque	hideous	impressive
innovative	modern	monstrous
unique		

2 Choose the correct alternative to complete the sentences.

1 Love or hate her, she always *starts / provokes* a reaction.
2 The design of this website is just awful. There's no other way I can *put / get* it.
3 Many people hate it, but it also has its share of fervent *admirers / fans*.
4 The new design of the building was *greeted / spoken* with outrage.
5 Although critics were sceptical at first, the film *decided / proved* to be very popular.
6 The building opened to *positive / critical* acclaim.
7 Opinion was *divided / separated* over the new wing of the museum.

3 Choose two of the sentences in exercise 2. Think of real examples of what they could refer to.

You decide ...

A multinational company wants to build its headquarters in your neighbourhood. They have suggested two possible designs for the building.

Speaking and Writing

1 Work in pairs. Read *You decide ...* and discuss which design you prefer. Give reasons for your choice.

2 Write a short message to the public relations department explaining which building you prefer, and why.

3 Exchange messages with another pair in the class. Read the messages. Did you have a similar reaction to the designs?

Chance & Design

Part 4

Speaking
Conspiracy theories

Reading
Ruled by Design

Grammar
Passive reporting

Writing
Conspiracy theories

Speaking

1 Look at three popular conspiracy theories in American culture. With a partner, write a definition of the term 'conspiracy theory'. Then check your ideas in your dictionary.

> The Apollo Moon landing of 1969 was a hoax. It was filmed at a film studio by NASA and used as propaganda.

> In 1947, a UFO was recovered at Roswell air base, New Mexico by the American army. The discovery was subsequently covered up.

> The American president, John F Kennedy was assassinated by a shadowy organisation including agents quite possibly within the American government itself.

2 Work in pairs and discuss each theory. Answer the following questions:

- Have you heard of these theories? Do you know anything else about them?
- How likely or unlikely do you think they are? Why?

Useful phrases

- *I've heard of this and … / I haven't heard of this, but …*
- The one about … sounds quite *credible / plausible*
- *I'm sceptical about … / I don't think this is very likely / convincing.*
- It strikes me as being *rather over the top / completely ridiculous.*

Reading

1 Read *Ruled by Design* quickly. Work in pairs. Close your book and explain what all conspiracy theories have in common.

2 Read the text again. Match these words from the text with the correct definitions.

1	randomness (paragraph 2)	a	take part in
		b	therefore
2	willed (paragraph 3)	c	although
3	coherent (paragraph 3)	d	lack of pattern or purpose
4	albeit (paragraph 5)		
5	hence (paragraph 5)	e	inconsistent
6	engage in (paragraph 5)	f	organised
7	arbitrary (paragraph 6)	g	intended

3 Are the following sentences true (*T*) or false (*F*), according to the author?

1 There are few definitions of the term 'conspiracy theory' because people don't know what it means.
2 Conspiracy theories are about people or organisations trying to do good things.
3 In the conspiracy theorist's world, there is no chance and coincidence.
4 The conspiracy theorist's world is less organised than the real world.
5 In a conspiracy theory, everyone who looks innocent, is innocent.
6 A conspiracy theorist is always trying to work out how everything is linked.

4 Discuss the questions.

- Do you think a world without coincidence is possible? Would it make the world a better or worse place?
- What makes conspiracy theories attractive to many people?
- Do you agree with the author that 'the conspiracy theorist's view is both frightening and reassuring'? In what ways?
- How might having a definable enemy 'give life purpose'?

Ruled by Design

Conspiracy theories were frequently discussed at the end of the second millennium. However, the term conspiracy has often been left undefined, as though its meaning were self-evident.

In essence, a conspiracy belief attempts to explain evil. For our purposes, a conspiracy belief is the belief that an organisation made up of individuals or groups was or is acting secretly to achieve some malevolent end. A conspiracist worldview implies a universe governed by design rather than by randomness. The emphasis on design is shown in three principles found in virtually every conspiracy theory.

Nothing happens by accident. Conspiracy implies a world based on intentionality, from which accident and coincidence have been removed. Anything that happens occurs because it has been willed. At its most extreme the result is a 'fantasy [world] ... far more coherent than the real world'.

Nothing is as it seems. Appearances are deceptive because conspirators wish to deceive in order to disguise their identities or their activities. Therefore, the appearance of innocence is considered no guarantee that an individual or group is benign.

Everything is connected. Because the conspiracists' world has no room for accident, pattern is believed to be everywhere, albeit hidden from plain view. Hence the conspiracy theorist must engage in a constant process of mapping hidden connections.

In an odd way, the conspiracy theorist's view is both frightening and reassuring. It is frightening because it magnifies the power of evil. It is reassuring for it promises a world that is meaningful rather than arbitrary. Not only are events non-random, but a clear identification of evil gives the conspiracist a definable enemy against which to struggle, giving life purpose.

Grammar

1 Complete the rules 1–3 with descriptions a–c below. Then answer the questions.

a   the focus is on the reported information at the end of the sentence

b   the focus is on *who* is reporting / believing the information

c   the focus is on the subject of the reported information

> *Conspiracy theorists* **believe that** *pattern is everywhere.*
> *Pattern* **is believed to be** *everywhere.*
> *It* **is believed that** *pattern is everywhere.*
>
> - use an active verb + clause when (1) _____ b
> - use a passive verb + infinitive when (2) _____ c
> - use an impersonal passive verb + clause when (3) _____ a

2 Three of the verbs below cannot be used in the passive sentences above instead of *believe*. Cross them out.

allege	claim	comprehend	gossip
know	regard	report	rumour	say
think	understand		

3 Read the sentence below. Match each alternative to the description a) ongoing or temporary, b) permanent, c) past situation.

He is said to **be working** *for / to* **have worked** *for / to* **work** *for NASA.*

4 Rewrite each sentence in two ways so that the sentences have a similar meaning. Use the correct infinitive.

1   People say that the two governments are in secret talks.
   The two governments are said to be in secret talks.
   It is said that the governments are in secret talks.

Glossary

malevolent *(adjective)* – evil-minded

intentionality *(noun)* – deliberate plans

benign *(adjective)* – not harmful

2   It is alleged that the opposition party belongs to a terrorist organisation.   *The opposition party ...   People ...*

3   People claim that large companies are collecting private information on the internet.
   Large companies ...   It ...

4   It is believed that the actor worked in secret for the government. *The actor ...   People ...*

5   There is a rumour that the head of state is dead.
   The head of state ...   It ...

Ⓖ Grammar focus – explanation & more practice of passive reporting on page 146

Writing

1 Work in pairs. Choose one of the sentences from Grammar exercise 4 or use your own idea. Brainstorm some ideas on how this could be a convincing conspiracy theory.

2 Use your ideas to write a short paragraph outlining your theory. Begin your paragraph with the sentence you chose.

3 Work with another pair. Read each other's conspiracy theories. How plausible are they?

Michael Barkun is professor emeritus of political science at the Maxwell School of Syracuse University. His book *A Culture of Conspiracy* examines the origins of conspiracy ideas and how they spread.

Function globally giving a presentation

Warm up

1 Work in pairs. Make a list of features of a good presentation (eg have a strong opening, keep an eye on your watch, use visual aids).

2 Work in small groups. Compare your lists.

3 Can you think of any good or bad presentations, lectures or speeches you have heard? What was good or bad about them?

Listening

1 You are going to listen to someone giving a presentation on 'How to design a website'. Work in pairs to predict the kind of information he might include.

2 🔊 **3.18** Listen to the presentation, and check your answers. Which of the features that you discussed in Warm up exercises 1 and 2 does it demonstrate?

3 Listen again and say if the following statements are true (*T*) or false (*F*). Note down the words or phrases that tell you.

1 Grant Fisher is an expert on IT.
2 Most of the audience have some knowledge of website design.
3 The speaker wants to make his topic accessible to laypeople.
4 His talk is divided into four sections.
5 The woman in the audience answered his question correctly.
6 The speaker illustrated his talk with slides.
7 The speaker overran at the end.
8 He concludes by stressing that website design is a complex process.

Language focus

1 🔊 **3.19** Work in pairs. Complete a shortened version of the introduction to the presentation. Then listen and check your ideas.

It's a (1) _____ to be here today. The (2) _____ of my talk today is website design, and my (3) _____ is to take the mystery out of designing a website. So, my presentation will be (4) _____ into three parts. I'm going to (5) _____ outlining the steps you need to take to set up a website. I'll (6) _____ mention some features of a good website, and I'll (7) _____ that with some slides. And finally, I'll (8) _____ on troubleshooting. If anything is not clear, (9) _____ interrupt me as we go along, otherwise if you have any questions, I'll (10) _____ to answer them at the end.

2 Match these expressions to their function.

1 to elaborate on that …   a finishing the talk
2 to conclude …   b giving more details
3 turning now to …   c giving a summary
4 to recap …   d introducing the next section

Pronunciation

1 🔊 **3.20** Listen to two people reading the passage in *Language focus* exercise 1. What is different about the speed, volume, intonation and delivery?

2 Practise reading the section to your partner. Give each other feedback on their delivery.

Speaking

1 You are going to give the introduction to a presentation on one of the following topics. Choose the topic and make notes on the sections and information you will include.

- a process (eg opening a bank account, writing a poem)
- a hobby, craft or skill (eg photography, golf)
- a country / town that your audience is not familiar with

2 Work in small groups. Using your notes, give the introduction. Ask and answer questions at the end.

Useful phrases

- I have a question. Can you tell us *why / what / when* …?
- You mentioned … Could you possibly expand on that?
- Could you say a bit more about …?

Global voices

Warm up

1 Look at the list of places below. Choose four and think of one example of each that you know or have visited.

- a cathedral or mosque
- a castle
- a concert hall
- a famous street
- a museum
- a monument
- a natural park
- a shopping mall

2 Work in pairs. Find out if your partner has visited the places you were thinking of in exercise 1 and what your partner thinks of them. Try to do this in one minute.

Listening

1 🔊 3.21 Listen to Beth from the US and Tim from Northern Ireland talk about places they have visited. Answer the questions.

1 Where did they go? 3 What did they think?
2 What did they visit?

2 Listen to Beth and Tim again. Check you understand the phrases below. Which refer to The Museum of Modern Art and which to York Minster? Which phrase relates to many buildings that Tim saw?

1 airy and spartan
2 archetypal multicoloured stained-glass window
3 full of sculptures and angles and arches
4 huge circle with red bricks
5 just as pretty as inside
6 built on huge ball bearings
7 openness and whiteness

Beth, US Tim, Northern Ireland

Silvia, Catalonia Evgenia, Belarus

3 🔊 3.22 Now listen to Silvia from Catalonia and Evgenia from Belarus talk about the Alhambra in Spain and buildings in Oxford. Complete the gaps in the sentences below.

Alhambra
… it's also because of the (1) _____ and the (2) _____ and the (3) _____, these elements that make it a special place. There are a lot of fountains and the (4) _____ of the sun on the water …

Oxford
I like classical buildings because they really took into account the light and the air because there wasn't (5) _____ or artificial (6) _____ …

Language focus: incomplete sentences

1 Look at the sentences below from the listening. What do you think the next word or words are? Think of one or two possibilities for each.

1 A lot of the buildings are built on huge ball bearings so that they move …
2 It's just brick on the outside and there is not a lot …
3 Yes, the whole …
4 These elements that make it a special place …
5 There wasn't ventilation or artificial lighting so it was …

2 Now match the sentence beginnings in exercise 1 to the endings below. Check your answers on the audioscript on pages 162–163.

a they made the most of these elements.
b the foundations move when there's an earthquake.
c the decoration is more inside, but that one was … is both outside and inside.
d actually the town of York, all the buildings are quite nice.
e like magic place.

3 In spoken English leaving sentences unfinished and starting sentences over again is very common. What does the speaker do in each of the examples above?

- rephrase an idea
- pause because of an interruption
- change focus

Speaking

Work in pairs. Look back at the places you talked about briefly in the Warm up. Discuss them more in detail. Look at the following questions to help you:

- Is there anything special about the design?
- What is the area like around this place?
- Do you like going there?
- Have you seen any other areas that are similar?

Writing an article

Reading

1 Read Chiara's article. What's the meaning of the title?

The road **not travelled**

I closed the door behind me, my mind buzzing with doubts and confusion. The professor had talked about joining a group of young anthropologists to conduct research in Nepal. 'But I don't even know where Nepal is! ... And besides, I've hardly ever been outside my country. How can I abandon my boyfriend, my friends and my family to live in a country where the tap water is polluted and there is malaria?'

Deep down, I sensed that this invitation marked a radical change in direction that would continue for years to come, and – as I felt with a sort of wrench in my stomach – would have major implications for the rest of my life. And yet, curiously, something inside me was intrigued at the whole idea – travelling, exploring, maybe it would be exciting too ... And so I accepted the invitation even though I felt homesick at the very thought.

That visit proved to be a decisive turning point in my life. In short, I fell in love with Nepal and its culture, and since then I have been back ten times to do fieldwork. Sixteen years later, I find myself in a foreign university with a job as a researcher in anthropology, specialising in Nepalese religion and society. I have lived in several different countries and the experience has opened my eyes to a great deal about the world outside my small, beloved but problematic country.

I often ask myself what might have happened had I declined that invitation. Naturally, it is hard to visualise what life would have been like, but I feel it would have been more stable. I would not have travelled so much; I would have got married, had children and cooked meals for my family. And now I would be leading a quiet life in my own house, sitting in front of a fireplace, with a book in my hands and a cat on my lap ... or would I?

I have met a great many wonderful people on my travels, but I think that any period of living abroad is a bitter-sweet experience, and involves a degree of loneliness, isolation and nostalgia for home. But do I regret it? No. Every path has both advantages and limitations, and I cannot imagine myself without the experiences I have had, even the most painful ones.

2 Decide if the statements are true (*T*) or false (*F*). Find evidence for your answers.

1 Chiara had mixed feelings about accepting the invitation.
2 She weighed up the pros and cons carefully.
3 It turned out to be a life-changing decision.
4 Her decision to go to Nepal did not impact on her relationships.
5 Her travels have broadened her horizons.
6 In retrospect, she wishes she had made another decision.

Writing skills: adding interest to your writing

1 Using synonyms can help make your writing more interesting. Match the words and phrases below with the more interesting alternatives that Chiara chose, highlighted in the text.

1	affect	5	taught me
2	am living	6	interested
3	good and bad	7	imagine
4	feeling confused	8	felt

2 Find examples of the following features in Chiara's article.

1 an attention-grabbing start
2 personal opinions
3 feelings
4 direct speech or thoughts
5 questions
6 concrete details
7 a decisive ending

Linking ideas: attitude

1 Complete the sentences from the text.

1 And yet, _____, something inside me was intrigued at the whole idea.
2 _____, it is hard to visualise what life would have been like.

2 Match the attitude adverbs in exercise 1 with ones with a similar meaning below.

- clearly
- oddly
- surprisingly
- obviously
- strangely
- of course

Study skills

3 Delete the least appropriate alternative below.

1 I had to go to hospital, but *thankfully / worryingly / luckily* I made a good recovery.

2 I had no time to study and *predictably / understandably / ironically* I failed the exam.

3 *Sadly / Quite rightly / Unfortunately*, we missed the plane.

4 The journey took ten hours and *amazingly / inevitably / not surprisingly* we were exhausted when we finally arrived.

Preparing to write

Work in pairs. Think about a decision you, or someone you know, has made (eg a career or study choice, travel plan or relationship) and discuss the questions.

- How difficult was it to make the decision, and how did you make it?
- What were or are the consequences of taking that path?
- How might things have been different, or be different now, if you had made another decision?
- What regrets, if any, do you have, and why?

Looking back at the past

- It marked a *radical change of direction / decisive turning point*.
- It proved to be a(n) *life-enhancing / enriching / difficult / painful* experience.
- *I'm glad I went to ... / I have no regrets about going to ...*
- *With hindsight, I regret (not) going to ...*
- Looking back, I *would have liked to go to ... / wish I had(n't) gone to ...*

Writing

Write an article called *The road not travelled* based on your discussions in *Preparing to write*.

Extensive reading

1 Work in pairs and discuss the questions.

1 Which of the following extended texts have you read in your own language in the last month? Can you add any others to the list?

- a novel or other work of fiction
- a non-fiction book
- a newspaper
- a magazine article
- a textbook
- an online article or blog

2 Which have you read in English ...
- in the last month?
- in the last year?
- ever?

2 Tick (✔) any statements that apply to you.

1 I quite often read extensively in English ...
- ☐ for my work or study.
- ☐ for pleasure.
- ☐ for language practice.

2 I don't read extensively in English because ...
- ☐ I don't have time.
- ☐ it feels too difficult.
- ☐ I don't know where to start.
- ☐ I'm not in the habit of doing so.

3 Read about extensive reading. Then discuss the questions in small groups.

> Research shows that extensive reading in a foreign language can not only improve reading skills and fluency, but can also facilitate language acquisition and both spoken and written communication. You should choose texts related to your interests, and read for enjoyment as much as possible. You should not stop to look up words, though you can, if you want, note down or mark words as you read to research later.

- Can you recommend any short, contemporary novels to read in English? Add to those featured in this book.
- Which news or current affairs websites have you found interesting?
- Where can you buy, borrow or read books, magazines and newspapers in English near where you live?

4 Find a partner or partners who share similar interests and agree together on a book or article in English that you will read and discuss.

Time & Motion

Speaking

1 Read a text about the passing of time. Work in pairs. Guess the word that goes in each gap, to rhyme with the word in the previous line.

When as a child, I laughed and wept,
Time ___crept___.

When as a youth, I dreamt and talked,
Time _____.

When I became a full-grown man,
Time _____.

When older still I daily grew,
Time _____.

Soon I shall find when travelling on –
Time _____.

2 🔊 **3.23** Listen to check your ideas. What point about time does the writer make?

- Why might we perceive the passage of time differently depending on our age?
- Can you think of times when time has gone particularly slowly, or quickly, for you?

Listening and Speaking

1 🔊 **3.24** You are going to listen to someone talk about how time is conceived in different societies. As you listen, label each diagram with one of the terms in the box. Which sorts of societies typically view time in these ways?

> cyclical   linear   monochronic
> polychronic

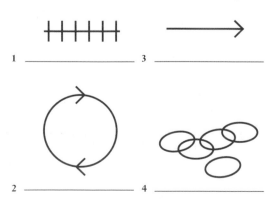

1 _____ 3 _____

2 _____ 4 _____

2 Listen again and answer the questions.

1 Which kind of time is associated with the following?
   a a never-ending river   d prosperity
   b female   e reincarnation
   c male   f schedules

2 How do polychronic and monochronic time differ with regard to time management?

3 Discuss the questions with a partner.

- Which of the concepts of time described by the speaker is closest to your own views, and why?
- How is timekeeping (eg punctuality, meeting deadlines) viewed in your country?
- How good are you at time management? Give examples.

Useful phrases

- Punctuality is *regarded / viewed / seen* as ...
- Multitasking is considered (*to be*) ...
- It is *good manners / bad manners / (un)acceptable* to ...

Extend your vocabulary – collocations with *time*

1 Match the two parts of the sentences to make time expressions.
1 If you *squander* or *fritter away* time
2 If you *take your time* over something
3 If you *kill time*, or do something *just to pass the time*,
4 If something *takes up a lot of time*,
5 If you *make* or can *spare the time* to do something,
6 If you *spend time* doing something,

a you do it slowly.
b you waste it.
c you use it to do an activity.
d you make sure you do it, as it is important.
e you fill time with something you are not really interested in.
f it is time-consuming.

2 Write questions using some collocations to ask a partner, eg:
How do you kill time when you're waiting for a bus or plane?

Grammar

- in the English tense system, as in most Western cultures, time is viewed as a line going from past to future:
PAST ⟶ PRESENT ⟶ FUTURE
- past events can be represented as:
  - single completed events: X
  - repeated events: XXX
  - continuing activities or states: ∿

1 Match the following sentences to a timeline below. Compare with a partner.

1 I started school at the age of six.
2 We lived in Buenos Aires for six years.
3 We went to the seaside for our holidays every summer.
4 I got married while I was living in India.

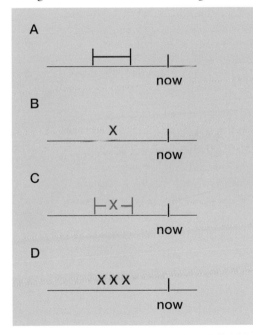

2 ⬤ **3.25** Listen to some short dialogues. After each one, decide who might be speaking to whom, and what or who they are talking about.

They could be talking to … She offers to … because …

3 Work in pairs. Try to finish the sentences from the dialogues. Then listen again to check your answers.

1 If only I _____ walk home.
2 Actually, I'd rather you _____, if you don't mind.
3 It's time you _____ a haircut.
4 I wish you wouldn't speak to me as if _____ a child.
5 I _____ if you'd like to go out tomorrow night.
6 Stuart told me she _____ swimming on Tuesdays.
7 I _____ I could take tomorrow off.
8 I wish _____ agreed to work overtime.

4 Read about uses of past forms in English, and match each rule to one of the sentences in exercise 3.

Use the past simple:
a after *It's time* (*you / he /* etc) … to say that an action is urgent or overdue
b after *I'd rather* (*you / he /* etc) … to indicate a preference about someone or something else
c after (*she*) *said / told me that* … in reported speech, even if a fact is still true in the present
d after *as if* or *as though* to describe a present action or state that is not actually true
e after *I wish* or *if only* to express a desire for something that is unlikely or impossible in the present

Use the past simple or past continuous:
f to make a statement more polite by distancing yourself from a present state or action

Use the past perfect:
g after *I wish* or *if only* to express a regret about something that happened or did not happen in the past

5 Complete the sentences so they are true for you. Read your sentences to a partner, and give more details.

- If only I didn't have to …
- It's time I …
- I'd rather [*name*] didn't …
- I wish I were …
- I was hoping that …
- I wish I'd …

Ⓖ **Grammar focus** – explanation & more practice of unreal past time on page 148

Time & Motion

Reading and Speaking

1 How many hours a week do you, or members of your family, work? How many days holiday a year do you take? Is that typical for people in your country?

2 Read *Working Time Around The World*, and answer the questions.

1 What point do all three texts make about working time?

2 What do you think the *international standard on working time* is?

3 Where do you think each text is taken from, and why?

3 Work in pairs. Explain the meaning of the underlined words and phrases.

4 Find answers to the following questions in the texts indicated.

1 reasons for working long hours (texts A, B)

2 the impact of overwork on family life (texts B, C)

3 a possible result of not working long enough (text B)

4 reasons why people shouldn't need to overwork (text C)

5 consequences of not having enough work (text A)

6 a suggestion for how long people should work, and why (text C)

5 Find words or phrases with the following meanings.

Text A

1 20% of the global workforce

2 very many

3 approximately 60%

4 about one third

Text C

5 one in fifty

6 approximately 30,000,000

6 Discuss the following questions with a partner.

• How does the work culture in your country compare with those described in texts A and B?

• *Overworked and underpaid. Underworked and overpaid.* Can you think of examples of both categories of worker in your country? What could account for the differences?

• Do you think a four-hour day is feasible, or desirable? If so, what would need to change? What would you personally do with more leisure time?

Vocabulary

1 Read text B again, and underline eight uses of *get*. Which of the uses fall into these categories?

1 *get* in a multi-word verb

2 *get* + past participle

3 *get* + infinitive

4 *get* + noun

2 Which could be replaced by the following words in a more formal text?

arrive	be	leave	manage	receive
rise				

3 Match each of the question beginnings with the most appropriate ending.

1 What makes you get really

2 When did you last get

3 What would you do if you got

4 How long does it take you to get

5 In your job, do you ever get to

6 In your household, who gets

7 Does your boss ever get you to

a travel abroad / attend conferences / travel first class?

b the meals ready / the shopping done / things organised?

c stressed / annoyed / bored?

d work overtime / entertain guests / conduct interviews?

e a promotion / a pay rise / a day off?

f dressed / showered / shaved in the morning?

g sacked / made redundant / transferred abroad?

4 Work in pairs. Ask and answer some of the questions.

Working Time Around The World

A Nearly a century after the adoption of the first international standard on working time, a new study estimates that one in five workers around the world – or over 600 million persons – are still working more than 48 hours a week, often merely to make ends meet. At the same time a considerable number of short-hours workers in <u>developing and transition countries</u> may be underemployed, and thus more likely to fall into poverty. In <u>the informal economy</u>, which provides at least half of total employment in all regions of the developing world, with about three-fifths of it self-employment, some 30 per cent or more of all self-employed workers work more than 49 hours a week.

B If you thought *you* worked long hours, consider 39-year-old Lee from South Korea. A civil servant at the ministry of agriculture and fisheries, Lee gets up at 5.30am every day, gets dressed and makes a two-hour commute into Seoul to start work at 8.30am. He typically gets out of the door at 9pm, or even later, and by the time he gets home, it's just a matter of jumping in the shower and collapsing into bed, before starting the whole routine all over again, about four hours later. This happens six days a week, and throughout almost all of the year, as Lee gets just three days of vacation. 'I get to see my kids for 10 or 15 minutes a week, and then just on the weekend,' he says, before adding that, on weekends, he usually gets interrupted to go to the office. Lee's schedule is completely normal in South Korea, where <u>the average employee</u> works 2,357 hours per year – that's six-and-a-half hours for every single day of their life. Leaving at the official time of 6pm could mean not getting a promotion or raise. 'It's very <u>bad form</u> to leave the office before the boss does, so people will <u>hang around</u> doing nothing,' says Lee. 'But we are changing.'

C At the beginning of the last century, the tractor and <u>the assembly line</u> revolutionised the American economy. The eight-hour workday and the forty-hour week soon prevailed as a natural consequence of these innovations. The computer and other minor miracles have since opened glorious opportunities for a further reduction of our <u>drudgery</u>, yet nothing of the kind has happened. Modern life remains a headlong rush into long commutes, two-income families, late nights at work, and <u>exhausting recreation</u>. How could this be? What is it about our collective personality that drives us into this endless <u>rat race</u>? Two per cent of Americans now grow all of our food and then some. Another thirty million or so do all the mining, manufacturing, and construction. If this minority can produce our modern cornucopia, then the four-hour day is within easy reach.

Glossary

cornucopia *(noun)* – large variety of something good

Grammar

1 Read about quantifiers and answer the questions.

> Quantifiers are a group of words which say how much or many of a particular noun we are talking about. They include:
> - words like *all, most, many, much, both, several, various, some, (a) few, (a) little, (very) few, (very) little, (hardly) any, no*
> - common expressions with *of*, eg *lots of, a lot of, loads of, a great deal of, a large amount of, plenty of, a bunch of, the (vast) majority of, a number of, a percentage of, a proportion of, a minority of, half of, three-fifths of, 30% of, hundreds of*

1 Which of the common expressions above are not usually used in formal texts?
2 What is the difference in meaning between the options in bold?
   All workers / All (of) the workers *need holidays.*
   Most women / Most of the women *take maternity leave.*
3 What adjectives are commonly used in the expression *a _____ _____ number of*?

2 Delete the grammatically incorrect alternative in the sentences below. Is there a difference in meaning or register between the two correct alternatives? Which sentences are true?

1 Footballers typically earn *several / a great deal of / loads of* money.
2 *A great many / A considerable number of / A large amount of* working days are lost each year due to people taking sick leave.
3 There are *plenty of / lots of / very much* employment opportunities in the IT sector.
4 *Much / A huge number of / A lot of* unemployment is due to the global economic situation.
5 There is *virtually no / hardly / scarcely any* state childcare provision for working mothers.
6 *Very little / Few / A few* men take paternity leave to look after their children.

3 In small groups, choose three of the topics below to discuss. Compare patterns in your country and others that you know about.

- maternity / paternity leave
- casual employment
- changing work patterns
- employment opportunities
- childcare
- retirement
- job security
- unemployment

G **Grammar focus** – explanation & more practice of quantifiers on page 148

Part 3

Reading
Traffic

Extend your vocabulary
UK / US English

Grammar
Comparisons

Speaking
Congestion problems

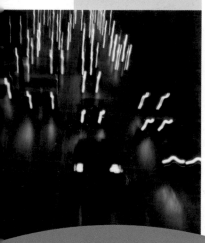

Reading

1 Write three or four sentences on the topic of traffic. Then compare your sentences with a partner. How far did you write about the same things? Were your comments positive or negative?

2 You are going to read extracts from a book called *Traffic* by the US author Tom Vanderbilt, in which he mentions the topics below. Work in pairs and predict what he might say about each.

1 a traffic problem in the time of the Roman Empire
2 the leading cause of death in London in 1720
3 the introduction of the bicycle
4 the speed limit for the first cars
5 cities with severe congestion and traffic problems
6 reasons for increased congestion
7 new jobs that have developed to ease congestion
8 road fatalities in 2020

3 Work in pairs. Student A: read *Traffic Problems* and check your predictions to points 1–4 in exercise 2. Student B: read *Traffic: A Universal Condition*, and check your predictions to points 5–8. Then share information with your partner.

4 Read both texts. Find evidence to suggest that the writer thinks that traffic …

1 has always been regarded as a problem.
2 has developed faster than our capacity to understand it.
3 has become more problematic with increased urbanisation.
4 travels at unnatural speeds.
5 shares similar features all over the world.
6 can shatter the peace of a traditional way of life.
7 can be avoided by rich people.
8 is becoming increasingly dangerous.

5 Work in pairs. Do you share the writer's views? Choose two or three of the statements in exercise 4 to discuss.

Extend your vocabulary – UK / US English

Look at the words connected with vehicles and driving, and match the UK word with its US equivalent. Which are more familiar to you?

car caravan	automobile
car park lorry	gasoline highway
motorway	license plate
number plate	parking lot
pavement	sidewalk
petrol	trailer truck
windscreen	windshield

Traffic Problems

Traffic problems of all varieties are as old as traffic itself. Ever since humans began to propel themselves artificially, society has struggled to catch up with the implications of mobility, to sort out technical and social responses to the new demands. Visitors to the ruins of Pompeii, for example, will see rutted streets marked by the tracks of chariot wheels – but many are wide enough for only one set of wheels. As early as 1720, 'furiously driven' carts and coaches were named the leading cause of death in London; and in the New York of 1867, horses were killing an average of four pedestrians a week. The larger the cities grew, and the more ways people devised to get around those cities, the more complicated traffic became, and the more difficult to manage. And just when it seemed as if things could not get more complicated, along came a novel and controversial machine, a newfangled contrivance that upset the fragile balance of traffic: the bicycle. Bicycles were too fast, they spooked horses and they caused accidents.

Before the dust kicked up by the bicycles had even settled, the whole order was toppled again by the automobile. When driving began, it was like a juggernaut, and we have rarely had time to pause and reflect upon the new kind of life that was being made. When the first electric car debuted in mid-nineteenth-century England, the speed limit was hastily set at 4 miles per hour – probably the last time the automobile existed at anything like human speed or scale. The car was soon to create a world of its own, a world in which humans, separated from everything outside the car but still somehow connected, would move at speeds beyond anything for which their evolutionary history had prepared them.

Glossary

chariot *(noun)* – vehicle with two wheels, pulled by a horse

newfangled *(noun)* – modern and complicated

juggernaut *(noun)* – something large and powerful, often with a bad effect

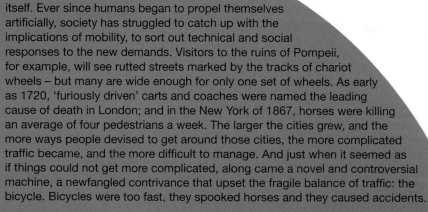

Traffic: A Universal Condition

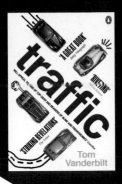

Traffic has become a universal condition, inflected with regional accents. In Moscow, the old images of Russians waiting in line have been replaced by images of idling cars stuck in heavy congestion. Ireland has seen its car-ownership rates double since 1990. The once tranquil Tibetan capital of Lhasa now has jams and underground parking garages. In Caracas, Venezuela, traffic is currently ranked 'among the world's worst', thanks in part to an oil-fuelled economic boom – and in part to cheap gas (as low as seven cents a gallon). In São Paulo, the wealthy shuttle between the city's more than three hundred helipads rather than brave the legendary traffic. In Jakarta, desperate Indonesians work as 'car jockeys', hitchhikers of a sort who are paid to help drivers meet the passenger quota for the faster car-pool lanes.

Another traffic-related job has emerged outside Shanghai and other Chinese cities. There, one can find a new type of worker: *Zhiye dailu*, or professional road guides, who for a small fee will jump into one's car and provide directions in the unfamiliar city – a human 'nav system.' But with opportunity comes cost. In China, the number of people being killed on the road every year is now greater than the total number of vehicles the country was manufacturing annually as recently as 1970. By 2020, the World Health Organisation predicts, road fatalities will be the world's third-leading cause of death.

Glossary

shuttle *(verb)* – travel a short distance, usually by air

car-pool lanes *(noun)* – road lanes with use restricted to car owners travelling together in one car

Grammar

1 For each sentence, delete two words or phrases that cannot be used in the gap.

a Cars are _____ **faster than** they used to be.
   *a bit   a great deal   a little   a lot
   considerably   far   infinitely   much
   quite   relatively   slightly   way*

b Congestion in Lhasa is _____ **as bad as** that in Caracas.
   *almost   equally   just   not
   nothing like   not nearly   nowhere near
   rather*

c Motorways are _____ **the worst** roads in terms of traffic fatalities.
   at all   by far   far   far and away

d **The more** roads we build, **the** _____ congestion will become.
   *heavier   more problematic
   more worse   worse   worst*

e Cars with smaller engines produce **less** pollution and are _____ expensive to run.
   least   less   the less   the least

2 Which words for sentence *a* are formal, and which informal, in register?

3 Complete the sentences in an appropriate way, using a comparative structure.

1 Far _____ people walk to school nowadays than in the past.
2 Traffic nowadays is _____ than it used to be.
3 Congestion in developing countries is _____ as in developed ones.
4 The speed limit nowadays is _____ in 19th century Britain.
5 The car is by far _____ cause of traffic jams in the present century.
6 The larger cities become, the _____.

4 Work in pairs. Add two or three more items to each of the lists below. Then choose two words from one of the lists, and try to make as many comparisons as possible, as in the example.

1 lorries, taxis, trams, zero-emission cars
2 built-up areas, country roads, motorways, residential streets
3 early morning, midnight, the rush hour
4 bus drivers, motorists, pedestrians, taxi drivers

Zero-emission cars cause far less pollution than lorries.

(G) **Grammar focus** – explanation & more practice of comparisons on page 148

Speaking

1 Read the following ways of dealing with congestion problems. Check you understand the meaning of each one. Then choose the five that you consider most effective.

- building more roads
- car pool schemes
- congestion charging
- creating more bus and cycle lanes
- increasing car parking charges
- Park and Ride schemes
- passenger quota schemes
- road tolls
- satellite traffic information systems
- subsidising public transport

2 Compare your ideas with a partner giving reasons for your opinions. Then answer the questions.

- Which of these measures have been implemented where you live?
- How successful have they been?
- Can you think of other ways to solve traffic problems?

Tom Vanderbilt writes on design, technology, science and culture, among other subjects, for many publications. He is the author of the *New York Times* best-seller *Traffic: Why We Drive the Way We Do (and What It Says About Us)*, which has been published in many different languages.

Time & Motion

Part 4

Reading
The Secret Life of Bees

Listening
The dance of the honeybees

Vocabulary
Formal and informal language

Speaking
Animal behaviour

Reading

1 Look at the photos below and explain what is happening using these words.

> bee   frame   hive   honey
> honeycomb   veil

2 Read the information about *The Secret Life of Bees*. Then read the extract and answer the questions.

1. What is Lily (the narrator) doing?
2. What advice does August give Lily? Does Lily follow this advice?
3. What do the bees do?
4. How does Lily react?

3 Read the text again. Look at the sentences below, used to describe the movement of the bees in the text. Which words or phrases tell you about …

1. the direction they move in?
2. their speed?

The bees poured out, rushing up all of a sudden in spirals of chaos and noise.
A bee flew straight at my forehead, collided with the net and bumped against my skin.
The bees spun round us, gathering strength till they made soft wind on our faces.
The bees began to light on my shoulders the way birds sit on telephone wires.

4 Describe the relationship August has with her bees with reference to the text. Can you give other examples of the strong bond that often exists between humans and animals? Do you think these bonds are changing in the modern world?

Listening

1 Look at these photos which show different versions of what is called the 'dance language' of honeybees. Compare them. What type of information do you think the bees might be communicating?

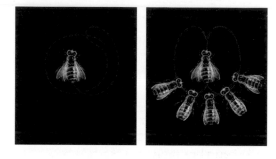

2 ⬤ **3.26** Listen to the first part of a lecture about the dance of the honeybees and check your answer from exercise 1. Complete the information.

1. Honeybee dances are performed by _____.
2. The dances tell other bees _____.
3. They communicate two items of information: _____.

3 ⬤ **3.27** Listen to the second part of the lecture. Label the photos above with the correct names.

4 Match words 1–8 to words a–h to form collocations from the listening.

1	spell out	a	direction
2	emit	b	straightforward
3	run	c	information about distance / direction
4	complete		
5	represent	d	a figure of eight
6	relatively	e	around in narrow circles
7	reverse	f	from side to side
8	wag	g	the angle of the Sun
		h	a buzzing sound

5 ⬤ **3.27** Listen again to the second part. Which of the features of the dance in exercise 4 refer to which dance? List them under the correct dance. Then compare with a partner and discuss how each feature works.

Vocabulary

1 Look at some examples of formal or academic language from the listening. Match the words and phrases in italics to their everyday equivalents in the box.

basically   changing   compared with
enough   gives out   important   justify
make up   pieces   place   position
shows   stands for

1 The dancer 'spells out' two *items* of information … *In essence*, the dances *constitute* a language that 'tells' other workers where the food source is.
2 When a bee returns to the colony with nectar or pollen that is *sufficiently* nutritious to *warrant* a return to the source …
3 … and then suddenly *reversing* direction to her original course. She may repeat the round dance several times at the same *location* … After the dance she often *distributes* food to the bees following her.
4 The *orientation* of the dancing bee … is *significant* because it *represents* the angle of the Sun. This *indicates* to the other bees where the food source is, *relative to* the Sun.

2 Decide which of these everyday phrasal verbs has a single verb equivalent. Use a dictionary to help you.

1 Remember: don't *take off* the veil when you're near the hive.
2 She never *puts on* gloves when she collects honey.
3 A bee stung me and my face *swelled up* like a balloon.
4 I can't *put up with* insects in the house, especially flies.
5 I'm trying to *find out* where that wasp went.
6 When I was *growing up*, I loved to collect creepy crawlies.
7 I thought she was *making up* that story about a giant cockroach until she showed me the book.
8 Don't eat that worm! *Put* it *down* this minute!

Speaking

1 Work in pairs. Read the sentences about animal movement and try to complete them by discussing ideas.

1 Kangaroos don't walk, they hop because …
2 Birds migrate to other countries in order to …
3 Ants find their way to food and back to their nests by …
4 Bats look for their prey in the dark using …
5 Despite having no legs, snakes manage to move quite quickly by …
6 Mature salmon find their way back thousands of kilometres from the ocean to their birth stream using …

2 Check your answers. A: turn to the answers to questions 1, 3 and 5 on page 128. B: turn to the answers to 2, 4 and 6 on page 131. Take it in turns to explain the answers to your partner without reading out the answers in the book.

Glossary

brood frames (noun) – removable frames at the bottom of a hive where the queen bee lays eggs

The Secret Life of Bees

I put on my helmet as August lifted the lid. The way the bees poured out, rushing up all of a sudden in spirals of chaos and noise, caused me to jump.

'Don't move an inch,' said August. 'Remember what I told you. Don't be scared.'

A bee flew straight at my forehead, collided with the net and bumped against my skin.

'She's giving you a little warning,' August said. 'When they bump your forehead, they're saying I've got my eye on you, so you be careful. Send them love and everything will be fine.'

I love you, I love you, I said in my head. *I LOVE YOU*. I tried to say it thirty-two ways.

August pulled out the brood frames not even wearing her gloves. While she worked, the bees spun round us, gathering strength till they made soft wind on our faces. It reminded me of the way the bees had flown out of my bedroom walls, stranding me at the centre of a bee whirlwind.

I watched the different shadows on the ground. The funnel of bees. Me, still as a fence post. August bent over the hive, inspecting the frames, looking for wax buildup on the honey comb, the half moon shape of her helmet bouncing along.

The bees began to light on my shoulders the way birds sit on telephone wires. They sat along my arms, speckled the bee veil so I could scarcely see through it. *I love you. I love you.* They covered my body, filled the cuffs of my pants.

My breath came faster and something coiled around my chest and squeezed tighter and tighter, until suddenly, like somebody had snapped off the panic switch. I felt myself go limp. My mind became unnaturally calm, as if part of me had lifted right up out of my body and was sitting on a tree watching the spectacle from a safe distance. The other part of me danced with the bees.

Function globally being interviewed

Warm up

1 Work in pairs. Make a list of some questions that are often asked in job interviews by …

1 the interviewer.
2 the interviewee.

2 Are there any questions you would not be comfortable answering, or that would not be acceptable in an interview?

3 What qualities and skills would be needed for the jobs below? Which would you most and least like to do?

- a librarian
- a PA
- a nanny
- a security guard
- a sports coach
- a tour guide
- a vet
- the CEO of a law firm

Listening

1 🔊 3.28 Listen to the first part of a job interview and answer the questions.

1 What kind of job is the woman being interviewed for?
2 What was her previous job?
3 Which questions from Warm up exercise 1 did the interviewer ask?

2 🔊 3.29 Listen to the second part of the interview and mark the statements true (*T*) or false (*F*).

1 The woman will hear the outcome of the interview at the end of the day.
2 She will be able to observe the current receptionist when the job starts.
3 Her workload will be increased progressively.
4 She may have to work more than 37.5 hours.

3 Would you offer the job to the woman? Why / Why not?

Language focus

1 🔊 3.30 Work in pairs. Complete the questions from the interview you heard. Then listen again to check your answers.

1 Perhaps you could start by saying why _____?
2 What previous experience _____ work?
3 Can you perhaps tell me about _____ in your last job?
4 What other qualities _____ this position?
5 Could you perhaps tell me about _____, as a person?
6 Are there any questions _____?

2 Read some more questions. Which are asked by the interviewer, and which by the interviewee?

1 Why did you want to leave your present job?
2 What's the next stage in this process? Will I receive feedback from this interview?
3 How will my performance be monitored?
4 What are my promotion prospects?
5 What are your outside interests?
6 In the first six months, is there anything specific that will be expected of me?
7 What are your career goals? Where do you see yourself in ten years' time?
8 When I first start, will I be given a mentor to oversee my development?

3 🔊 3.31–3.32 Listen to six answers from another interview. Which of the questions from exercise 2 do you think they were answering? Then listen to the full interview to check your answers.

Pronunciation

1 When do we use expressions like these?

- Well, …
- Let me see, …
- That's a tough one.
- I'll have to think about that one.

2 🔊 3.33 Listen and practise repeating the intonation.

Speaking

1 Work in pairs. Each choose a job you would like to do and briefly describe it to your partner.

2 Interview for their job. Then swap roles.

3 Give each other feedback on the interviews. What was good, and what could be improved?

Global English

Changing English
by David Crystal

'Be prepared' is the motto of the scouting movement; but it could equally well be the motto of the English learner, for one never quite knows what changes are going to be encountered as time goes by. Vocabulary, pronunciation and grammar all change. Vocabulary moves quite rapidly: a new word can become widely used within a few days, especially when it moves around the globe via the internet. Pronunciation moves rather more slowly. And grammar moves slowest of all.

We tend not to notice grammatical change, but it is happening all around us. The trends become apparent only when we look back in time, as we can now do using the large collections (corpora) of English usage. The growth in the use of the present continuous verb form is a good illustration. This construction developed in the Middle Ages, but took a long time to settle down. Shakespeare shows us simple and continuous usages competing: in *Hamlet* Polonius asks the Prince 'What do you read?' while in *Troilus and Cressida* Achilles asks Ulysses 'What are you reading?'.

There was a significant growth in the use of the continuous during the 17th century, and it became increasingly frequent over the next 300 years. Even so, during the 19th century it's possible to find many examples which differ from what is standard today. 'It rains', says the poet John Keats in one of his letters (1818). 'He really behaves very well,' writes novelist George Eliot in *Middlemarch* (1871).

The onward march of the continuous isn't over. Before the 20th century, it was uncommon to find it used with verbs expressing a state of mind. In the 1960s, people typically said *I need a holiday, They recognise the issue, Jane hopes to visit her mother, I think you're right, She misses John*, and *I love it*. Fifty years on, we are more likely to hear people saying *I'm needing a holiday, They're recognising the issue, Jane's hoping to visit her mother, I'm thinking you're right, She's missing John*, and *I'm loving this weather.* Some state verbs, such as *know* and *understand*, have been slower to accept the change, but it can surely only be a matter of time before such sentences as *I'm understanding your point* become part of standard British and American English, especially as they are commonplace in one of the fastest growing parts of the English-speaking world: India.

I'M LOVING YOU

Warm up

1 Languages change over time. What changes do you think happen the quickest? What changes are slower? Number the following from 1 (changes most quickly) to 3 (changes most slowly).

Vocabulary _____ Grammar _____ Pronunciation _____

2 Can you think of any examples of changes in your own language in any of the above areas?

Reading

1 Read *Changing English*. What is the answer to Warm up exercise 1, according to the author?

2 Read the text again and answer the questions.

1 Why does the author suggest that the vocabulary of a language changes most quickly?
2 How can we track grammatical changes?
3 Which did they use in Shakespeare's time: the simple, the continuous or both?
4 How has the use of the continuous form changed in the last 100 years?
5 What examples are given of the use of the continuous form that have not yet become standard in British English usage?

3 Look at the following examples. Put the verb in the present simple and then present continuous. Does the meaning change? Does one sentence 'feel' more correct?

1 Perhaps they weren't under pressure before, but they _____ (*feel*) it now. (in a sports commentary)
2 I _____ (*love*) this new look of yours! (a woman complimenting a friend)
3 She _____ (*be*) a bit difficult today as she hasn't had her nap. (two people talking about a baby)
4 We _____ (*have*) lunch in the garden. (a person answering the phone)
5 Let me make sure I _____ (*understand*) all this correctly … (one engineer to another)
6 He _____ (*not miss*) it at all. (two workers talking about a friend who has retired)

Speaking

• Does this distinction between progressive and simple aspect exist in your language? How would you translate the sentences in Reading exercise 3?
• Are there examples of your language changing? Can you think of any?
• The English suffix *-ing* is sometimes used to make new words in other languages. Can you think of or invent new words or expressions in your language by combining words with *-ing*?

Writing a proposal

a Reports indicate that the number of bicycles in Beijing reached ten million at the end of 2001. This figure has continued to increase over the past ten years, making Beijing one of the world's foremost cycling cities. Improving conditions for cyclists in Beijing should therefore be a high priority. While some progress, such as providing extra bicycle parking spaces around subway stations, has been made in recent years, it is vital that more should be done in order to make Beijing a safer and more pleasant city for cyclists. The following two measures would go a long way towards achieving this objective.

b Traffic conditions in Beijing are very dangerous, hence the need for further safety measures. At present there is no legislation on the use of bicycle helmets, reflective vests or lights, and so very few cyclists in the city use them. Consequently, cyclists' chance of injury, especially on poorly-lit streets, is greatly increased. Given the large population of Beijing, it may be neither feasible nor realistic for the city council to enforce the wearing of helmets and vests or the use of lights. Nevertheless, they could subsidise the purchase of such equipment so as to encourage more cyclists to invest in their own safety. In addition, they should hold more educational events to increase cyclists' awareness of traffic rules and the possible consequences of breaking them.

c Most current cycling lanes in Beijing are built alongside the traffic lanes, thus creating a dangerous environment for cyclists. Whereas this may be necessary in the central urban area due to space limitations, the situation could certainly be improved in suburban areas or rural areas. Wherever funding and other resources are available, the council should build special lanes for cyclists that are separated from the traffic. In this way, they would both promote the general safety of cyclists in Beijing and also encourage more people to choose a bicycle as their preferred means of transport. Demand for private cars would thus decrease, and so fewer greenhouse emissions would be discharged into the air. As a result, Beijing would not only become a more cycle-friendly city, but also a more pleasant environment for residents and tourists alike.

Reading

1 Read Yu's description of cycling in Beijing and choose the best title.

1 The disadvantages of cycling in Beijing
2 A proposal for improving conditions for cyclists in Beijing
3 Why we should all get on our bikes

2 Match each paragraph to one of the headings.

1 Upgrading infrastructure
2 The current situation
3 Enhancing cyclists' safety awareness

3 For paragraphs b and c, find this information:

1 the situation being described
2 the problem
3 a solution
4 the outcome

Linking ideas: results

1 Complete the sentences with all the words or phrases from the box that are possible in each case. Which is the only link expression that can join two clauses together?

| accordingly | as a result | because of this |
| consequently | for this reason | so |

1 The council has improved safety. _____, more people are taking up cycling.
2 The council has improved safety, _____ more people are taking up cycling.
3 The council has improved safety, and _____ more people are taking up cycling.

Language note: *thus, therefore* and *hence* are used in more formal writing. *Thus* and *therefore* are commonly placed mid-position in a sentence:
Accidents have increased. There is therefore / thus a need to review the situation.
Thus can also introduce a participle clause:
The council has improved safety, thus creating a safer environment for cyclists.
Hence is often followed by a noun phrase:
Accidents have increased, hence the need for a review of the situation.

2 Look again at Yu's essay and find the link expressions.

3 Complete the sentences in a suitable way.

1 Cycling is currently perceived as dangerous by many people. As a result, ...
2 The cycle lanes are poorly-lit. The council should therefore ...
3 Cyclists and motorists use the same roads, hence ...
4 Cycle lanes should be built on major roads. More people would thus ...
5 The number of cars on the roads has dramatically increased, thus creating ...

Writing skills: impersonal style

1 Find sentences or parts of sentences in the text that express the following ideas in a more impersonal way.

1 We need to do a lot more.
2 We should make things better for cyclists.
3 We don't have any laws at the moment.
4 We could certainly improve things in the suburbs and the countryside.
5 We wouldn't need so many cars.

2 Match your answers from 1–5 above to one or more of the impersonal structures a–e.

a a passive structure
b *there is / there are*
c *it is* + adjective
d a gerund as subject
e a noun or noun phrase as subject

Preparing to write

With a partner, discuss ways to improve one of the situations below. What concrete measures could or should be taken, and what would be the result?

- conditions for pedestrians in your town
- safety awareness for children or motorists
- conditions or facilities in your place of work or study

Useful language

- The council *could / should / needs to* ...
- They could also consider *introducing / improving* ...
- It is *vital / crucial / essential / of paramount importance* that this should be done.
- It might also be *useful / helpful / desirable* to ...
- *Another / A further possibility / option* would be to ...

Writing

Write a proposal based on your ideas in *Preparing to write*.

Improving listening

1 Tick (✔) the statements about listening to spoken English that are true for you. Then read the information below and discuss with a partner.

- [ ] I find it hard to sustain concentration for a long time, and 'switch off'.
- [ ] I have difficulty following fast conversation with several speakers.
- [ ] I often have problems understanding films and plays.
- [ ] If people speak with an accent, I sometimes only understand a little.
- [ ] I find it hard to understand humour and word play.
- [ ] I sometimes feel frustrated that I can't catch words and understand details.

If any of the statements were true for you, then you are not alone – these are some of the most difficult listening skills to master, even at advanced level. The best way to improve your listening is through practice – little and often is ideal, and it also helps to have a focus or reason for listening. Try to listen on good quality equipment, and at a time when you feel relaxed and able to concentrate.

2 Read a list of strategies for improving your listening and discuss with a partner any that you would like to try.

- ★ Listen regularly to clips on the internet or satellite television (eg news reports, weather, commercials), for interest and information.
- ★ Predict the kind of content or specific words that you might hear, or ask yourself questions.
- ★ Watch feature films and longer programmes. If it helps, listen with subtitles.
- ★ Listen to an audio book, eg when you are travelling or doing chores.
- ★ Read the news in English to understand the content and prepare key vocabulary. Then listen to a news broadcast.
- ★ Listen and take notes on a recording. Replay and add to your notes.
- ★ Listen to a short recording and stop at regular intervals. Try to repeat what you have just heard, or predict what will come next.
- ★ Listen to a very short piece and write down every word that you hear, replaying as often as necessary. If possible, check with a transcript.

Speaking

1 Which of the following shops and places can be found in your neighbourhood or close to where you live?

- butcher's
- estate agent's
- fast-food outlet
- fishmonger's
- florist's
- foreign food restaurant
- grocer's
- live-music venue
- pawn shop
- place of worship (eg church, mosque)
- tattoo parlour
- video rental store
- 24-hour supermarket

2 Work in pairs. Think of two or three shops in your neighbourhood that you visit regularly or that you like for a particular reason. Describe them to your partner and explain why you enjoy shopping there. You can include information about what kinds of products are sold there, the décor, the shop owners or assistants and the kinds of people who shop there.

Reading and Speaking

1 You are going to read an author's description of his neighbourhood. Look at the photos, the picture and the title of the text. What do you think the author is going to say about this area?

2 Now read *Isolarion*. How similar is the neighbourhood described here to your own?

3 Read the text again. Find these phrases and use them to choose the correct option in the statements below. Use a dictionary to help you.

a in its heyday (line 12)
b has been a magnet for (line 13)
c pilgrimage (line 34)
d preserved in aspic (lines 38–39)
e inordinate number (line 41)
f barometer of the health of the nation (lines 46)

1 The Cowley Works car factory employed over 20,000 people *at its height / when it first opened*.
2 The Cowley Works car factory *still attracts / no longer attracts* immigrant workers.
3 The author's journey is a *personal / business* venture.
4 The centre of Oxford *has changed a lot / has not changed much*.
5 One institution in the city owns *quite a large number / an extremely large number* of buildings.
6 The Cowley Road *contrasts with / mirrors* the changing state of the nation.

4 Work in pairs. Choose one question and discuss it with a partner.

- Have you been to other places in your country or abroad which have been 'preserved in aspic' for tourism? What did you think? Should such areas be protected like that?
- The road the author describes contains a real mix of cultures. Do you think that this kind of place is a good model for urban development? If not, what might some of the problems be?

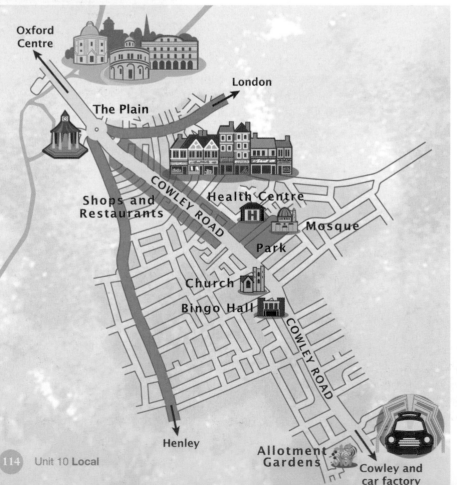

Extend your vocabulary – collocations with *road*

1 Look at collocations with the word *road*.
Verbs:

branch climb cross fork lead

Adjectives:

bumpy coastal congested dirt winding

Which word means …
1 it goes up? goes across? goes to?
2 it divides into two parts? into two or more parts?
3 it goes by the sea? there is lots of traffic?
4 it has a loose surface? isn't smooth? isn't straight?

2 Complete the sentences using some of the words above.
There is a crossroads where three roads meet.
The first road …
The second road …
The third road …

3 Work in pairs. Read your sentences to your partner and ask them to say which road they would rather take, and why.

Writing

You are going to write a description of an interesting area near where you live. It can be an area with appealing shops or buildings, cultural attractions or a particular landscape.

1 First sketch a rough map of the area and its points of interest.
2 Write about your area using your map, as if you are conducting a guided walk around it. Describe the places of interest and why you think other people should know about them.
3 Swap your description with a partner. Read your partner's description and say what you have learnt about this area or what you would like to see.

Isolarion: when local goes global

In the book Isolarion: A Different Oxford Journey, *the Oxford-based author James Attlee decides to go on a journey of global exploration. His trip takes him to many different countries, but none are far away. All of them are right on his doorstep, in his local neighbourhood.*

There is an old road in my neighbourhood that follows approximately the path that ran between the city walls of Oxford and the medieval leper hospital, and beyond it to the village of Cowley. Cowley Road is now the main thoroughfare through 10 East Oxford, connecting the academic and touristic heart of the city with the Cowley Works, the car factory that in its heyday in the 1960s employed over twenty thousand people and has been a magnet for immigrant workers since the 1920s. Today it is lined with businesses that seem to represent every nation on earth. Among them are Jamaican, Bangladeshi, Indian, Polish, Kurdish, 15 Chinese, French, Italian, Thai, Japanese and African restaurants; sari shops, cafés, fast-food outlets, electronics stores, a florist, a Ghanaian fishmonger, pubs, bars, three live-music venues, tattoo parlours, betting shops, 20 a Russian supermarket, a community centre, a publisher, the headquarters of an international NGO, musical instrument vendors, butchers (halal and otherwise), three cycle shops, two video-rental stores, 25 post offices, two mosques, three churches, a Chinese herbalist, a pawn shop, a police station, two record shops, two centres of alternative medicine, a 24-hour supermarket, an independent cinema, call centres, numerous 30 grocers, estate agents, and a bingo hall.

Why make a journey to the other side of the world when the world has come to you?

One aim of my pilgrimage will be to connect me to the neighbourhood in which I live. 35 At the same time, perhaps my journey will offer clues to a wider reality. Oxford is an untypical city, its centre preserved in aspic for tourists, its biggest landlord an ancient institution that still owns 40 an inordinate number of its buildings. Much of the change and diversity in the city has therefore been concentrated into a small area, along the length of Cowley Road. Paradoxically it is this place, often overlooked or omitted from 45 the guidebooks, that is a barometer of the health of the nation. It is both unique and nothing special. It could be any number of streets in your town. For that reason alone, it seems as good a place as any from which to start a journey.

Glossary

leper *(noun)* – a person with leprosy, a serious disease that can cause people's fingers and toes to fall off

thoroughfare *(noun)* – a main road through a place *(formal)*

vendor *(noun)* – a person who sells something

James Attlee lives in Oxford and works in art publishing in London. He is also author of *Nocturne: A Journey in Search of Moonlight*.

Part 2

Speaking and Reading

1 Work in pairs. Ask and answer the questions.

- What is the most recent meal you have had today? What did you eat?
- Do you know where the food came from?

2 Read the text *Why Eat Locally?*, written by a group of North Americans about their choice to become *locavores*, people deciding to only eat local food. Answer the questions.

1 On average how far does American food travel before a person eats it?
2 Why is the journey so long?
3 Why don't people think about this?
4 What are children ignorant of, according to the authors?

3 Do you think people have similar concerns in your country? Do you or anyone you know eat locally on principle? Do your children or children in your country know where their food comes from and how it is produced?

Listening

1 ⚇ **3.34–3.38** You are going to listen to five people talk about different choices. Match each speaker (1–5) to the correct description of the person (a–h).

a a vegan _____
b an advocate of fair trade _____
c a locavore _____
d a picky eater _____
e a vegetarian _____
f a convenience food addict _____
g an allergy sufferer _____
h a health fanatic _____

2 Match the speakers (1–5) to what is being expressed (a–h). Then listen again and check.

a the decision to eat or not eat some kinds of food _____
b an awareness of how animals are reared for food _____
c a desire to help agricultural producers _____
d a reluctance to eat fresh fruit _____
e a lack of interest in changing his or her diet _____
f a commitment to using local sources _____
g a preoccupation with weight and healthy eating _____
h health issues with a certain type of food _____

3 Listen to the first speaker again. Complete the sentences. How can you say these words or phrases more formally?

1 It can be a bit of a _____, eating, just because of my schedule.
2 Stock up on easy stuff, really … _____ it in the freezer.
3 I'll eat on the move and just _____ whatever I can really.
4 I would like to eat more healthily, but just can't be _____ really sometimes.

4 Work in pairs. Have you made similar food choices? What do you think of the other speakers' ideas and opinions?

Extend your vocabulary – *have*

1 Add five more food and drink expressions you can use with *have*:
have *a coffee, a sandwich, …*

2 Study these phrases with *have*. Replace the words in italics with your own ideas.
1 I have no intention of *eating meat ever again*.
2 We have a responsibility to *pay a fair price for agricultural products*.
3 I have no idea if *butter's good for you or not*.
4 I've had enough of *frozen food*.
5 I had a go at *baking bread once and it was a total disaster*.
6 I have high hopes for *genetically modified food*.

Why Eat Locally?

Our food now travels an average of 2,414 km before ending up on our plates. This globalization of the food supply has serious consequences for the environment, our health, our communities and our tastebuds. Much of the food grown in the breadbasket surrounding us must be shipped across the country to distribution centers before it makes its way back to our supermarket shelves. Because uncounted costs of this long distance journey (air pollution and global warming, the ecological costs of large-scale monoculture, the loss of family farms and local community dollars) are not paid for at the checkout counter, many of us do not think about them at all.

What is eaten by the great majority of North Americans comes from a global everywhere, yet from nowhere that we know in particular. How many of our children even know what a chicken eats or how an onion grows?

Grammar and Pronunciation

1 Look at the examples and answer the questions.

1 What is the singular form of the plurals in bold in examples a and b? Do you know other plurals with a similar form?
2 Is the noun in bold in examples c, d and e singular or plural? Is the verb in the singular or plural form?

a *Vegans don't wear wool from* **sheep***.*
b *They don't wear* **clothes** *made of silk either.*
c *The* **data** *never tells you where the food was sourced from.*
d *My* **family** *are all vegetarians.*
e *A large* **percentage** *of small local farmers struggle to survive.*

* although *media* and *data* are Latin plurals, they are sometimes treated as singular uncountable nouns and can be followed by a singular verb
* collective nouns, such as *family, government, company, police, class* and *team* can be followed by either a singular or plural verb form or pronoun
* we use a singular verb when the focus is on the group as a unit and a plural verb when the focus is on the individuals in the group
* in informal language, a plural verb is generally more common, but words such as *percentage, majority, half* and *rest* follow the same pattern

2 Look at the following lists of words. In each list one word is different from the others in its plural form. Delete the odd one out. Then make a rule about how the plurals of the other words are made.

1 deer, fish, pancake, salmon, species
2 headquarters, premises, products, scissors, works
3 goose, lamb, mouse, ox
4 avocado, buffalo, kangaroo, kilo, potato
5 analysis, crisis, oasis, tennis, thesis

3 Look at the plural forms of the words in exercise 2. Plurals ending in *-s* can have two pronunciations: /s/ and /z/. Decide on the pronunciation of …

* words that end in *-oes*.
* *-is* words whose plural ends in *-es*.
* the other words in this section that end in *-s*.

G **Grammar focus** – explanation & more practice of plurals and number on page 150

Speaking

1 Complete the sentences with the correct form of a verb from the box. Compare with a partner. If you have different forms, discuss why.

| release | say (x2) | show | start | throw |

1 One group _____ it's better to eat organic, another _____ local. So is it better to take an organic apple from abroad or a local apple?
2 If the majority of people _____ eating local food in richer countries, it will affect farmers in poorer countries who export food. What about their livelihoods?
3 Data _____ that up to 5% of children in the UK are hyperactive and that food additives play a role. So should food additives be completely banned?
4 The government _____ a report showing that only 10% of emissions related to food come from transport. If eating locally doesn't help the environment, why do it?
5 Some supermarkets give surplus food to homeless and needy people, but many supermarkets simply _____ it away. What can be done about this?

2 Discuss the questions in exercise 1.

Speaking and Vocabulary

1 Answer the questions below with your own ideas. Then work in pairs. How many items do you have in common?

What is the world's most popular …
- sport?
- drink?
- food?
- invention?
- type of music?

2 Read the following definitions of globalisation. Complete the gap with the correct form of the words in brackets.

Globalisation is …

1 the process by which _____ economies, societies and cultures have become integrated through a global network of _____, transportation and trade. (*communicate, region*)

2 a term used to describe the changes in societies and the world economy that are the result of _____ increased cross-border trade, and _____ in cultural exchange. (*drama, invest*)

3 a worldwide process which has resulted in increased _____ of trade and a _____ of wealth in the hands of fewer people. (*concentrate, liberal*)

4 an attempt to _____ consumer habits, values and ways of thinking that contributes to the development of global markets, but undermines local economies and traditions of _____. (*standard, self-sufficient*)

5 a complex series of technological, _____, social, cultural and political changes which have led to an increase in communication and _____ between a large _____ of nations on the planet. (*economy, major, understand*)

3 Look at the definitions again. Which ones seem to be in favour of, against and neutral about globalisation?

4 Do you think globalisation is connected to the popularity of the things you wrote down in exercise 1? Do you think globalisation is a good thing?

Listening

1 Work in pairs. Choose three of the following questions and discuss:

- Why do you think that football (soccer) is so popular?
- Do you ever watch football on television? Have you ever been to a match? If yes, give more details. If not, why not?
- Why is football called the 'beautiful game'?
- Has football changed? What is better or worse about the modern game?
- What do you think the world can learn from football?

2 🔊 **3.39** Listen to a talk about globalisation and football. Tick (✔) those statements which accurately reflect the speaker's comments and opinions. Mark those that do not with a cross (✘).

1 The number of people who watched the 2010 World Cup final on TV was disappointing.

2 Football cannot be considered a 'beautiful game'.

3 It is difficult to imagine a global movement of workers on the same scale as that of footballers.

4 Rich football clubs rob poorer nations of their best players.

5 FIFA (the International Federation of Association Football) does not do enough to support smaller footballing nations.

6 The movement of players and coaches between countries leads to an improvement in the quality of the game.

7 Workers from poor countries should not be allowed to work for more than five years abroad.

3 Listen again to check your answers. Then discuss with your partner what the speaker actually *does* say for those sentences you have marked with a cross.

4 Do you agree that 'everybody benefits and standards rise' as a result of the free movement of football players? Do you think this is a good model for other jobs and professions?

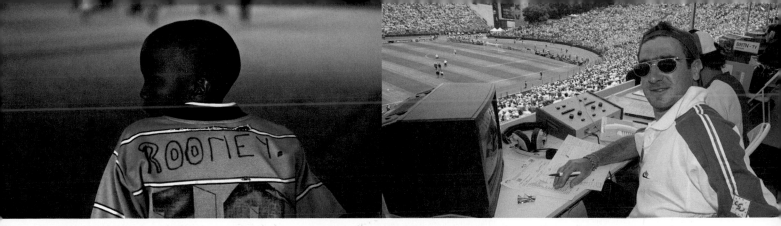

Grammar and Pronunciation

1 Look at the sentences below from the lecture and answer the questions. Then read the explanations.

> a Never before has a single activity captured the hearts and minds of so many people.
> b Not for nothing is it called the 'beautiful game'.
> c Not only do these players and managers bring skills and knowledge back home, they also become heroes in their adopted countries.
>
> • inversion after negative adverbials is used to emphasise that something is unique or rare. It is used in formal language, particularly in speeches and lectures
> • other negative adverbials which take inversion include *rarely, only, no sooner ... than* and *hardly ... when*

1 What words do the sentences a–c start with? What do they have in common?
2 What do you notice about the word order of the subject and verb in the sentences?
3 What is unusual about the verb structure in sentence c?
4 Do the sentences sound formal or informal?

2 🔊 **3.40** Listen to the sentences in exercise 1.

1 Which words are particularly stressed? Underline them.
2 In sentence c, where does the voice go up and down? Where is there a pause?

3 🔊 **3.41** Rewrite the sentences so they begin with the words in brackets. Then listen and check.

1 We rarely find out how decisions are made by FIFA. (*Rarely*)
2 Asian countries have only recently joined the top teams of football. (*Only recently*)
3 The 2010 World Cup had just finished when preparations started for the next one. (*No sooner*)
4 A country can only host the World Cup by paying huge amounts of money to FIFA. (*Only by*)
5 We should never allow countries to spend so much money on a sporting event again. (*Never again*)
6 Winning the World Cup is not only good for a country's self-esteem, but it also boosts its economy. (*Not only*)

4 You are giving a formal speech after winning a sports event. Choose three of the sentence stems below and complete with your own ideas. Read your sentences to a partner. Pay attention to stress and rhythm.

• Never in my life ...   • Rarely ...
• Not only ... but ...   • Never again ...
• At no time ...

ⓖ Grammar focus – explanation & more practice of inversion on page 150

Speaking

1 Work in groups. Your country is lobbying FIFA to be the host of the World Cup.

Group A: think of arguments **in favour of** hosting the World Cup. Consider the following aspects: costs, jobs, tourism, development.
Group B: think of arguments **against** hosting the World Cup. Consider the following aspects: costs, jobs, tourism, development.

2 Work in pairs with a partner from a different group. Present your arguments for or against hosting the World Cup.

3 Who do you think had the best arguments? If your real opinion was different to the one you argued, have you now changed your mind?

10 Local & Global

Part 4

Speaking
Technological inventions

Reading
A Treatise on the Astrolabe

Vocabulary
Using technology

Writing
A technical manual

Speaking

1 Make a list of at least eight technological inventions that have changed society and the way we live.

2 Work in pairs. Compare your lists. Then decide on your three most important objects. What are your criteria for choosing these items?

They are globally available, they help people communicate, they save lives ...

3 Work with another pair. Explain your list and the criteria you used to decide.

Reading

1 You are going to read an introduction to an instruction manual for the *astrolabe*, a technological object from ancient times.

- Look at the image of the astrolabe. Have you seen this image before? What kind of information do you think it gives?
- Turn to the back cover of your book and check your answers.

2 Now read *A Treatise on the Astrolabe*. When was the manual written, who was it written for and why was it written?

3 Read the text again and insert a–f below in the correct places in the text.

a so you can become familiar with your own instrument
b even though the original has been lost
c following the style of our scholars
d and in every sign from your almanac
e having observed the boy's ability and eagerness in science
f the majority of which come from the 15th century

4 Read the text and the information about Chaucer again and underline the following. Then work in pairs and explain the terms.

1 three geographical terms
2 four words connected to astrology

5 Here are some of the uses for the astrolabe, according to Chaucer's treatise. Do you think any of them are useful knowledge today? Can you do any of them?

- to find the four cardinal points (East, West, North, South)
- to find the Sun's altitude in degrees
- to find the length of the day from daybreak to twilight
- to find the coordinates of any visible star in relation to the Earth
- to find the latitude of where you are on the planet

Vocabulary

1 Look at the words below. Which of them are used to describe the astrolabe in the text? Could any of the other words be used?

1 **appliance**: a machine or piece of equipment in your home
2 **tool**: a piece of equipment that you hold in your hand
3 **gadget**: a small piece of modern equipment that does something useful or impressive
4 **device**: a piece of equipment that does a particular thing
5 **instrument**: a piece of equipment used in science, medicine or technology

2 Think of at least one example for each of the words in exercise 1.

A Treatise on the Astrolabe
The first technical manual for a global device

A Treatise on the Astrolabe *was composed in the years 1391–92 by the English writer Geoffrey Chaucer. It is regarded as the oldest English 'technical manual' or description of a scientific device. (1) ___, the text has survived in as many as at least 22 manuscripts, (2) ___.*

The work can be thought of as an initial book on astronomy. It was addressed to ten-year-old Lewis, apparently the author's own son. (3) ___, Chaucer gave him the instrument and wrote a manual to teach the child to use the device.

'Little Lewis, my son, I see some evidence that you have the ability to learn science, number and proportions, and I recognise your special desire to learn about the astrolabe. So, as the philosopher said, "he serves his friend who grants his friend's wishes," I propose to teach you some facts about the instrument with this treatise. There are several reasons for this treatise. First, no one in this region has complete knowledge of the noble astrolabe. Another reason is that there are errors in the astrolabe treatises that I have seen and some of them present material too difficult for a ten year old to understand.

This treatise is divided into five parts.

First part: The first part of this treatise presents the parts of your astrolabe (4) ___.

Second part: The second part teaches practical uses of previous facts, as much as possible for such a small portable instrument.

Third part: The third part contains various tables of longitudes and latitudes of fixed stars for the astrolabe, a table of declinations of the Sun, tables of longitudes of cities and towns, tables for setting a clock and to find the meridian altitude and other notable conclusions from calendars.

Fourth part: The fourth part contains a theory to explain the movements of the celestial bodies and their causes. In particular, the fourth part contains a table of the moon's motion for every hour of every day (5) ___.

Fifth part: The fifth part shall be an introduction, (6) ___, in which you can learn most of the general theory of astrology.'

Geoffrey Chaucer (c. 1343–1400) was the first great poet writing in English and is best known for *The Canterbury Tales*, a collection of stories in verse and prose recounted on a pilgrimage to Canterbury. However, he earned his living as a diplomat, a member of parliament and a judge – as well as being a keen astronomer.

---

3 Read the definitions for eight objects. Choose the correct option in the sentence. Then match it to the correct object in the box.

bar code reader	car alarm	CCTV
ear thermometer	GPS navigation	mp3 player
robot vacuum cleaner	USB memory stick	

1 _____ is a device that is used to *determine / evaluate* your position, wherever you are in the world.

2 _____ is an instrument that is used to *display / monitor* activity in public places.

3 A(n) _____ is a gadget that you can use to store and *access / approach* electronic documents and files on the move.

4 A(n) _____ is an appliance that can be programmed to *remove / dispose* dirt and dust all over your home.

5 A(n) _____ is a tool that can *calculate / measure* the body's temperature and show it on a small screen.

6 A(n) _____ is a tool that can *scan / control* visual representations of data such as prices.

7 A(n) _____ is a device which is used in order to *encourage / discourage* thieves.

8 A(n) _____ is a gadget that is used to *decode / encode* and play back audio files.

4 Which of these devices do you use or experience in your daily life? Which one would you say is the least useful?

Writing

Look back at the list of objects you talked about in Speaking exercise 2. Choose one of them. You are going to write a short introduction to a simple technical manual for this object.

1 Think first about what you are going to write. Use the following questions to help give you ideas:
- What is the function of your object and why is it important for global understanding?
- Who are you writing for and what is the purpose of your manual?
- Which functions will you include and how will you divide the manual into sections?

2 Write your introduction. When you've finished, exchange it with a partner. Is your partner's introduction clear and helpful? Has he or she left out any important information? Give your partner feedback.

Function globally making proposals and suggestions

Warm up

Work in pairs. Discuss these questions.

- Which of the following facilities do you have in your town? How often do you use them?

Swimming pool	Arts centre
Library	Football pitch
Park	Tennis courts
Children's playground	Zoo

- Which are subsidised by the town council or government?
- Do you think facilities like these should be publicly managed and subsidised, or should they be run and financed by the private sector? Why?

Listening

1 🔘 3.42 Listen to a meeting to discuss proposed local government cuts and answer the questions.

1 Which facility are they discussing?
2 What proposals are put forward to deal with the proposed cuts?
3 What advantages and disadvantages of the proposals are mentioned?
4 What time is agreed on for the next meeting?

2 Listen again and complete the sentences. What does each word or phrase mean?

1 I've _____ this meeting to discuss the local government spending cuts.
2 Has everyone got a copy of the _____ by the way?
3 I would just _____ with that from a safety point of view.
4 Can I just _____ something here?
5 I don't think we should get too _____ by the whole demonstration thing.
6 I would like to _____ what Nigel has just said about health and safety as well.
7 Who would be willing to _____ for the fundraiser?
8 OK, well, that _____ for today.

Language focus

1 Read some ways of making suggestions and choose the better alternative.

1 Can I *make / have* a suggestion, please?
2 I think it *is / would be* a great idea to write a letter.
3 We *could / can* write a letter.
4 I propose we *write / could write* a letter.
5 It *can be / might be* an idea to write a letter.
6 I'd like to suggest *to write / that we write* a letter.
7 How about *writing / we write* a letter?
8 I think we *have to / should* write a letter.
9 In *that / this* case, we could always write a letter.
10 What we need to do is *write / writing* a letter.

2 Which of the suggestions are …

a stronger? b more tentative? c more formal?

3 Read the responses to suggestions, and rank them 1–6 (1 = strong agreement, 6 = strong disagreement).

That's a good idea. _____
Yes, but the problem is … _____
That's ridiculous. _____
That's a brilliant idea. _____
I suppose we could. _____
With respect, I don't think that's feasible. _____

Pronunciation

1 Work in pairs. Look again at the responses to suggestions in *Language focus* exercise 3, and predict which word or words carry the main stress.

2 🔘 3.43 Listen to check your ideas. Then practise repeating the expressions.

Speaking

Work in small groups. Choose one of the situations below to roleplay. One person should chair the meeting, and everyone should offer suggestions.

- A local residents' meeting to discuss how to spend money to improve leisure facilities.
- A group of students or co-workers discussing how to improve facilities at their school or workplace.

Useful phrases

- Let's get started.
- Could we *start with / move on to* item 2 on the agenda?
- Does anyone have anything else to add?
- Are we in agreement on this?
- Can we set a date for the next meeting?

Global voices

Warm up

🔊 **3.44** Listen to Evgenia talk about a typical task she had in English class in Belarus. Did you ever have to do this in language classes at school?

Listening

1 🔊 **3.45–3.46** Listen to Harshula from Sri Lanka and Jiawei from China talk about towns they remember from their childhood. Who says what? Write *H* for Harshula or *J* for Jiawei.

1 Travelled from one part of the town to another as a child. _____
2 Has decided to go back home to this town. _____
3 Always wanted to visit this town during the holidays. _____
4 Has a cousin in this town. _____
5 Has memories of activities that cost very little. _____
6 Wants to do something for the community. _____
7 Thinks that people have become more interested in material things. _____

2 Work in pairs. Use the notes below to take turns retelling what you remember of Harshula's and Jiawei's stories.

Harshula
- Ratnapura
- summer vacation
- Oxford
- London law firm
- go back home
- do something

Jiawei
- Pudong
- eastern and western side
- ferry
- round structure
- sitting
- father
- river

3 🔊 **3.47–3.48** Now listen to how Harshula and Jiawei say their towns have changed. Answer the questions.

1 What reason does Harshula give when he says that Ratnapura has been neglected?
2 What disappointed Jiawei about the Shanghai exposition?

Language focus: *the thing is*

1 Read Jiawei's sentence. What is the best explanation for the use of the phrase in bold?

*But **the thing is** they charge admission fee, right, and so it becomes a little bit different, it becomes like a commercial.*

1 to avoid a specific mention of something
2 to focus attention on a problem
3 to list the order of things

2 Complete the sentences with your own ideas.

1 I'd love to go out without everyone this Saturday, but the thing is …
2 Thanks for calling about the job interview. The thing is …
3 A: So, did you call your boss?
   B: No, ummm, the thing is …
4 A: Hi, I'm here to pick up my car.
   B: Your car? Oh yes. Well, the thing is …

Speaking

1 Think about a local area you remember while you were growing up. Look at the following questions to help you:

- What was the area like?
- Did you enjoy living there? What was good about it?
- Do you still live there?
- If you don't live there now, have you returned?
- Has it changed? Are the changes for the better or worse?

2 Work in pairs. Discuss your answers to the questions.

Evgenia, Belarus   Jiawei, China   Harshula, Sri Lanka

Unit 10 Writing a website entry

Reading

1 Read Davide's website entry about his village. Suggest a heading for each paragraph.

2 Here are some answers from the text. What could the questions be?

1 In the north-west of Italy.
2 By bus, train or car.
3 To relax and get away from it all.
4 Spectacular.
5 About 1,200.
6 You can visit churches and take part in sporting activities and cultural events.
7 The *Antico Bistrot* bar.
8 Yes, several, including the *Festa dal pais c'me nà vota* in June.

Writing skills: register

1 Read an informal email to a friend about Mirabello. Match the words and phrases in italics with formal equivalents in the website entry.

Hi Gina

It's great you're planning to visit Mirabello. (1) *It's* only an hour from Milan – (2) *you can easily get there* by train or by car (3) *coming off* the A21 at Alessandria Sud. You'll love all the old buildings. (4) *It's got* four gorgeous churches – plus (5) *you don't need to book in advance* if you fancy just having a look around. (6) *You can do loads of sports too*. The festivals (7) *are a bit touristy* – but the one in June is (8) *great fun*! Hope you enjoy your stay anyway!

Cheers, D.

1 Mirabello Monferrato is situated in the Piedmont region in the north-west of Italy, one hour by car from cities such as Milan, Turin and Genoa. Public transport consists of a bus service connecting the village with a small town called Alessandria located ten miles to the south; alternatively, it is easily reachable by train from mainline stations. If coming from abroad, it is best to rent a car at Turin airport and take the A21, leaving at Alessandria Sud and following signs to the village.

2 Mirabello is a perfect place to spend a relaxing weekend or week away from the crowds. The countryside in the surrounding area is spectacular and the whole village steeped in a history dating back to the Middle Ages. Whereas in the past the population reached 3,000, nowadays there are only about 1,200 inhabitants.

3 Despite its size, the village boasts four magnificent churches, each with its own particular architectural style, reflecting the history of Mirabello during medieval times. These churches can be visited every day from 8am to 6pm; no reservation is required and no entrance fee is charged. Sporting activities are also well provided for in Mirabello; it is possible to take part in activities such as football, tennis, cycling, jogging, basketball and volleyball.

4 When lunchtime comes, I strongly recommend a visit to the *Antico Bistrot* bar, in the main village square. Delicious local dishes including ravioli, polenta and the traditional *bagna cauda* (hot sauce in English) are served from 10am to 2pm. Sandwiches are available all day long, up to 1am when the bar closes.

5 There are also several cultural events throughout the year that attract a large number of tourists. The first week of June, for example, is notable for the so-called *Festa dal pais c'me nà vota* which in the local dialect means 'village festival like in the past'. The event takes place in the main square where traditional food (and wine) is served and ancient local music played. It is a hugely enjoyable occasion that should not be missed!

2 Which of these would you normally include in a more formal piece of writing?

- *a lot of / a bit*
- complex sentences
- contractions, eg *don't*
- exclamation marks
- non-specific words, eg *thing, stuff*
- *get / got*
- informal words and expressions
- many phrasal verbs
- noun phrases instead of verbs
- passive verbs
- precise details

Language note: in formal language it is common to use words derived from Latin, eg *obtain / discover / construct* instead of *get / find / build*.

Linking ideas: alternatives and examples

1 Which of the words or phrases in the box introduce ...

1 an alternative?   2 an example?

alternatively   eg   equally   for example
for instance   including   like   likewise   otherwise
similarly   such as   whether ... or

2 Complete the sentences thinking of places that you know.

1 You can sample a variety of local dishes, *such as* ...
2 It is an ideal spot for relaxing and unwinding; *equally*, you can ...
3 The town boasts several luxury hotels; *alternatively*, there are ...
4 You can take part in a number of outdoor pursuits *including* ...
5 It is an excellent location, *whether* you are looking for a cultural experience *or* ...
6 Cities *like* ... are often packed with tourists in summer.
7 Adults are well catered for; *similarly*, ...

3 Which other words or phrases from the box (if any) could replace the words in italics?

Preparing to write

Choose a place that you know to write a visitors' introduction. Working in pairs, use the questions from Reading exercise 2 to find out about your partner's place.

Describing a place

- It is *one hour / easily reachable* from Milan by *bus / train*.
- It is a perfect *place to ... / base for visiting ...*
- The village boasts *four churches / a modern shopping centre*.
- It is *notable / famous / worth visiting* for its annual music festival.
- *Sporting activities / Cultural events / Outdoor pursuits* are well *provided for / catered for*.

Writing

Write a visitor's introduction using the headings you wrote for Reading exercise 1.

Celebrating your achievements

1 Congratulations – you have reached the end of the course! Becoming an advanced user of English entails hard work. This is a good time to celebrate and enjoy your achievements as an advanced learner. As you read the list of skills and abilities below, tick (✔) the ones that apply most to you, and add other ideas of your own at the end.

- [ ] I have a sound knowledge of English grammar and can answer questions about several aspects of English usage.
- [ ] I can get information quickly and accurately from newspapers and fact sheets.
- [ ] I can watch a television programme or film in English and understand nearly all of it.
- [ ] I can enjoy reading novels or other works of fiction in English.
- [ ] I have developed language learning skills that can help me learn another language more efficiently.
- [ ] I can help others by translating or interpreting.
- [ ] I can be creative in English, expressing my ideas in writing or playing with words.
- [ ] Knowing another language in depth has taught me other ways of looking at the world.
- [ ] I can fully appreciate and enjoy listening to songs in English.
- [ ] I can express different sides of myself in a different language.
- [ ] I can enjoy listening or reading in English and understanding humour and subtleties.
- [ ] I can take an advanced qualification in English.
- [ ] I can use English effectively in my work or studies.
- [ ] I have increased my employment opportunities.
- [ ] I can teach English to other people with confidence and enjoyment.
- [ ] I can communicate fluently and confidently with native and non-native speakers of English, in my own country or abroad.
- [ ] I can participate fully in the global conversation.

2 Compare your ideas with a partner. What have been the highlights of this English course for you?

3 In small groups, share ideas on ways in which you can keep up your English after the course.

Communication activities: Student A

Unit 1, Reading and Speaking (page 8)

Read the text and match your museum to one of the photos on page 8. Then make notes on these questions:

1 What is on display at the museum?
2 What is unusual or adventurous about the museum?
3 Is the aim of the museum stated? If not, what do you think it could be?

Museum in the Clouds, Dolomites, Italy

Over 2,000 metres above sea level, the Dolomites' Museum in the Clouds is an ambitious exercise in mountaineering and unique landscape art. Part of the ongoing Messner Mountain Museum project, the site exhibits paintings and sculptures of the Dolomite range. All collections are from the private memorabilia of pioneering climber Reinhold Messner – and are a celebration of the thrills and challenges that adventurers face on the range.

Glossary

memorabilia *(noun)* – objects you collect that interest you

Unit 1, Grammar (page 13)

Read out the sentences and questions to your partner and listen to their replies. Then listen to your partner's sentences and questions and answer as quickly as you can using one of the phrases below.

- I think horoscopes are total rubbish.
- Can you explain to me what quantum physics is?
- Would you like to come to the opera with me on Saturday?
- I love country music.
- Everything was better in the old days.
- Looks like interest rates are going to go down.

I think so (too). / I don't think so.
I hope so. / I hope not.
I'd love to. / I'd really like to, but I can't.
I do too. / I'm afraid I don't.
I'll try to. / I don't think I can.

Unit 2, Listening and Speaking (page 18)

1 Study your work of art. Then describe it to your partner, using some of the questions in exercises 1 and 2 to guide you. Your partner should try to form a mental image of the work of art. Swap over.

2 Now look at the original. How does it compare with the image you had in your mind's eye? Which of the works of art do you prefer, and why?

Unit 2, Speaking (page 20)

Read information about the Sun and write three quiz questions. Ask your partner the questions. Which facts surprised you most?

The Sun is actually a very large star, and is the closest star to the Earth in the solar system. The distance between the Sun and the Earth is approximately 150 million km. The Earth rotates around the Sun every 365.26 days, and the Sun rotates on its own axis every 27 days. It takes about 8 minutes 18 seconds for light from the Sun to reach the Earth. Sunlight helps release vitamin D in the body, which can enhance a person's mood.

How long does it take light from the Sun to reach the Earth?

Unit 3, Vocabulary and Pronunciation (page 33)

1 Read the facts about the Great Depression in the United States. Tell your partner about this event.

The Great Depression of the 1930s

- Began 29 October 1929 with a stock market crash.
- By 1933, 11,000 of the 25,000 banks in the US had failed.
- 273,000 families had been evicted from their homes by 1932.
- Unemployment in the United States reached 25%.
- Depression spread quickly to the world, with international trade falling by over a half.

2 Ask your partner to retell you the story of the Great Depression. Have they got their facts right? Is the pronunciation of the numbers correct?

3 Listen to your partner tell you about another 'Great' event. Make notes, but only of the numbers you hear. When you've finished, retell your version of the event using only the numbers to help you.

Unit 1, Reading and Speaking (page 8)

Read the text and match your museum to one of the photos on page 8. Then make notes on these questions:

1 What is on display at the museum?
2 What is unusual or adventurous about the museum?
3 Is the aim of the museum stated? If not, what do you think it could be?

Chichu Art Museum, Naoshima, Japan

Japan's Chichu Art Museum is worth visiting for its adventurous architecture alone: its entire collection is exhibited below ground. Dubbed the 'art museum in the earth', the venue displays artwork by the likes of Claude Monet, Walter De Maria and James Turrell – and is lit only by strategic pools of natural light. A 400 sq metre garden has been planted above ground, and it's hoped that the overall experience will encourage visitors to explore man's relationship with nature.

Communication activities: Student A

Unit 4, Reading (page 44)

1 Read the film review. You have three minutes to read and remember details about your film, including the plot, theme, setting, ending and reviewer's opinion.

2 Compare notes with a partner. What extra information does each person have? Do the reviews make you want to see the film or not? Why?

Italian For Beginners (2000)
Lone Scherfig

There's some mileage yet in the Dogme franchise. Shot on some of the same locations as *Dancer in the Dark*, this immensely likeable movie about six unhappy loners eking out an existence in a dead end town starts in bleak fashion, but once the losers start attending evening classes in Italian, the mood begins to lighten. By the final reel, the film has turned into something approaching a conventional romantic comedy. Scherfig (the first woman to direct a Dogme movie) denies that she was trying to serve up a fairytale ending. 'I just hope people who see the film can see the possibility of turning a not so good fate into a slightly better one,' she says.

Unit 5, Grammar (page 61)

1 Complete the sentences in a suitable way. Use a participle clause if the sentence does not contain one already.

2 Read the sentences you have written to your partner. Are any the same?

1 The prisoners _____ trying not to wake the guards.
2 _____, he turned to a life of crime.
3 While eavesdropping on the conversation, he _____.
4 Seeing the pirate ship approach, the captain _____.
5 The prisoners escaped from the jail, _____.
6 _____, she started to scream uncontrollably.
7 Having been convicted of murder, she _____.
8 _____, the psychologists started to analyse the results.

Unit 9, Speaking (page 109)

Read the answers to questions 1, 3 and 5. Take it in turns to explain the answers to your partner without reading them out.

1 Kangaroos don't walk, they hop because their feet are too big and their legs are simply unsuited to walking. Kangaroos have four toes on each foot and the fourth toe propels them off the ground. They also have strong elastic tendons in the legs which mean they move like a spring. Kangaroos can hop at up to 40–50 km an hour.
3 Ants find their way to food and back to their nests by storing and activating memory images. Ants have very poor eyesight and first follow a chemical trail left by other ants on a journey. At the same time they store memories of the trip based on certain landmarks.
5 Despite having no legs, snakes manage to move (or slither) quite quickly by using their muscles and their scales to push off the ground. There are four different types of snake movement or 'locomotion' and for each one the snake uses a different part of its body – head, tail or belly.

Communication activities: Student B

Unit 1, Reading and Speaking (page 8)

Read the text and match your museum to one of the photos on page 8. Then make notes on these questions:

1 What is on display at the museum?
2 What is unusual or adventurous about the museum?
3 Is the aim of the museum stated? If not, what do you think it could be?

Museo Subaquático de Arte, Moilinere Bay, Grenada

The clue's in the name: entry to Museo Subaquático de Arte requires a wetsuit ... and a full oxygen tank. Art knows no boundaries for British sculptor Jason de Caires Taylor – his exhibition of 65 life-size sculptures lies in the Caribbean Sea, accessible only by boat from mainland Grenada. Visitors must scuba dive to the site, which lies up to 25 metres below sea level. It's hoped that the installation will encourage marine life to develop, and encourage travellers to reflect upon their impact on the coast.

Glossary

wetsuit *(noun)* – a rubber suit worn for water sports

Unit 1, Grammar (page 13)

Read out the sentences and questions to your partner and listen to their replies. Then listen to your partner's sentences and questions and answer as quickly as you can using one of the phrases below.

- I think the speed of technological change is just crazy.
- Has the price of petrol gone down?
- How about going out for lunch on Sunday?
- I think there's going to be a bad storm later.
- Telepathy is complete nonsense.
- Do you think you could help me put up some shelves?

I think so (too). / I don't think so.
I hope so. / I hope not.
I'd love to. / I'd really like to, but I can't.
I do too. / I'm afraid I don't.
I'll try to. / I don't think I can.

Unit 2, Listening and Speaking (page 18)

1 Study your work of art. Then describe it to your partner, using some of the questions in exercises 1 and 2 to guide you. Your partner should try to form a mental image of the work of art. Swap over.

2 Now look at the original. How does it compare with the image you had in your mind's eye? Which of the works of art do you prefer, and why?

Unit 2, Speaking (page 20)

Read information about the Sun and write three quiz questions. Ask your partner the questions. Which facts surprised you most?

The Sun was formed over 4.5 billion years ago. It will probably continue shining for at least another 5 billion years. Its diameter is 109 times wider than the Earth's diameter. It is composed of about 92% hydrogen, 7% helium and 1% other gases. The temperature at the core of the Sun is about 15 million degrees Celsius. Sunlight contains UV (ultraviolet) light, which can harm the skin and the eyes if they are exposed to too much sunshine.

What is the temperature at the core of the Sun?

Unit 3, Vocabulary and Pronunciation (page 33)

1 Listen to your partner tell you about a 'Great' event. Make notes, but only of the numbers you hear. When you've finished, retell your version of the event using only the numbers to help you.

2 Now read the facts below about the Great Fire of London. When you're ready, tell your partner about this event.

The Great Fire of London

- Started on 2 September 1666 and lasted five days.
- Almost 80% or four-fifths of the city was destroyed, including 13,200 homes and 84 churches.
- Made an estimated 100,000 people homeless, 1/6 of London's population and caused £10 million worth of damage.
- The rebuilding started in 1667 and lasted nearly 50 years.
- Only four officially recorded deaths.

3 Ask your partner to retell you the story of the Great Fire of London. Have they got their facts right? Is the pronunciation of the numbers correct?

Unit 4, Reading (page 44)

1 Read the film review. You have three minutes to read and remember details about your film, including the plot, theme, setting, ending and reviewer's opinion.

2 Compare notes with a partner. What extra information does each person have? Do the reviews make you want to see the film or not? Why?

Italian For Beginners (2000) Lone Scherfig

This beautiful, understated film from Danish director Lone Scherfig uses natural lighting, muted cinematography and a partially improvised script. The film is not about learning Italian, though the film's six thirtysomething characters all meet each other through an Italian class at the community centre in their quiet, rainy town. The film is about real life and hardship and hope. A nurturing hair stylist, a clumsy bakery clerk, a committed pastor, a foul-mouthed waiter, a friendly hotel manager and a lonely waitress all struggle with the banality of daily life, while dealing with their own unique challenges. But as they begin to reveal themselves and their problems to each other, they form a bond and a network that is both a safety net and a new reason to live.

Unit 5, Grammar (page 61)

1 Complete the sentences in a suitable way. Use a participle clause if the sentence does not contain one already.

2 Read the sentences you have written to your partner. Are any the same?

1 The prisoners tiptoed out of the cell, _____.
2 Not knowing how to support his family, he _____.
3 While _____, he overheard a plot to assassinate the dictator.
4 _____, the captain radioed for help.
5 _____, causing widespread panic.
6 Seeing the burglar break into her room, _____.
7 _____, she was sentenced to life imprisonment.
8 The experiment concluded, the psychologists _____.

Unit 9, Speaking (page 109)

Read the answers to questions 2, 4 and 6. Take it in turns to explain the answers to your partner without reading them out.

2 Birds migrate to other countries in order to find a plentiful and reliable food supply. They also migrate in order to find a suitable place to breed with longer daylight and away from predators. Birds that forage for food in flocks are less likely to migrate, as are birds that live in all-year climates such as the Amazon rainforest.

4 Bats look for their prey in the dark using sonar sound or 'echolocation'. Bats produce sounds using their voice box or clicking their tongues. The resulting echoes of insects or other animals are heard and interpreted by the bats, whose ears and brain cells are fine-tuned to hear minimal differences in sound.

6 Mature salmon find their way back thousands of kilometres from the ocean to their birth stream using their ability to detect the Earth's magnetic field. This enables them to sense direction. Once they are near their target area, they use their sense of smell to guide them over the final section of their journey.

Student D

Unit 1, Reading and Speaking (page 8)

Read the text and match your museum to one of the photos on page 8. Then make notes on these questions:

1 What is on display at the museum?
2 What is unusual or adventurous about the museum?
3 Is the aim of the museum stated? If not, what do you think it could be?

Pitcairn Island Museum, Pitcairn Island, South Pacific

A visit to Pitcairn Island, a volcanic outcrop stranded in the South Pacific between New Zealand and South America, is not for the faint-hearted. It's a 30-hour, $4,000 boat trip from the island of Mangareva in the French Polynesian Gambier Islands, but should you find yourself there on a wet afternoon, be sure to pay the island's museum a visit. You'll find Polynesian artefacts, and probably encounter most of Pitcairn's residents – the descendants of the *Bounty* mutineers and their Tahitian 'companions'. A recent headcount reported a population of just 50.

Historical note

The *Bounty* mutineers took over the naval ship The *Bounty* in 1789, in response to the alleged cruelty of the ship's captain. They were attracted to the islanders' lifestyle.

Additional material

Unit 3, Study skills (page 41)

Looking up unknown words: this is not a good general strategy. It may increase your vocabulary, but it will slow you down. Often you do not need to know the meaning of every word in order to understand what you need from a text, though there are some texts (eg instructions, legal documents) where you need a detailed understanding. Reading aloud slows most people down and can distract from understanding, although a few auditory readers may find it beneficial.

In general, you should experiment with reading strategies to find what works best for you, as no two readers are exactly the same.

Unit 7, Study skills (page 89)

1–5 F. Native speakers normally rely on fixed expressions and a reduced range of language when speaking and frequently repeat themselves, use fillers, and make false starts and grammatical errors. In many conversational situations it is not necessary to be precise, and even preferable to use general words and 'vague language'. Studying a transcript of real speech will soon confirm this!

6–7 T. It is hard to concentrate on content, accuracy, fluency and range of language at the same time, given the natural constraints of speaking in real time. Research suggests that both task rehearsal and task repetition can improve and enrich aspects of speaking by reducing what speakers have to concentrate on, especially if they can analyse their performance.

Unit 8, Speaking (page 91)

1 No, the chance still remains 50%.
2 Yes. Statistically speaking, your chances increase from 1/3 to 2/3.

Grammar focus

Unit 1

Present simple and continuous for facts and trends

We use the present simple ...
- to describe states, routines and habits
  I *love* visiting museums.
  I *usually do* my research on the internet.
- for well-established facts
  Museums *keep* many of their exhibits in storage.

We use the present continuous ...
- to describe a temporary situation
  Sorry, *I'm using* this computer. I won't be long.
- to describe a trend or new development, often with verbs describing change, eg *change, increase, get* + adjective. Comparative adjectives often occur in this type of sentence.
  The number of people reading using electronic readers is increasing.
  More and more young people are visiting our museum.
- with certain state verbs which also have a dynamic, progressive meaning
  Science *is appealing* to younger audiences nowadays.
  I'm loving every minute! (colloquial)

Simple or continuous?
Some time adverbials may be more common with either simple or continuous, or can be used with both, but with a different meaning.

Most people get their information from the internet *nowadays*. (established fact)
Nowadays, more and more people are reading books electronically. (new development)

Frequency adverbs *always, forever* and *continually* can be used with present continuous to emphasise an emotional reaction to a regular activity.
He's *continually making* a nuisance of himself! (This annoys me.)

Position of adverbials
Single word time adverbials can be placed between subject and verb. They normally come after auxiliary verbs *be, have*, etc, and after *be* as a main verb, but after a negative auxiliary.
I *usually* look up information on the internet.
You're *always* interrupting me when I speak.
He's *generally* at home by 6.00.

Longer adverbials are placed at the beginning or end of the sentence or clause.
Most of the time I do my research on the internet.
I read modern novels *from time to time*, but I prefer watching films.

Currently, at the moment, temporarily, at present and *for the time being* describe a <u>temporary</u> situation.
The museum is *currently* being refurbished.

Ellipsis

Words can often be left out to avoid repetition ...
- the main verb and its object can be left out after an auxiliary verb
  The museum *should abolish* entrance charges.
  Yes, they *should*, but they *can't*.
  I think the book has presented some interesting facts and figures.
  Yes, it *has*.
- infinitive clauses can be reduced to the word *to*
  He was told *to read* both books, but he decided *not to*.
- in answers to questions
  Do you know much about science?
  I'm afraid *I don't*.   Yes, *I do*.

- in opinion questions
  Is there human life on other planets?
  I think *there is*.   I think *so*.
  I don't think *there is*.   I don't think *so*.
  (NB *I think not* is considered old-fashioned.)
  I suppose *so*.   I suppose *not*.
- in spoken English where the context is clear, unnecessary words can also be left out
- at the beginning of a sentence, subject pronouns can be left out before all verbs
- in questions the auxiliary verb can be left out when the subject is clear (except before *I* and *it*)
  Want some coffee?   Sorry, *don't have* the time.

Future forms: plans

There is no future tense in English. To express intention, various different forms are used.
- use the present continuous, *have / has arranged to do* or *be due to do* to express fixed personal arrangements
  I'm seeing Pete tomorrow.
- use the present simple for a formal timetabled arrangement
  My plane *gets in* at six.
- use *be going / planning / intending / hoping to do* or *be thinking of doing* to express a clear intention
  I'm going to clean the house tomorrow.

- use *might / may do* or *will* qualified with *maybe, perhaps* or *probably* to express a less certain intention
  I might go to the cinema, or *maybe* I'll watch a DVD.
- use *will* for plans formed at the moment of speaking
  The rain's stopped – I think *I'll go* for a walk.
- the continuous aspect distances the speaker from the plan
  I'm going to be working late this evening.

Unit 1 Exercises

Present simple and continuous for facts and trends

1 Choose the more likely option for the context.

1 Sorry, could you wait a moment? *I speak / I'm speaking* to someone on the phone.
2 Can you put the heating on? *It gets / It's getting* cold in here.
3 All the lights have gone out. What *happens / is happening*?
4 This book *tells / is telling* the story of a man lost in the mountains.
5 Unfortunately, more and more second-hand bookshops *close down / are closing down*.
6 After many years of research, most scientists are in agreement that the world's climate *changes / is changing*.

2 In which sentences are both options possible?

1 Stop ordering me about! *You're always telling me what to do! / You always tell me what to do.*
2 This was such a good idea! I *am really enjoying / really enjoy* myself.
3 *I find / I'm finding* this book really interesting.
4 I'm pleased with your work. *You're trying very hard. / You try very hard.*
5 The air on Earth *is containing / contains* about 78% nitrogen.
6 Most students *prefer / are preferring* to research projects on the internet.
7 Fewer and fewer people *use / are using* libraries.

3 Choose the best time adverbial to complete the sentence.

1 _____, many people feel that space exploration is a waste of money.
  a Every other week   b Generally speaking   c Rarely
2 _____, I wonder whether life exists on other planets.
  a From time to time   b At present   c These days
3 We don't _____ go to art exhibitions unless it's someone really famous.
  a most of the time   b increasingly   c normally
4 _____, people are finding that information on the internet is incorrect.
  a Temporarily   b Increasingly   c Once in a blue moon
5 This part of the library is _____ closed, while new computer terminals are being installed.
  a rarely   b these days   c currently
6 _____, children's books are enjoying great popularity.
  a At the moment   b Normally   c From time to time

Ellipsis

4 Rewrite the sentences deleting or replacing any unnecessary words.

1 A: Do you feel like seeing a film tonight?
  B: No, I don't want to see a film.
  _____

2 A: Is the gallery open tomorrow?
  B: No, I don't think it's open tomorrow.
  _____

3 A: I'm taking a break now.
  B: Yes, I think I'll take a break too.
  _____

4 A: Are you getting a new computer?
  B: No, I can't afford to buy a new computer.
  _____

Future forms: plans

5 Delete the least likely alternative.

1 *I'm going to retire / I'll retire / I'm retiring* next year.
2 I'm *planning / hoping / thinking* to buy a new car.
3 I think *I'll be playing / I'll play / I play* tennis on Sunday.
4 What time *does the film start / is the film starting / has the film arranged to start*?
5 What *do you do / are you doing / will you be doing* tonight?
6 *I've arranged to / I'll / I'm due to* take my driving test tomorrow.

Unit 2

Future predictions

Will is used in a definite prediction, when we know or believe that an event is certain.
*The cost of oil **will continue** to rise.*

We can make the prediction less or more certain by using ...
*   adverbs such as *definitely (not)*, *certainly (not)* and *probably (not)* and modifiers such as *almost*, *quite*
    *The cost of oil **will (almost) certainly continue** to rise.*
*   It is + *certain*, *(un)likely*, *(im)possible*, *probable*, etc + *that* clause
    ***It is (highly) likely that** the cost of oil **will continue** to rise.*
*   There is + *(a) (strong, etc) chance / likelihood / possibility, no way / no doubt* + *that* clause
    ***There is a slim chance that** more oil supplies will be discovered.*

Be bound / certain (not) to do describes something that will definitely happen, or not happen, in the future. *Be (highly) likely / unlikely to do* describes a probable or improbable future event.
*There is **bound to be** a lot of interest in this exhibition, and tickets **are likely to sell out** fast.*

May, might or *could* are used for uncertain predictions, when we are not sure what will happen. We do not use *can* in this way. There is no difference between *may* and *might* in this context, but *well* adds a greater degree of probability.
*We **may / might (well)** run out of oil before the end of the century.*

Should is used to say that you think something positive will probably happen, based on what you already know.
*He **should** pass the exam – he's been working hard. We **should** have enough coal to last the winter.*

Would is used to make a prediction based on a condition. This means that something would have happened if something else happened. The *if* part of the meaning is often left out, or stated in another way, but understood.
*More help from the government **would encourage** people to install solar panels. (This means the same as: If the government gave more help ...)*

We can also use *will* with *be doing* or *have done* to make predictions.
*   we use *will have done* to describe looking forward to a future point, and then looking back to say what has happened (we often use a time point with *by* = not later than)
    *We are starting to install the solar panels tomorrow. We'll install four panels every day, and so **by** the end of the week **we will have fitted** panels to all the houses in the street.*
*   we use *will be doing* to describe continuing events in the future
    *This time next year **we'll be generating** our own electricity with our new solar panels.*

Narrative tenses

We use the past simple for the main events, or the finished actions, in a narrative.
*She **got up** and **walked out** of the room.*

Language note: We often use present tenses in spoken narratives such as jokes.

We use the past continuous for temporary situations and repeated or unfinished actions or states. These can contrast with finished actions and are often background description in a story.

*She **was leaving** the house when she saw him.*

The past simple is used with stative verbs.
*She **did not know** that he wanted to speak.*

We use the past perfect simple only if we need to show clearly that one event in the past happened before another event in the past. In a narrative, it may not be necessary to use the past perfect if the context explains the order of events. It may be possible to express the same idea using *before* or *after*. Sometimes the choice of tense depends on the sense especially with *when*.
*When she arrived, it was too late. **He had already left** the house.* (no connection between the actions)
***When she sat down**, she heard a crack.* (one action led to another)
*He left the house **before she got there**.*

The past perfect continuous is used in the same way as the past perfect simple, but to describe an ongoing situation or repeated action.
*She looked at his desk. There were sheets of paper half-covered in writing. **He had been trying** to write her a letter.*

Different forms are used to describe a future event viewed from a point in the past.
Would do / be doing, was / were going to do, was / were doing, etc describe a future event or plan.
*I went to bed early because we **were catching** a train at 6.00 the next day and I knew I **would feel** tired otherwise.*

Was / were about to do, be on the point / verge of doing describe an imminent action or event, often interrupted.
*She **was just about to leave** when the phone rang.*
*I **was on the verge of diving**, but suddenly felt afraid.*

Unit 2 Exercises

Future predictions

1 Complete the sentences with one suitable word. More than one answer may be possible.

1 The hero is _____ to save everyone in the end.
2 Unfortunately, it seems very _____ that nuclear power will ever be completely safe.
3 It may not be possible to arrange, but I'm sure an exhibition of her paintings _____ attract a lot of people.
4 I'm not sure, but I think this _____ well be what we are looking for.
5 Readers _____ definitely enjoy this story for many years to come.
6 I'm afraid there is a strong _____ that he will lose his sight completely.

2 Rewrite the sentence so it contains the word in brackets. More than one answer may be possible.

1 This book has a good chance of winning the prize. (*probably*)
_____
2 This painting certainly won't sell for a million. (*way*)
_____
3 It's certain that solar power will replace other forms of domestic power. (*bound*)
_____

4 She will almost certainly win the Nobel Prize for Literature. (*likelihood*)
_____
5 It's possible scientists will discover a new way of producing energy. (*well*)
_____
6 There's little chance that people will learn to use less electricity. (*highly*)
_____

3 Complete the sentences with *will* and the correct form of the verb in brackets.

1 No, three o'clock on Monday isn't a very good time. I _____ (*give*) a talk in a meeting then.
2 I'm hoping that we _____ (*finish*) by the time it gets dark.
3 He _____ (*complete*) his first novel by the end of the year.
4 See you at 5.30. I _____ (*wait*) outside the cinema.
5 We'd better hurry up, or else the play _____ (*already start*).

Narrative tenses

4 Choose the correct option.

1 I *wanted / was wanting* to buy the painting, but I *didn't bring / hadn't brought* enough money with me. I asked if he *would accept / was about to accept* a cheque.
2 When the lights *went out / had gone out*, people *were starting / started* screaming.
3 She *had visited / was visiting* the town once before, several years earlier, but she *hadn't forgotten / didn't forget* how to reach the town centre.
4 He *wasn't arriving / didn't arrive* at work one Friday morning, and nobody knew he *had had / had* an accident.
5 She *opened / was opening* the window. A cold wind *was blowing / had blown*, and she was glad that she *had packed / was packing* some warm clothes.
6 He *was glancing / glanced* into the room. A cat *was sleeping / had slept* on the sofa and a small girl *was sitting / had sat* on the floor, reading a comic.
7 I *was going to accept / would accept* the job, but I had second thoughts.
8 They *were building / were on the verge of building* an extension, but planning permission was refused.

5 Complete the sentences with suitable past tenses of the verb in brackets.

1 He _____ (*stand*) by the window when he _____ (*begin*) to realise that someone else _____ (*come*) in through the door, and _____ (*stare*) at him.
2 The sun _____ (*grow*) stronger all the time, and sweat _____ (*now drip*) down her face, but when she _____ (*open*) her backpack and _____ (*start*) to look for the water bottle, she _____ (*realise*) that she _____ (*leave*) it in the car.
3 He _____ (*wake up*) suddenly in a dark room. Some noise _____ (*come*) from outside. People _____ (*shout*), and cars _____ (*hoot*). He _____ (*try*) to get up, but he couldn't move. What _____ (*he do*) here? How long _____ (*he sleep*)? How _____ (*he end up*) in this place?
4 She first _____ (*notice*) the small silver box as she _____ (*walk*) to the bus stop. There it was, on the top of a low garden wall by the side of the pavement. Perhaps someone _____ (*carry*) it and _____ (*drop*) it in the street, and then a passerby _____ (*notice*) it and _____ (*put*) it on the wall, so that the owner could find it again. She _____ (*pick*) it up and _____ (*look*) at it more closely. It _____ (*seem*) quite valuable. The street was deserted, and she _____ (*think*) of putting it in her pocket when suddenly she _____ (*realise*) something odd. Her name, Helen, was written on the top of the box.

Unit 3

Relative clauses

A defining relative clause describes exactly which person or thing we mean. It cannot be separated from the main clause, and there is no comma in front of it.
Bleak House *is considered to be the greatest novel* **which / that Dickens wrote**.

A non-defining relative clause contains extra information and has a comma in front of it, or on both sides if it is in the middle of the sentence.
The Pickwick Papers, **which he wrote early in life,** *is one of his most popular books.*

In a defining clause we can use either *which* or *that*. *Which* is thought to be more formal. In a non-defining clause we normally only use *which*. See the examples above.
Colloquially we can use *that* instead of *who*.
She is the character **who / that** *interests me most.*

Relative clauses refer either to the object or the subject.
Whom is the object form of *who* and is used only very formally.
They all liked **her**. (object)   *She is the character* **whom** *everyone likes.* (very formal)
She is the character **who** *everyone likes.*

Whose means 'of whom' and can be used in both defining and non-defining clauses.
One of Pip's friends, **whose name I can't remember,** *gets him into trouble.*
A man **whose house had been broken into** *called the police.*

In defining clauses referring to the object, we often leave out the relative pronoun, especially in everyday speech.
She is the character **everyone likes**.
The first novel **Dickens wrote** *was called* The Pickwick Papers.

In non-defining clauses *of whom* and *of which* can be used with quantifying determiners such as *some, any, none, all*, etc, and with superlatives and ordinal numbers, especially in more formal use.
Dickens wrote 14 complete novels, **most of which** *first appeared in magazines in serialised form, and* **the most successful of which** *was* A Tale of Two Cities.
He had ten children, **nine of whom** *survived.*

A non-defining clause can refer to the situation mentioned in the clause before it.
Pip has to learn how to live as a member of the wealthy class, **which he finds difficult.**

In relative clauses with a preposition + *whom / which* there are two possible word orders. Sentences are often made more informal by putting the preposition at the end of the sentence, and using *who* instead of *whom*.
That's the club to **which** *I belong.* (very formal)
That's the club **(which / that)** *I belong to.*
For **whom** *are you waiting?* (very formal)
Who *are you waiting for?*

Compound nouns

Noun + noun is generally used for commonly accepted compound nouns which refer to familiar things. The second noun shows the main class of noun, the first noun shows the type.
a waiting room   a police inspector
a bottle opener   a water bottle

The first noun is used as a kind of adjective, so is normally singular only.
a **pencil** *case* (the first 'adjectival' noun is singular, although this is *a case for pencils*)

Other relations include: where something is found, when it is used, the thing it is part of.
a garden chair   (where)
morning coffee   (when)   *a door handle* (part)
Language note: although some noun + noun compounds can be joined with a hyphen, it is increasingly common for them to be either written as two words, eg *window seat* or as one word, eg *daylight*.

Noun + 's/s' + noun is generally used for things loosely belonging to or related to people.
the school's policy   my sister's car   Peter's hair   the boys' father

Noun + of + noun is generally used where no common compound exists, for units and parts and for certain fixed expressions. It is also used to describe things belonging to other things, not to named people.
the end of the film   a glass of milk   the corner of the street

There is sometimes a difference of meaning between noun + of + noun and noun + noun.
a cup of tea = a cup containing tea   *a tea cup* = a cup used for tea

In some cases, noun + 's/s' + noun and noun + of + noun are both used.
the decision of the author / the author's decision
the publication of the book / the book's publication

Unit 3 Exercises

Relative clauses

1 Complete the sentences using one word, where necessary. If a sentence is already possible, leave it blank. Look at the example to help you.

The person who left their bag behind can reclaim it from the college office.

1 He is the last person I would want to ask for advice.
2 Roy, mother was a political activist, is prominent in Indian politics.
3 Pip is not the kind of hero you can completely admire.
4 The main characters, are twins, spend many years without seeing each other.
5 She is one of those people for one can only feel sympathy.
6 Dickens' last novel, was unfinished, is a murder mystery.
7 Most of the people have read this book value it highly.
8 Last summer I went trekking in the Himalayas, was a great experience.

2 Make one sentence from each pair of sentences.

1 My teachers gave me some good advice. This helped me to decide my future.

_____

2 She met an enthusiastic publisher. The publisher believed she had talent as a novelist.

_____

3 The main character's parents died when he was young. He was brought up by his sister.

_____

4 At the end of the book Pip works to pay back the money. The convict had given him the money.

_____

5 There are many interesting characters in the book. Some of them are comic characters.

_____

6 Dickens wrote two different endings for the book. This makes it more interesting.

_____

7 There are five Great Lakes in North America. The largest lake is Lake Superior.

_____

3 Rewrite the sentence informally so it ends with the word underlined. Leave out the relative pronoun where possible.

1 Esther is the person with whom Pip is in love.

_____

2 Everyone needs something in which they can believe.

_____

3 He is someone for whom Pip has great respect.

_____

4 It's a book with which I was impressed.

_____

5 Is this someone to whom you are related?

_____

6 She is someone on whom you can rely.

_____

Compound nouns

4 Choose the correct or most likely option.

1 He spent the afternoon gazing into *shops' windows / shop windows / the windows of shops*.
2 She was so thirsty that she drank a whole *water bottle / bottle of water / water's bottle*.
3 I'll wait for you at the *end of the lesson / lesson's end / lesson end*.
4 In their back garden they've got a *court of tennis / tennis's court / tennis court*.
5 Don't put paper in the *bin of rubbish / rubbish's bin / rubbish bin*. You can recycle it.
6 Do you know the *office phone's number / office phone number / office's phone number*?
7 You'll need a *knife of the kitchen / kitchen's knife / kitchen knife* to cut that.
8 Is this the right *stop of bus / bus's stop / bus stop* for the city centre?
9 Have you got *yesterday newspaper / yesterday's newspaper / the newspaper of yesterday*?
10 They are the *president's children / the presidents' children / the president children*.

5 Make a noun + noun compound from the definition.

1 a program used in a computer _____
2 a shelf on which books are put _____
3 a paper which is published in the evening _____
4 a pocket in a pair of trousers _____
5 the bell found on a door _____
6 the desk at an airport where you check in _____
7 a show where new fashions are presented _____
8 an assistant who works in a shop _____
9 a dog that is trained to guide people who cannot see _____
10 a box containing paints _____

6 Delete the noun that does not make a compound noun when it follows the noun in bold.

1 **house**	work	boat	husband	agent
2 **travel**	writer	truck	guide	experience
3 **life**	style	cost	span	jacket
4 **bike**	ride	travel	lane	lock
5 **tourist**	operator	destination	attraction	visa
6 **book**	mark	case	library	seller

Unit 4

Modals: language functions

Modal auxiliaries are used in many language functions:
- offering to do something
  Can / Shall I carry *that for you? /* **I'll carry** *that.* *Thanks.*
- asking for permission
  Can / Could / May / Might I leave *early today?* *Yes, OK.*
  Might in this context is very formal.
- making an unenthusiastic suggestion
  I suppose **we may / might as well** *go home, now.*
- making a promise
  I'll pay *you the money on Monday!*
- making a request
  Can / Could / Will you *help me, please?*
- making a recommendation
  You *really* **should / must / have to visit** *the Greek Islands.*

- suggesting a moral obligation
  You should / ought to reply *to her letter.*
  We use *could / might* in this context to make a reproach.
  You could / might listen / have listened *to me.*
- making a suggestion with *I* or *we*
  Shall / Should we sit *here by the window?*
  Should in a suggestion carries the sense of asking whether the action is a good idea or not.
- complaining about an annoying habit
  He **will** **keep arriving** *ten minutes late!*
  Will is often used with keep in this context and is stressed.
- refusing to do something or explaining that something is not working
  I won't do *it!*
  My car **won't start**.

Modals of obligation

Modal	Use for	Example
must(n't)	Rules and obligations by the speaker enforcing the rule	*You mustn't use your phone in class.*
have to	Passing on information about others' rules	*You have to bring a passport to the exam.*
don't have to	To show something isn't necessary	*You don't have to answer all the questions.*
should(n't) / ought to	Recommendations	*They should tell her what they think.*
can / can't	Describing what is(n't) allowed in the rules (informal)	*You can't eat in class.*
may / may not	Describing what is(n't) allowed in the rules (formal)	*Members of the library may borrow up to five books.*
need(n't) / need not	Describing what is necessary / unnecessary	*You needn't worry about my friends – they're lovely.*

Past modal forms: obligation, need and ability

There is no past form of *must* or *mustn't*. Use *had to do* or *couldn't / wasn't allowed to do*.
She **wasn't allowed to leave** *– she* **had to stay**.

Use *should(n't) have done, ought to have done, could(n't) have done* or *needn't have done* to imagine the opposite of what really happened.
I **should have practised** *the violin more.* (desirable, but I didn't)
I **needn't have arrived** *early.* (unnecessary, but I did)
We **could have played** *football.* (possible, but we didn't)

Use *didn't need / have to do* for something that was unnecessary and probably not done.
I **didn't need to arrive** *early.* (so I didn't)

Use *could do* or *was / were able to do* to say something was possible more than once. If something was possible on one occasion only, use *was / were able to do* or *managed to do*.
We **could play** *football at the weekends at secondary school.*
We **were able to play** *football on Saturday despite the rain.*

Determiners

Determiners are a group of words which include *a(n)*, *the*, *this*, *that*, *each*, *every*, *some*, *no*, *any*, *either*, *neither*, *one*, *another* and possessive adjectives, eg *my*, *her*. Singular nouns must be preceded by a determiner. Uncountable and plural nouns can be used without a determiner.
A film *needs* **a director**. **Films** *need* **directors**.

Each, every, either, neither are used with a singular verb.
Neither film was *particularly interesting.*
Every film *he makes* **is** *the same.*

Every emphasises 'all'. *Each* emphasises individuals.
Every *child needs encouragement.* **Each** *child is different.*

No means the same as *not … any*, but can be more emphatic and formal.
We **don't have any** *money. / We* **have no** *money.*

Any is used with *if* and *not* to express a slightly negative idea or expectation.

Some in a question (often an offer or invitation) indicates a more positive idea or expectation.
Would you like **some** *milk?*

Any can also mean 'it doesn't matter which'.
Choose **any** *book you like.*

Each other / one another means something is done reciprocally.
You should encourage **one another**.

Unit 4 Exercises

Modals: language functions

1 Complete the sentences with one modal verb. More than one answer may be possible.

1 Excuse me, _____ you open the door for me, please?
2 I feel really hungry. _____ we have a sandwich?
3 I don't think it's even worth asking her. I'm sure she _____ agree.
4 If your tooth really hurts, I think you _____ go to the dentist's.
5 She _____ keep interrupting! It's very annoying!
6 All the restaurants are closed. I suppose we _____ as well go back to the hotel.
7 You really _____ listen to this track! It's a great song!
8 You _____ have told me you'd be late! I've been waiting for ages!
9 This pen _____ write. I think it's run out of ink.
10 You've really upset Sabine. I think you _____ apologise.

2 Rewrite the sentence so that it contains a modal form. More than one answer may be possible.

1 I promise to finish the work by Friday.
_____
2 Is it all right if I leave my bike here?
_____
3 I suggest we take the bus.
_____
4 I agree to do the washing-up.
_____

5 It would be a good idea for you to take a holiday.
_____
6 She just refuses to listen to anyone!
_____
7 I'd like you to open the window, please.
_____
8 She refuses to pay for anything!
_____

3 Rewrite the sentence so that it contains a modal form. More than one answer may be possible.

1 Eating in the classroom is forbidden.
_____
2 It's a good idea not to eat too much late at night.
_____
3 You are not allowed to park here.
_____
4 Wearing a tie is not obligatory.
_____
5 You are allowed to bring two guests free of charge.
_____
6 It's a good idea to get there early.
_____
7 Driving on the right is obligatory.
_____
8 My doctor told me to lose weight.
_____

Past modal forms: obligation, need and ability

4 Rewrite the sentence so it contains a past modal (or related) form. More than one answer may be possible.

1 The journey didn't take long, so it wasn't necessary for us to leave so early.
_____
2 It would have been a good idea if I'd discussed it with her.
_____
3 She was obliged to show the police officer her licence.
_____
4 I worried unnecessarily, as she phoned me soon afterwards.
_____

5 It wasn't necessary for me to pay an extra charge.
_____
6 I argued with her, which was a bad idea.
_____
7 In the end, they managed to rescue her from the burning building.
_____
8 We had the chance to stay an extra day, but we didn't.
_____

Determiners

5 Say whether each sentence is grammatically correct or incorrect. Correct the incorrect sentences.

1 Any person with talent can succeed.
_____
2 We didn't have no training.
_____
3 Every student needs to practise.
_____
4 The children play well with each another.
_____
5 The government has introduced programme to eliminate drug addiction.
_____

6 Can I have some time to think about it?
_____
7 I didn't enjoy either concerts.
_____
8 Teamwork and practice are the secret of success.
_____
9 Does the orchestra have new members?
_____
10 Neither student have conducted an orchestra before.
_____
11 Musicians need perseverance and patience.
_____

Unit 5

Present perfect simple and continuous

We use the present perfect for indefinite events in the past, with no exact time reference, and which have some relevance to the present. We use the past simple for definite completed events which may have a past time reference – either explicitly stated, or understood from the context.
*Pirates **have seized** an oil tanker.* (indefinite: no time reference, some time before now)
*Pirates **seized** an oil tanker in the Indian Ocean last week.* (definite past event)

The present perfect is used in relation to an unfinished time frame. The past simple is used when the time period is ended.
*I've **visited** ten countries this year.* (this year has not ended)
*I **visited** ten countries last year.* (last year is in the past)

The present perfect is often used with indefinite time expressions, eg *just*, *recently*, *ever*, *before*, etc.
*The birth rate **has fallen** significantly in **recent years**.*

In news reports, the report often starts with a general point (what has happened) and then moves to describing definite details (what happened).
*Pirates **have seized** an oil tanker in the Indian Ocean. A group of men **approached** the ship on Monday, and **ordered** the captain to stop.*

Using the continuous form emphasises the length of time and we often include a time adverbial.
*I've **been sitting** at my desk **all day**.*

The continuous form can also indicate a repeated activity. The simple form is used with a single event, or when a definite number is mentioned.
*They **have been digging** wells recently.*
*They **have dug** a well / ten wells recently.*

Using the present perfect simple can emphasise completion, while the present perfect continuous can indicate the ongoing nature of an activity.
*I've **painted** my bedroom.* (complete)
*I've **been painting** my bedroom.* (recent activity, possibly finished)

With state verbs such as *live*, *work*, etc there is little contrast because the verb refers to a continuing state.
*How long **have you worked** here? How long **have you been working** here?* (no difference)

When the present perfect is used in the negative with *for* or *since*, it is normally in the simple form.
*It **has not rained for** six months.*

Other ways to express the same idea are:
It is / has been six months since it rained.   It last rained six months ago.

Some state verbs are used only in the simple form. These include verbs of …
* knowing, believing, etc: *understand, know, believe, remember, realise, think*, etc
* liking, etc: *like, hate, wish, prefer*, etc
* possession: *own, belong to, contain, include*, etc
* imagination: *seem, appear*, etc
  *I've **known** about this for a long time.*
  *Have **you understood** this point?*

There may be action meanings with the continuous, but these have a different meaning or are colloquial.
*I've **thought** this for a long time.* (believe)
*How long **have you been thinking** about this?* (consider)

Participle clauses

The subject of the participle clause must be the same as the subject of the main clause (unless a noun comes before the participle – see examples below).
***After throwing his spear**, he charged at the enemy.* (he threw, he charged)
~~*After throwing his spear, the enemy charged towards him.*~~
(different subjects)

To form the negative, use *not* before the participle.
*After **not** talking for ten years, they signed the treaty last week.*
The present participle can be used …
* to show one action which happens just before another or almost at the same time
  ***Leaving the cabin**, she ran across the deck.*
* with certain time conjunctions, eg *after, before, while, on, since*, etc
  ***Since leaving school**, he has had three jobs.*
* to show the result of an action
  *He played his guitar, **producing** a soulful melody that we loved.*
* to show events happening together
  *She listened carefully, **trying** to make sense of his story.*
* with a subject for the participle. This is common in descriptive writing
  ***Sweat running down his face**, he struggled to carry the heavy bag.*

A past participle can be used to refer to a previous event in the passive.
***Locked** in the cabin, he couldn't get out.* (after he had been locked in)

The perfect participle shows an action which clearly happens before the action in the main clause.
***Having put** the gun in the desk drawer, she left the cabin.*

A noun in front of the participle is also possible. In this case, the main clause can refer to a different subject. This is more common in writing.
***The pirates having left the ship**, the men were able to escape.*

With + noun + present participle / past participle – in this case, *with* emphasises that one event results from another.
***With the ship sinking**, the crew were forced to jump into the water.*

A present or past participle clause can be used as a reduced relative clause.
*There were two men **holding guns**.* (= who were holding …)
*There was wreckage **scattered across the water**.* (= which was scattered …)

Unit 5 Exercises

Present perfect simple and continuous

1 Choose the better option.

1 Since two men *stole / have stolen* over €5M from the National Bank yesterday, police *carried out / have been carrying out* searches throughout the city.
2 The activity of pirates in the Indian Ocean *increased / has increased* recently even though warships of several nations *patrolled / have been patrolling* the area.
3 Last Friday the trial *finished / has finished*, and the court *sentenced / has sentenced* all three men to ten years in prison.
4 According to news sources, in recent years the pirates *seized / have seized* over 200 ships and *received / have received* several million dollars in ransom money.
5 Two masked men *came / have come* into the shop and *grabbed / have grabbed* the jewels, and we *had / have had* no chance of stopping them, I'm afraid.
6 I *have read / have been reading* an interesting book about pirates, but so far I *didn't find / haven't found* any mention of Captain Kidd.
7 It *is / was* ten years since the river *last flooded / has last flooded*.

2 Complete the sentences with the past simple, present perfect simple or present perfect continuous form of the verb in brackets.

1 Ever since she _____ (*finish*) at university she _____ (*look for*) a job, but she _____ (*not have*) any luck finding one so far.
2 Nobody _____ (*ever discover*) where Captain Kidd _____ (*bury*) his treasure, even though people _____ (*search*) for it for hundreds of years.
3 The story of the Trojan War _____ (*be*) the subject of many films, though historians are not sure that the events in Homer's poem actually _____ (*happen*).

4 I _____ (*think*) all day about what you _____ (*say*) last night, and I _____ (*change*) my mind about the film.
5 The UN _____ (*recently send*) more aid to the country which is still recovering from the earthquake which _____ (*cause*) over a thousand deaths last year.
6 I'm sorry I _____ (*not attend*) lessons last Friday, but I _____ (*have*) problems with my health recently and I _____ (*go*) to see a specialist at the hospital.

3 Complete the sentences with the present perfect simple or present perfect continuous form of the verb in brackets. Use the present perfect continuous if both are possible.

1 I _____ (*wait*) here for you for hours! What _____ (*you do*) all this time?
2 She _____ (*run*) really well this season, and _____ (*win*) three races so far.
3 I hear that you _____ (*look*) for a new flat. _____ (*you find*) one yet?
4 I _____ (*know*) her for several years, but we _____ (*only go out*) together since January.
5 I _____ (*just stop*) to have a rest. I _____ (*study*) all afternoon, and I _____ (*not finish*) yet.
6 According to statistics, the amount of violent crime _____ (*rise*) over the past three years and _____ (*reach*) a serious level.
7 I _____ (*not read*) a newspaper for ages.
8 This is the first time I _____ (*have*) a free moment today.

Participle clauses

4 Remove two words from each sentence to make it correct.

1 After having inspecting the damage, later the team reported their findings.
2 There were three people being in the boat who waving flags.
3 She having lost her wallet and she was unable to pay for the ticket.
4 Being with both legs broken so he was unable to move.
5 While he robbing the bank which he shot and killed two people.
6 The fire was having gone out while the rescuers were able to search the ruins of the house.
7 On his seeing the fire, he then immediately phoned the fire brigade.
8 Her not having anything to eat, so she was forced to beg.
9 Because it rained heavily, and causing extensive flooding.

5 Rewrite the sentence so that it contains a present participle or past participle form of the verb underlined.

1 She <u>opened</u> the box and looked inside.

_____

2 They repaired the building and <u>opened</u> it as a health clinic.

_____

3 As the bank <u>was surrounded</u> by police, the robbers were forced to surrender.

_____

4 There was a long line of people who <u>were waiting</u> to see the doctor.

_____

5 As the level of the water <u>was rising</u>, the villagers were unable to cross the river.

_____

6 Since she <u>appeared</u> in a TV documentary, she has become well known.

_____

Unit 6

The passive

An active or a passive verb can change the focus of interest in a sentence. In these two sentences, the information is the same, but in the first the focus is on the people using the road (the doers), and in the second it is on the road itself (the object of the action).
Many different kinds of travellers **used** *the Silk Road.* (active verb)
The Silk Road **was used** *by many different kinds of travellers.* (passive verb)

To form the passive, use the appropriate form of the verb *be* + the past participle of the main verb. Certain long forms are unlikely in the passive.
They **have been building** *the road for ages.*
The road **has been being built** *for ages.* (unlikely)

In speech, *they* + an active form is often used instead of a passive form.
The bridge **has been demolished**.
They've demolished *the bridge.* (informal)
Note that we can only make a verb passive if it is a verb with a direct object. This sentence cannot be made passive as *arrive* has no direct object:
The travellers arrived at the caravanserai in the evening.

The agent is not always mentioned, as it may not be an important piece of information, or may be unknown or obvious.
Travellers **will be supplied** *with food and lodging.* (obviously by sellers of food, innkeepers, etc)
Some caravanserai **were destroyed** *during the war.* (by people unknown – or obviously by soldiers)

In some cases, not mentioning the agent is a way of generalising, or being impersonal and avoiding saying who was responsible for an action.
Camels **are still widely used** *as a form of transport all over the Middle East.* (generalisation)
It has been decided *that no further action will be taken.* (impersonal)

In informal language, *get* is sometimes used instead of *be*.
I'm afraid a glass has **got** *broken.*

The passive is also used when we describe scientific or technical processes, where the focus is on the action, not on the people who perform it.
After inspection, the cars **are sealed** *in containers, which* **are loaded** *onto ships.*

With certain verbs that have a direct and indirect object (eg *give*, *lend*, *teach*, etc) the indirect object often becomes the subject in a passive sentence.
He gave her *a new car.*
She was given *a new car.*

Cleft sentences

We use cleft sentences as a way of adding emphasis to part of a sentence and giving it more stress in speech. These are some ways of stressing the information **in bold** in the first sentences.
- *It is / was* + noun phrase + relative clause (with *that / which /* etc)
  Travellers need **shelter for the night**. → *It is* **shelter for the night** *that travellers need.*
  Unpredictable oil prices *cause most trouble.* → *It is* **unpredictable oil prices** *that cause most trouble.*
- *It* + adverbial / prepositional phrase + *that* + clause
  The trade route became less important **after railways were built**.
  → *It was* **after railways were built** *that the trade route became less important.*
  Everything changed **in the middle of the century**. → *It was* **in the middle of the century** *that everything changed.*
- *It is / was (only)* + *when / because* + *that* + clause
  They only realised the goods were missing *when they opened the boxes.* → *It was only when they opened the boxes* **that they realised the goods were missing**.

What-clauses perform a similar function. Some common forms are:
- *What* + clause + *is / was* + clause / noun phrase
  She wanted to find **the old donkey path**. → *What she wanted to find was* **the old donkey path**.
- *What* + verb + object
  The cost of a hotel room *surprised me.* → *What surprised me was* **the cost of a hotel room**.

- *What* + subject + *do / did* + *is / was* + infinitive without *to*. Here the auxiliary *do / did* can be used to emphasise actions.
  They **invested the money**. → *What they did was* **invest the money**.
- *What happen / happened* + *is / was* + *that* + clause. This is another way to emphasise the action.
  The bank raised interest rates. → *What happened was that* **the bank raised interest rates**.

Other ways of adding emphasis are:
- *All* + clause + *is / was* (Here *all* means *the only thing*.)
  The building only needed **minor repairs**. → *All the building needed was* **minor repairs**.
- *The thing that / which* instead of *what*
  What / The thing that shocked them was **the cost of saving the banks**.
- *The reason that / why* at the beginning of the sentence to emphasise a purpose clause with *to / in order to / so as to* or a result clause with *because*
  The banks borrowed more money in **order to avoid complete collapse**. → *The reason why the banks borrowed more money was* **to avoid complete collapse**.

NB Cleft sentences are more common in writing. In spoken language, important information is emphasised using stress and intonation.
The **banks** *raised interest rates.*
The banks **raised** *interest rates.*
The banks raised **interest rates**.

Unit 6 Exercises

The passive

1 Rewrite the sentences in the passive. Include the agent where appropriate.

1 Their masters gave all the slaves their freedom.
All the slaves _____.
2 A French film company is making a documentary about the Silk Road.
A documentary about the Silk Road _____
_____.
3 The local authority has built a new business park.
A new business park _____
4 The government should have taken over responsibility for the bank's debts.
Responsibility for the bank's debts _____
_____.
5 Some large supermarket chains were exploiting small farmers.
Small farmers _____.
6 A UN report to be published next week will highlight the problem of modern slavery.
The problem of modern slavery _____
_____.

2 Rewrite the sentence so that it contains a passive form, if possible. Leave out the agent where its use would be unlikely or inappropriate.

1 The company is going to cut the number of employees by 20%.
_____
2 Some have suggested that the banks have not been telling the truth.
_____

3 Nomads have been using camels for carrying goods for centuries.
_____
4 They should keep the bars of gold deep below ground in secure rooms.
_____
5 Fishermen catch these fish off the shores of the south island.
_____
6 People might have used shells as currency.
_____
7 Decorators will be painting the classroom next week.
_____
8 Schools should teach children how to manage their money.
_____

3 Rewrite the sentences with a passive form of the verb in brackets.

1 There are no rooms left in the hotel. (*take*)
All the rooms _____.
2 The company no longer has the same name. (*change*)
The name _____.
3 Since 2008 the government has owned this bank. (*take over*)
This bank _____.
4 The Silk Road is a centuries-old trade route. (*use as*)
The Silk Road _____.
5 Since the earthquake in 2011, nobody has been living in the village. (*abandon*)
The village _____.
6 An investigation into slavery is currently going on. (*carry out*)
An investigation _____.

Cleft sentences

4 Complete the sentence by putting one suitable word in each space.

1 _____ _____ uncertainty about the future which poses the greatest problem for business.
2 _____ worries me most _____ that we are running out of water.
3 _____ _____ why the town was built in this way _____ to protect it from pirates.
4 _____ the company _____ to get out of trouble _____ to cut the price of all its cars.
5 _____ _____ _____ we left the next day that we noticed our car had been damaged.
6 _____ I wanted to do was sleep for as long as possible.
7 _____ _____ I noticed first was the long hours that everyone worked.
8 _____ _____ the weight of the gold bars that I remember most.

5 Rewrite the sentences.

1 The cost of transporting the goods adds to the price.
It _____.
2 The cost of transporting the goods adds to the price.
What _____.
3 After I looked more closely, I saw the difference.
It _____.
4 The speed of the camels surprised me.
What _____.
5 The government stopped the ships which transported the slaves.
What _____.
6 The length of the Silk Road is surprising.
It _____.
7 Sales rose to record levels.
What happened _____.

Unit 7

Articles

Use the zero article to make a generalisation about uncountable and plural nouns.
Love is more important than money.

Use the indefinite article *a(n)* …
- to mention something for the first time
  *There's **a swimming pool** quite near here.*
- to generalise about a singular noun
  *It is important to have **a balanced diet**.*
- with a noun which describes a person's job or character
  *She's **an airline pilot**.   He's **a fool**!*

Use the definite article *the* …
- when a noun, or a characteristic or property of the noun has already been mentioned
  *In the painting there's a tiger. **The tiger** is about to attack.*
- when it is clear from the context what you are talking about
  *Could you pass **the salt**, please?*

- for a formal generalisation about one member of a class
  ***The tiger** is a member of the cat family.*
- when a noun is defined to make it clear what is being talked about, for example with a defining relative clause, prepositional phrase or adverbial phrase
  *She was **the girl he wanted to marry**.*
  ***The discovery of penicillin** was an important medical advance.*
- with items seen as unique   *the Government   the Sun*
  (However, some nouns can also have a general meaning and so can be used with *a(n)*. *Every star in the night sky is **a sun**.*)
- with superlatives   *This is **the best way** to keep fit.*
- with ordinal numbers   *This is **the first time** I've been here.*
- with unique adjectives, eg *same, main, right, maximum*, etc
  *These two houses look exactly **the same**.*
- with a limited group of adjectives, eg *rich, young, blind*, to make generalisations about a group
  ***The rich** should pay more taxes than **the poor**.*

Unreal conditionals 1

If conditional sentences about the present / future (Conditional 2) describe an unlikely or impossible state or event. Use the past simple in the *if*-clause, and *would / 'd wouldn't, could(n't)* or *might (not)* in the result clause.
***If I owned a car**, I probably **wouldn't use it** very much / **I could get** to work more easily.* (but I don't own a car)
*I **might take** the job **if he offered** it to me.* (but I don't believe he will)

When we use *be* in this kind of *if*-clause, we use *was / were*. *Was* is informal.
***If I were** a doctor, I **wouldn't like** working for such long hours.*

Use *were* + subject without *if* in formal sentences.
***Were I** a doctor, I **wouldn't like** working for such long hours.*

Use *if I were you* for giving advice. Put the stress on *I*.
***If I were you**, I'd see a doctor.*
*I wouldn't worry about it **if I were you**.*

Use *If* + *were* + infinitive or *were* + subject + infinitive in formal sentences where we imagine an event is less likely, or we want to be more indirect.
***If you were to take** the job, we would provide accommodation.*
***Were I to be offered** a place, I would gladly accept.*

Gerund and infinitive

If a verb is the subject of a sentence, use the gerund.
***Acting** has never interested me.*

If a verb comes after a preposition, it is always a gerund. Sometimes *to* is a preposition, and not part of an infinitive, eg *look forward to, be / get used to, object to*.
*I'm not interested in **acting**.   I can't **get used to living** in a big city.*

Put *not* before a gerund to make it negative.
*I hate **not knowing** the answer.*

Form a past gerund with *having* + past participle. This use is often more formal, and a present gerund is often used instead.
*I apologise for **having arrived / arriving** late.*

Form a passive gerund with *being* + past participle (present) or *having been* + past participle (past).
***Being interrupted** doesn't bother me.*
*She complained about **having been interrupted**.*

Use *my / your / his* (formal), or *me / you / him* before a gerund to refer to another person.
*I remember **his having** said that.   I remember **him saying** that.*

In formal discourse, use *the* + gerund + *of* + noun to make a noun phrase.   ***The burning of the city** lasted for three days.*

Use the infinitive to express purpose, use *to do, so as (not) to do* or *in order (not) to do*.
*He joined the gym **to lose weight**.*

Form a passive infinitive with *to be* + past participle (present) or *to have been* + past participle (past).
*The car needs **to be cleaned**.   My bike seems **to have been stolen**.*

Certain verbs and expressions (eg *suggest, enjoy, mind*) are followed by a noun or gerund, and certain verbs and expressions (eg *offer, allow, seem*) are followed by the infinitive.
*Would you **mind following** me?*
*He **encouraged** me **to take up** the piano.*

Some verbs can be followed by either a gerund or an infinitive. Sometimes this changes the meaning.
*He **continued talking / to talk**.* (no difference)
*I **regret telling** him that.* (It was the wrong thing to do.)
*I **regret to tell** you that you didn't pass the exam.* (I am sorry that I have to tell you.)

Some verbs and expressions (eg *make, let, would rather*) are followed by an infinitive without *to*.
*He didn't **let** me **finish** what I wanted to say.*

Unit 7 Exercises

Articles

1 Choose all possible words.

1 *The / A / -* health is *the / a / -* most important thing in *the / a / -* life.
2 This is *the / a / -* second time *the / a / -* police have made *the / an / -* arrest.
3 *The / A / -* liver is *the / an / -* organ in *the / a / -* body that cleanses *the / a / -* blood.
4 *The / A / -* answer to this question is not *the / a / -* same as *the / a / -* previous answer.
5 *The / A / -* heart surgeon is necessarily *the / a / -* specialist in *the / a / -* field of cardiology.
6 Are you *the / a / -* person who left me *the / a / -* message on *the / an / -* answerphone?
7 *The / A / -* love is *the / an / -* important part of *the / a / -* close relationships.
8 Anna is *the / a / -* teacher and works in *the / a / -* school in *the / a / -* centre of *the / a / -* city.
9 *The / A / -* young know a lot more about computers than *the / an / -* old.
10 *The / A / -* cup of coffee would be nice, if we can find *the / a / -* café.

2 Read a text about heart surgery and add 'the' 15 times.

World's first heart transplantation was carried out by Christiaan Barnard in 1967, on 53-year-old Lewis Washkansky. Operation was a success; however, medications that were given to patient to prevent his immune system from attacking new heart also supressed his body's ability to fight off other illnesses and 18 days after operation, Washkansky died of double pneumonia. Since then, scientists have been trying to develop an artificial heart that can completely replace functions of human heart. In August 2010, Angelo Tigano had his failing heart removed and replaced with a totally artificial heart after a five-hour operation conducted at Heart Transplant Unit at St Vincent's Hospital in Sydney. This was first case of an artificial heart being implanted into a living human in southern hemisphere. In many countries, cost of a heart transplant is too high for majority of patients, so use of an artificial heart could be a way of reducing costs involved in such operations.

Unreal conditionals 1

3 Delete the incorrect alternative.

1 If they *gave / would give / were to give* me the award, I *would / could / 'd* be very surprised.
2 If I *were / was / were to be* young again, I *would / might / may* do things differently.
3 *Would / Did / Might* you take the job if we *offered / would offer / were to offer* it to you?
4 *Were he / Would he be / If he were* in better health, he *could / couldn't / would* be able to travel by himself.

4 Rewrite each sentence so that it has the same meaning.

1 If he had the operation, it might save his life.
   If he were _____.
2 If you applied for this post, we would support your application.
   Were _____.
3 You should take more exercise.
   If I _____.
4 Were he to ask me to marry him, I would say no.
   If _____.

Gerund and infinitive

5 Complete the sentence with the correct form of the verb in brackets.

1 There is no point _____ (*pretend*) that things will improve.
2 I regret _____ (*inform*) you that you have not passed.
3 I'm afraid he isn't very fond of _____ (*help*) others.
4 She stayed behind after school _____ (*speak*) to her teacher about her work.
5 This bag seems _____ (*leave behind*).
6 _____ (*take*) to see the play in the National Theatre appealed to them greatly.
7 _____ (*leave*) home was a difficult thing to do.
8 I am really looking forward to _____ (*see*) the ballet.
9 She suggested _____ (*take*) the train instead of the plane.
10 I'd rather not _____ (*go*) out tonight, if you don't mind.
11 Everyone wants _____ (*take*) seriously.
12 My parents made me _____ (*study*) for university and school and didn't let me _____ (*apply*) for art school.

6 Complete the sentences by writing one word in each space.

1 The rebuilding _____ the town took over a year.
2 She kept the keys in a drawer so _____ not _____ lose them.
3 The house appears to have _____ broken into.
4 He was not aware of _____ _____ given any instructions.
5 Do you mind _____ asking you what the matter is?
6 I came here _____ ask you for some advice.
7 I'm sorry, but I object _____ _____ ignored like that.
8 What can be done in _____ _____ stop this happening?
9 Her worst experience was of _____ punished severely as a child.
10 I apologise for _____ _____ written to you before now.
11 I'm sorry, but I'm not used _____ _____ up early in the morning.
12 I'm surprised at _____ arriving late – he's normally so punctual.

Unit 8

Real conditionals

Zero conditionals are *if*-sentences which describe general truths or scientific facts. The *if*-clause is in the present tense, and the second clause is in the present tense or is an imperative. *If* can have the same meaning as *when* or *whenever*.
If / When you boil *water,* **it turns** *into steam.* (scientific fact)
If / When you choose *four correct numbers,* **you win** *€500.* (general truth)
If you want *more chance of winning in the lottery,* **buy** *more tickets.* (instruction)

In real conditions (Conditional 1) the *if*-clause is in the present tense and the second clause uses the *will* future or *going to*, or a modal form. It is called a real condition because the situation is real not hypothetical (imaginary), and the second clause is a prediction. The second clause can be a suggestion or a request.
If we catch *a bus,* **we'll get** *there faster.*
If we don't finish *work too late,* **let's go** *for a meal.*

Alternatives to *if* can be used. *Supposing (that)* means 'just imagine that'; *providing / provided, on condition that* and *as long as* mean 'if and only if'; *assuming (that)* means 'if it is true that'; and *unless* means 'if not'.

Supposing you don't get *the job,* **what will you do** *then?*
Assuming *the train is on time,* **we should have** *enough time to catch it.*
Unless you help *me, I* **won't be able** *to do it.*
Provided that you take *the medicine as instructed,* **you should be** *fine.*

We can use *will* in the *if*-clause when it expresses politeness, or for emphasis when it means the same as *insist on*.
If you'll wait here *for a moment, I'll go and see.* (polite)
If you will eat *so much chocolate, of course you'll feel sick!* (insist on – *will* is stressed in speaking)

The use of *should* in the *if*-clause implies that the action is unlikely and is often used for suggestions and advice. It is used in more formal contexts. *Should* + subject + verb (without *if*) is an even more formal way to express this.
If you see her, give her *this message.*
If you should see her (less likely), *give her this message.*
Should you see her, *give her this message.* (very formal)

Unreal conditionals 2

In hypothetical (imaginary) past conditions (Conditional 3), we are thinking about past events, and imagining the opposite of what actually happened. The *if* clause uses the past perfect, and the second clause uses *would have done* (past conditional). Modal forms are also possible in the second clause: *might have done, could have done*. Continuous forms are also possible.
If he'd stayed *in a different hotel, they* **would not have met**.
If she hadn't been waiting *outside, she* **would have missed** *him.*
If they hadn't rescued *him, he* **might have died**.

Had + subject (+ *not*) + past participle (without *if*) is a more formal alternative form.
Had I known *it was your birthday, I would have baked you a cake.*

It is also possible to mix the different kinds of conditionals. A common mixed condition imagines a past event with a possible result in the present.
If they hadn't met *by chance (in the past), they wouldn't be together* (now).
I'm visiting London now. **If I hadn't found** *a job in New York,* **I would still be living** *here.*

Passive reporting

Passive forms can be used to report events, or what is said about them. They are sometimes called 'hearsay reports', as they are used to say what is reported, rather than stating definite facts.
The palace **was built** *in three months.* (definite fact)
The palace **is said to have been built** *in three months.* (what people say is the fact)

Report verbs used in this way include: *say, think, believe, rumour, report, allege, assume, understand, expect* and *know*.

We use a passive verb + infinitive when the focus is on the subject of the reported information, rather than who believes or thinks it.

In passive reporting, the infinitive can be continuous, perfect or simple.
- present reference
  He is thought **to own** *several buildings.* (simple)
  They are reported **to be working** *in China.* (continuous)

- past reference
  He is assumed **to have left** *the country.* (perfect)
  She is alleged **to have been working** *as a spy.* (perfect continuous)
- past passive reference
  He is understood **to have been dismissed**. (perfect passive)
- future reference
  The president **is expected to make** *a statement later today.*

For negative statements, *not* can be used in either part of the sentence.
There **is not thought to be** *any danger.*
There **is thought not to be** *any danger.* (more formal)

These reports can also be made impersonal by using *It* + passive form of the report verb + *that* + verb form.
He is thought **to own** *several buildings.*
It is thought that he owns *several buildings.*
She is said **to have been working** *too hard.*
It is said that she was working *too hard.*

Unit 8 Exercises

Real conditionals

1 Say whether the sentences are grammatically correct or incorrect. Correct the incorrect sentences.

1 Supposing nobody turns up to your party, what would you do?

2 Unless you don't explain how the machine works, I won't be able to use it.

3 If it will rain tomorrow, we may not go for a picnic after all.

4 I think I'm going to scream if you say that once more.

5 Many people get frustrated if they have to queue for a long time.

6 If you should see him, can you tell him I was looking for him?

7 If you will go to bed so late, naturally you'll feel tired!

8 Assuming your theory is correct, we may not have any problems.

9 Should you begin to feel tired, you'll take a 15-minute break.

10 If you'll get into difficulties, I help you.

11 I'll lend you my key on condition that you won't lose it.

12 You shouldn't have any problems providing you follow the instructions.

Unreal conditionals 2

2 Rewrite each sentence beginning with *If* or *Had*.

1 They searched the room and found the missing money.
If _____.

2 She only met him because she took the 5.00 train.
If _____.

3 Perhaps the bridge only collapsed because the storm was so powerful.
If _____.

4 She wasn't looking where she was going and so she fell over.
If _____.

5 She was driving dangerously because she was feeling stressed.
If _____.

6 I couldn't speak Italian so I wasn't able to explain what had happened.
If _____.

7 He reacted quickly, so there wasn't an accident.
If _____.

8 She didn't look carefully at him and didn't recognise him.
Had _____.

9 I couldn't get a flight so I wasn't able to attend the meeting.
If _____.

10 The architect changed the plans – maybe that is why the building survived the earthquake.
Had _____.

3 Use the verbs in brackets to make a mixed conditional sentence about a past event with a result in the present. Write NO next to sentences which can't be formed in this way.

1 If I _____ (*save up*) more money, I _____ (*be able*) to afford this new bike.

2 If you _____ (*hold*) the glass more carefully you _____ (*not drop*) it.

3 If I _____ (*not decide*) to take music lessons, I _____ (*have*) more free time.

4 If the company _____ (*manage*) its finances more successfully, it _____ (*not need*) a loan from the bank.

5 If she _____ (*not fall*) from the balcony, she _____ (*not break*) her leg.

6 If I _____ (*not argue*) with my boss, I _____ (*still work*) with her.

7 If you _____ (*not lie*) so many times before, I _____ (*believe*) what you are saying.

8 If the car _____ (*stop*) at the red light, it _____ (*not hit*) the bus.

Passive reporting

4 Rewrite the sentence so that it has the same meaning, but leave out any unnecessary words.

1 People believe that she is one of the richest women in the country.
She _____.

2 People report that the President has resigned.
It _____.

3 They say that the architect earned more than $2 million.
The architect _____.

4 It is understood that the council refused planning permission.
The council _____.

5 People think the prisoner has escaped.
It _____.

6 People think the weather has been the worst for a decade.
The weather _____.

7 They know that the police are looking for two men.
The police _____.

8 There is a rumour that bank officials stole the money.
It _____.

9 They allege that Marilyn Monroe was murdered.
Marilyn _____.

10 We expect that interest rates will rise.
Interest rates _____.

Unit 9

Unreal past time

We use the past simple in some expressions as an unreal tense …
- after *It's time* … to say that an action is urgent or overdue
  *It's time **we left***. (If we left it would be better …)
- after *I'd rather* + pronoun to indicate a preference about someone or something else
  *I'd rather you **didn't smoke***.

As if / as though is used with a past tense form to describe a present action or state that is not actually true.
*He walked in **as if he owned** the place.* (but he doesn't)

We use the past simple with *I wish* or *If only* to talk about wishes about the present, when these are the opposite of what is actually true. With *be*, we use *was / were*. *Were* is more formal.
*I wish he **was / were** better qualified for the job.*

We use a past perfect form after *I wish* or *If only* to express a regret about something that happened or did not happen in the past.
*I wish he **hadn't said** that!*
*If only I **had known** about it.*

In reported speech, we use a past tense verb even if a fact is still true in the present.
*She **explained** that **he was** an architect.* (he is still an architect)

We also use past tenses for distancing. These are polite forms as they are less direct.
*I **was wondering whether** you felt like going out tonight.*
What did you have in mind?

Quantifiers

Quantifiers are a group of words which say how much or how many of a particular noun we are talking about. They include:
- countable or uncountable: *all, most, (not) many, both, some, (hardly) any, no*
- uncountable only: *(not) much, (a) little*
- countable plural only: *both, several, various, (a) few*
- common expressions with *of*: eg *lots of, a great deal of, a number of, the majority of, half of, hundreds of*

Plenty of has a positive meaning, indicating 'there is no shortage'.
*There are **plenty of** places to park in the city centre.*
A few and *a little* have a positive sense, but *(very) few* and *(very) little* are negative.
*We have **a little** time. I have **a few** ideas.* (not a lot, but some)
*We have **very little** time. They have **few** ideas.* (not enough)
A great deal of and *a large amount of* are used with uncountable nouns.
*A **great deal of attention** has been paid to childcare provision.*

We use *a (huge / large / small / tiny / significant / growing, etc) number of* and *the majority of* with countable nouns. They are both usually followed by a plural verb.
*A **growing number of women work** in the caring professions.*

Lots of / a lot of are very similar in meaning, and are generally used in positive statements. *Many* and *much* are generally used in negative statements and questions, but can be used in positive statements in more formal contexts.
Many workers were made redundant. (more formal)
A lot of people lost their jobs. (more informal)

Plural or uncountable nouns used without quantifiers often have a general meaning.
Unemployment is a growing problem. (in general)

Use quantifier + *of* if a definite article is used, or if it is combined with another pronoun.
Many women stop working when they have children.
Many of the women in my country stop working when they have children. Some of them find it hard to return to work later in life.

Most quantifiers can also be pronouns, except for *no* which becomes *none*.
*A **lot of** our students took a gap year after university. **Many** got full-time jobs; **a number** travelled abroad; and **some** did voluntary work. **None** felt that their year had been wasted.*

Comparisons

In general most one-syllable adjectives and two-syllable adjectives ending in *-y* make a comparative form ending in *-er /-ier* and a superlative in *-est / -iest*. Some two-syllable adjectives (eg *clever, common, gentle*) can use either this form or *more / most*. Otherwise, adjectives with two or more syllables use *more / most*.

We can use intensifiers to qualify comparative adjectives. These include *considerably, far, a great deal, infinitely, a lot, much* (large amount) or *a little, a bit, slightly*, etc (small amount).
*In a city, cycling can be **a lot faster than** driving.*

We can qualify *as* + adjective + *as* with words such as *almost, nearly* and *just* (= equally).   *Cycling is **almost as fast as** driving.*

We can qualify negative comparisons (*not as / so* + adjective) with *not nearly, nothing like, nowhere near* or *quite* (a little less).
*Walking is **not nearly as fast as** cycling.*

We can also use intensifiers to qualify superlatives, eg *by far*.
*This is **by far the most congested** road in the area.*

We can use *the* + (comparative based phrase) … *the* + (comparative based phrase) to show that two things change in relation to each other.
*The **more roads** we build, **the greater** the amount of traffic there is.*

Note that *less, the least, more, the most* are irregular forms.
*This car is **the least / the most economical** of them all.*

More / fewer and *most* are also used to describe number. *Most* is not used with *the* in this case. *Less* is used for uncountable nouns, and *fewer* with countable nouns.
*More / Fewer people here commute by car **than** use public transport.*

Unit 9 Exercises

Unreal past time

1 Complete each sentence with a suitable word.

1 It's _____ you had a haircut.
2 I'd _____ you left your dirty boots outside.
3 He treats his employees as if they _____ servants.
4 I really wish I _____ there in Tahiti with you!
5 _____ only the Metro station wasn't so far away.
6 Sorry, but I'd rather you _____ leave your bag there.
7 I wish I _____ the answer, but I don't!
8 I was _____ whether you needed anything.
9 If only you _____ told me earlier.
10 It's time you _____ some serious work for a change!
11 What _____ you have in mind to do tonight?
12 He told me he _____ a writer.

2 Rewrite the sentence so that it has a similar meaning and includes the word or phrase in brackets.

1 From the way he acts, he thinks he's the boss! (*as if*)
_____

2 We forgot the map – which was a mistake. (*if only*)
_____

3 I think you should go home now. (*time*)
_____

4 I have to work tomorrow, but I don't want to! (*wish*)
_____

5 It is a pity that he lost the keys! (*if only*)
_____

6 I'd prefer you not to sit there. (*rather*)
_____

Quantifiers

3 Say if the sentences are grammatically correct or incorrect. Correct the incorrect ones.

1 They tried various ways of solving the traffic problem.
_____

2 Unemployment is a problem in a great deal of countries.
_____

3 Most of economists claim that the economy is recovering.
_____

4 The majority of commuters uses the train to get to work.
_____

5 There is hardly any room on the roads here for more traffic.
_____

6 When the police found the security van, most of money was still inside.
_____

7 Hurry up! There is very little time left.
_____

8 A considerable number of new jobs has been created in the private sector.
_____

9 I'm sorry, but there are a few seats available on that flight.
_____

10 There are not plenty of really good restaurants open in this area.
_____

11 The most people in this area have casual jobs.
_____

12 We had loads of fun on holiday.
_____

Comparisons

4 Complete the sentences with one word.

1 The more cars there are on the road, the _____ pollution they cause.
2 In some areas, walking is _____ faster than taking a bus.
3 The traffic here is not _____ as bad as it once was.
4 Electric cars are less damaging to the environment _____ conventional cars.
5 Motorbikes are almost as damaging _____ cars.
6 Walking in a city can be a _____ more dangerous than riding a bike.
7 This car is by far the _____ economical of all small cars.
8 Travelling by bus can be only _____ slower than travelling by metro.
9 Nowadays the roads in the centre are _____ near as crowded as they used to be.
10 It's a _____ easier to get around than it once was, but it's still difficult.

5 Rewrite the sentence so that it has the same meaning and includes the word or phrase in brackets.

1 I didn't use to spend as much time on my work. (*less*)
_____

2 I've never done a harder job. (*hardest*)
_____

3 Travelling by train is a lot more expensive than travelling by bus. (*much cheaper*)
_____

4 No company in Oman is larger than this one. (*by far*)
_____

5 My journey to work was once much longer. (*deal*)
_____

6 The roads were more crowded than they are now. (*nothing*)
_____

7 No form of commuting is cheaper than cycling. (*far and away*)
_____

8 The buses and the trains here are equally crowded. (*just*)
_____

Unit 10

Plurals and number

Some nouns have identical singular and plural forms (eg *sheep, aircraft, deer*).

Some nouns have irregular plurals, eg *ox – oxen, tooth – teeth, child – children*. Some nouns coming from Greek or Latin use the original plural forms, eg *phenomenon – phenomena, medium – media, crisis – crises, fungus – fungi*. English plurals are used in some cases, eg *syllabus – syllabuses*.

Media and *data* are Latin plurals, but they are sometimes treated as singular nouns and can be followed by a singular verb.

Some nouns are normally plural and have no singular form (eg *clothes, headquarters, goods, congratulations*). *People* is normally a plural noun (the plural of *person*).
People in my country are very fond of football.

Some nouns ending in *-o* have the plural form *-os* (eg *pianos, kilos, radios*) and others have the plural form *-oes* (eg *tomatoes, heroes, echoes*).

Other nouns referring to pairs (*scissors, jeans*, etc) are normally plural. They are used with a plural verb and have no singular form.
*Those **trousers** are too big.*
*These are my new **pyjamas**.*

Some nouns ending in *-s* are used with a singular verb, eg *news*, some games or sports (eg *athletics, aerobics*), academic subjects (eg *mathematics, economics*) and some words for illnesses (eg *mumps*).
*Here is **the news** from Moscow.*
***Darts** is a popular game in the UK.*
***Measles** is a serious childhood illness.*

Some words ending in *-s* can be used as both singular and plural nouns without changing form, eg *means, species, headquarters, series*.
*This is **a** useful **means** of testing for infection.*
*There was / were no other **means** available.*

Some nouns which can be countable or uncountable are uncountable as portions of food so use a singular verb.
***There are some chickens** in the garden.* (birds)
*There **is some chicken** in the fridge.* (food)

Some nouns which are normally uncountable can have singular or plural forms with a different meaning, eg *hair, wood, tea*.
***Tea** is my favourite drink. / Two **teas**, please.*

Collective nouns, such as *family, government* and *team* can be followed by either a singular or plural form or pronoun. We use a singular verb when the focus is on the group as a unit and a plural verb when the focus is on the individuals in the group.

In informal language, a plural verb is generally more common. Words such as *percentage, majority, half* and *rest* follow the same pattern.

Compound words can be formed with numbers and a noun before another noun. The preceding noun is used as an adjective, (and usually hyphenated) so has no plural form.
*a fifty-**euro** note   a three-**year**-old child   a ten-**kilometre** run*

In compound nouns, the first noun is often the one made plural.
*my **sister**-in-law / my two **sisters**-in-law*

We can use singular or plural verbs with *neither / neither of* and *either / either of, each of* and *none of*. Plural is considered to be more informal. Some people prefer to use singular.
***Neither of** the classrooms is / are large enough.*
*I don't think **either of** them is / are at home.*
***None of** my friends was / were there.*

To avoid using *his* or *her* with an unknown or generalised person, informally we can use the plural pronoun *their*. Some people prefer to use the phrase *his or her*.
*Each student has **their / his or her** own room.*
*Someone has left **their** bag behind.*
*Has anyone lost **their** phone?*

Inversion

We can invert the verb when a negative adverbial comes at the beginning of a clause. This also applies to adverbials which have a sense of restriction, eg *only, little, rarely, no sooner ... than, hardly ... when, not only ... but also*. Inversion is used to emphasise that something is unique or rare. These expressions are only used in very formal speech and writing and can be avoided by placing the adverbial in the normal position. In speech, we usually rely on intonation to stress important information.
***Never have I heard** such utter nonsense!* (I have never heard such nonsense.)
***Never again will there be** such a good opportunity to buy property in this area.*
***Not until** she tasted the dish **did she realise** how delicious it was.*
***Never before have food suppliers been faced** with such a serious crisis.*
***No sooner had we reached the house than** the rain began to fall.*
***Under no circumstances would I consider** living in that town.*
***Rarely does such a valuable painting come** onto the market.*
***Scarcely had she left the room when / than** we heard a scream.*

***Seldom has a new restaurant made** such a great impression.*
***Hardly had the lecture begun** when the fire alarm started ringing.*
***Not only did they win** the tournament, **but they also became** league champions.*

Only can be combined with *when, after, then* and *later*. Note that a past tense clause can follow the adverbial, giving more details about the event, but the verb in this clause is not the verb that is inverted.
***Only after** I took my first bite of the food **did I realise** that it was so hot!*
***Only when** we arrived at the hotel **did we discover** what had happened.*

Other examples of inversion include:
***Little did people realise / know / think** how expensive transport would become.*
***So powerful are** the supermarkets **that** many small farmers will go out of business.*
***Such was the enthusiasm** for the national team **that** hardly anyone went to work that day.*
***At no time / Under no circumstances** must the children be left unsupervised.*

Unit 10 Exercises

Plurals and number

1 Complete the sentence by putting the verb in brackets into the singular or plural. Write both when possible.

1 Billiards _____ (*be*) a popular game in many countries.
2 Each member of the team _____ (*receive*) the same payment for the match.
3 The news _____ (*be*) on Channel Five at half past nine.
4 None of these restaurants _____ (*be*) any good, I'm afraid.
5 There _____ (*be*) a new series of *Madmen* on Channel Six.
6 Neither of them _____ (*own*) a car.
7 The data _____ (*suggest*) that this is a growing trend.
8 The media _____ (*devote*) too much time to sport, in my view.
9 Politics _____ (*be*) boring, but economics _____ (*be*) even more boring.
10 Unfortunately, my jeans _____ (*be*) too tight for me now.
11 The organisation's headquarters _____ (*move*) to Geneva last month.

2 Complete the sentences with a suitable word.

1 I am still using a ten _____ old computer.
2 Someone has left _____ umbrella behind.
3 I always wear a _____ of pyjamas in bed.
4 We both love good food, but _____ of us actually likes cooking.
5 In this house, everyone makes _____ own breakfast.
6 The police were worried that _____ might be injured.
7 I don't think that _____ of these two flats is really suitable.
8 It was meant to be a 20-_____ programme, but it lasted over an hour.
9 My favourite means of transport _____ a motorbike.
10 My scissors _____ broken I'm afraid.

3 Write the plural of these words. If there is no plural, leave it blank. If it is already only a plural form, write *P*.

1 tomato _____
2 crisis _____
3 deer _____
4 sheep _____
5 clothes _____
6 kilo _____
7 aircraft _____
8 phenomenon _____
9 series _____
10 physics _____
11 coffee _____
12 congratulations _____

Inversion

4 Write one suitable word in each space.

1 _____ _____ had the goal been scored _____ the match ended.
2 Only _____ the product was advertised on television _____ it sell well.
3 _____ is the popularity of the restaurant _____ it is very hard to book a table.
4 Not _____ she started using the computer _____ she realise how easy it was.
5 _____ expensive is the neighbourhood _____ very few people can afford to live there.
6 _____ _____ people at the time realise how popular mobile phones would become.
7 _____ _____ such delicious food cost so little!
8 _____ _____ will we ever see such an exciting match in the World Cup!

5 Rewrite the sentence so that it means the same.

1 Hardly had the plane started to take off when there was an explosion.
The plane _____.
2 Rarely have I seen such a range of exotic fruit and vegetables!
I _____!
3 Not until we moved here did we realise what a lovely street it was.
We _____.
4 Spectators will not be allowed on the pitch under any circumstances.
Under _____.
5 The restaurant was so popular that you could wait a couple of hours for a table.
So _____.
6 I only realised how much I liked Indian food when I visited Delhi.
Only _____.

6 Rewrite the sentences.

1 This is the first time there has been such a violent match.
Never _____.
2 It is rare for a new product to sell so many examples in so short a time.
Seldom _____.
3 The power had only just been turned on when the fire began.
Scarcely _____.
4 We really didn't know what was in store for us at the new French restaurant!
Little _____!
5 There has almost never been such a universally popular appliance.
Rarely _____.
6 People were so interested in the new phones that they sold out very rapidly.
Such _____.
7 She is a professional violinist and she also sings beautifully.
Not only _____.
8 It was such an exciting match that we sat glued to the screen all evening.
So _____.

Phonetic symbols

Single vowels

/ɪ/	fish	/fɪʃ/	(build, busy, English, women)
/iː/	bean	/biːn/	(he, key, niece, people)
/ʊ/	foot	/fʊt/	(could, put, woman)
/uː/	shoe	/ʃuː/	(fruit, rule, through, two)
/e/	egg	/eg/	(breakfast, friend, many, said)
/ə/	mother	/mʌðə/	(arrive, colour, police)
/ɜː/	word	/wɜːd/	(learn, curly, skirt, birthday)
/ɔː/	talk	/tɔːk/	(four, horse, thought, water)
/æ/	back	/bæk/	(fat, cat, catch, bag)
/ʌ/	bus	/bʌs/	(blood, does, enough, onion)
/ɑː/	arm	/ɑːm/	(aunt, heart, laugh, past)
/ɒ/	top	/tɒp/	(what, stop, hot)

Diphthongs

/ɪə/	ear	/ɪə/	(here, Italian, theatre)
/eɪ/	face	/feɪs/	(break, eight, email, say, they)
/ʊə/	tourist	/tʊərɪst/	(plural, sure)
/ɔɪ/	boy	/bɔɪ/	(noise, toy)
/əʊ/	nose	/nəʊz/	(although, coat, know, no)
/eə/	hair	/heə/	(careful, their, wear, where)
/aɪ/	eye	/aɪ/	(five, buy, die, my)
/aʊ/	mouth	/maʊθ/	(town)

Consonants

/p/	pen	/pen/	(happy)
/b/	bag	/bæg/	(rabbit)
/t/	tea	/tiː/	(ate, fatter, worked)
/d/	dog	/dɒg/	(address, played)
/tʃ/	chip	/tʃɪp/	(natural, watch)
/dʒ/	jazz	/dʒæz/	(age, bridge, generous)
/k/	cake	/keɪk/	(chemistry, kitchen, toothache)
/g/	girl	/gɜːl/	(foggy, dog)
/f/	film	/fɪlm/	(different, laugh, photograph)
/v/	verb	/vɜːb/	(of, very)
/θ/	thing	/θɪŋ/	(thin, think)
/ð/	these	/ðiːz/	(that, those, mother)
/s/	snake	/sneɪk/	(city, message, race)
/z/	zoo	/zuː/	(has)
/ʃ/	shop	/ʃɒp/	(description, machine, sugar)
/ʒ/	television	/teləvɪʒən/	(garage, usual)
/m/	map	/mæp/	(summer)
/n/	name	/neɪm/	(sunny, knife)
/ŋ/	ring	/rɪŋ/	(sing, tongue)
/h/	house	/haʊs/	(who)
/l/	leg	/leg/	(hill, possible)
/r/	road	/rəʊd/	(carry, write)
/w/	wine	/waɪn/	(one, why)
/j/	yes	/jes/	(used)

Audioscript

Unit 1

🔊 1.02

A = Interviewer; **B** = Professor Arnold

A: So, Professor Arnold, are people still going to museums today?

B: Yes, well, more than ever in fact, so more people are going to public cultural institutions these days than are going to sporting venues, and in recent years attendance at many museums has in fact risen steadily.

A: So what sort of people are they? Is the audience for museums changing?

B: Well, it can be hard to tell actually, but I think museums are increasingly appealing to young adult audiences ... A number of museums have also experimented with the idea of opening up in the evening, and some have found themselves absolutely crowded with youngsters looking for I suppose what is for them a different but fun night out. So at Wellcome Collection, our biggest audience sector has ended up being in the years 20 to 30.

A: So, tell us something about the history of museums. Where have they come from?

B: Well, modern museums really started in the Renaissance and as you know, the Renaissance was a time when there was a massive blossoming of interest in the idea of knowledge, particularly gathering facts, and using scientific investigation and discovery to create knowledge and actually some historians have gone so far as to argue that museums helped establish the very notion of knowledge being based on evidence.

A: Can you explain a bit more by, what you mean by 'knowledge based on evidence'?

B: Well, I guess what I mean is this idea of facts that were publicly visible, that they were verifiable by anyone who wanted to question them so museums in this respect were particularly important because they provided places where this sort of factual evidence – so specimens and samples from parts of the world almost unknown to Europeans or, on the other hand, examples of extraordinary craftsmanship and ingenuity that very few people could see, all of that could be gathered together, it could be ordered, it could be made available for scientific study. And the important thing is, done in public.

A: Can you give us some examples of those kind of specimens gathered in these early museums?

B: Yeah, well, almost every Renaissance museum had a unicorn's horn. Lots and lots of them had human flesh which was believed to have medical properties. And then some of the first examples of what were then exotic fruits were brought into museums, so the very first banana in England arrived in a museum in the early 17th century.

A: Fascinating. What about now? I mean, we have the internet, we have so many other sources of knowledge now. What place is there now for museums?

B: Well, actually as far as I'm concerned, museums can still effectively perform the same sort of function, but now not just for a few people – it's for everyone, and that function is creating and engaging knowledge through experimental projects. So, for example, you can put on an exhibition about skin ... and you can bring together the scientific knowledge of how skin works – it's the biggest organ in our body – but also all the ideas that artists and historians have put together about the same topic. So through temporary exhibitions as well as through live events which museums play host to, I think museums hold up this notion of ideas for inspection, and this not so much by presenting dry information, through factual knowledge in books, but rather, really, sort of emotionally-charged facts, facts that you can, you can almost feel in your stomach.

A: And finally, do you think there'll still be museums in 100 years? And if so, what do you think they'll look like?

B: Yes, I'm pretty sure there will be museums. I'm sure in some respects they'll look and function very differently, though often, it's in ways that we simply can't tell at this stage. They'll look different in ways that we can't predict.

🔊 1.03

the Arabian Nights

Long ago, in the islands of India and China, there was a king called Shahriyar. He ruled over the lands, treating his subjects with justice and enjoying the affection of them all until one day the news reached him that his wife had been unfaithful to him. The king was furious, and overcome with rage and sorrow, he killed both his wife and her lover. And from that day on, he developed a deep hatred for all women. He would order his vizier to bring him a young girl every night, marry her, and after their wedding night he would kill her. The story continues ...

This led to unrest among the citizens; they fled away with their daughters until there were no nubile girls left in the city. Then, when the vizier was ordered to bring the king a girl as usual, he searched, but could not find a single one, and had to go home empty-handed, dejected and afraid of what the king might do to him.

This man had two daughters, of whom the elder was called Shahrazad and the younger Dunyazad. Shahrazad had read books and histories, accounts of past kings and stories of earlier peoples, having collected, it was said, a thousand volumes of these, covering peoples, kings and poets. She asked her father what had happened to make him so careworn and sad, quoting the lines of a poet:

Say to the careworn man: 'Care does not last, And as joy passes, so does care.'

When her father heard this, he told her all that had happened between him and the king from beginning to end, at which she said: 'Father, marry me to this man. Either I shall live or else I shall be a ransom for the children of the Muslims and save them from him.' 'By God.' He exclaimed, 'you are not to risk your life!' ...

Shahrazad listened to what her father had to say, but she still insisted on her plan, and so he decked her out and took her to King Shahriyar. Shahrazad had given instructions to her younger sister, Dunyazad, explaining: 'When I go to the king, I shall send for you. You must come, and when you see that the king has done what he wants with me, you are to say: "Tell me a story, sister, so as to pass the waking part of the night." I shall then tell you a tale that, God willing, will save us.'

Shahrazad was now taken by her father to the king, who was pleased to see him and said; 'Have you brought what I want?' When the vizier said yes, the king was about to lie with Shahrazad, but she shed tears and when he asked her what was wrong, she told him: 'I have a young sister and I want to say goodbye to her.' ...

Later that night, the king agreed to Shahrazad's request and Dunyazad was sat by her bedside ...

They then sat talking and Dunyazad asked Shahrazad to tell a story to pass the waking hours of the night. 'With the greatest pleasure,' replied Shahrazad, 'if our cultured king gives me permission.' The king was restless and when he heard what the sisters had to say, he was glad at the thought of listening to a story and so he gave his permission to Shahrazad.

Shahrazad said: 'I have heard, O fortunate king, that a wealthy merchant, who had many dealings throughout the lands, rode out one day to settle a matter of business with one of them ...'

Morning now dawned and Shahrazad broke off from what she had been allowed to say. 'What a good, pleasant, delightful and sweet story this is!' exclaimed Dunyazad, at which Shahrazad told her: 'How can this compare with what I shall tell you this coming night, if I am still alive and the king spares me?' 'By God,' the king said to himself, 'I am not going to kill her until I hear the rest of the story,' and so they spent the rest of the time embracing one another until the sun had fully risen.

🔊 1.04

1 shocked, pleased
2 enraged, incensed, upset, distraught, appalled
3 angry, speechless, puzzled, baffled
4 bewildered, delighted, euphoric
5 overjoyed
6 furious, heartbroken, horrified, mystified
7 devastated

🔊 1.05–1.09

1 **A:** I hope not. Well, I don't think so. I think we have some sort of duty, moral duty, to the future generations, our children, our children's children, to find out, you know, discover if we are alone in the universe or not. Or at least try to.

  B: I agree. I just think that we're, you know, we're exhausting all our resources here and we need to find things further afield.

  A: Exactly.

2 Don't know really. Hadn't thought about it. Suppose it's up to every generation to spend the money on the technology they think's worth spending it on. I grew up in the 60s so there was lots of space exploration stories around and it was exciting when I was a kid, but is it appropriate now? Not sure really. Don't really have an opinion.

3 **A:** No, I don't think so. I think it's important to find out about the things we know little about. I'd certainly go into space if I had the chance. Wouldn't you?

  B: Yeah, I mean, I would too and, you know, we have got to know more about our, you know, existence, you know.

  A: Exactly.

  B: I mean, marine exploration, they spend a lot of money on that.

  A: Yes, but space is so huge and we know so little about it.

  B: Exactly, so why not spend, I mean, what is the amount they're like billions ...

  A: Well, it's billions, but it's got to be inconsequential to the rewards of finding out about us as the human race and our environment and how to survive.

4 Well, no, I don't think it is actually because without it, well, I think all kinds of things wouldn't have been discovered and generally speaking, you know, we need to ... we need to invest in research, you know, if we want to make new discoveries and push back boundaries. Know what I mean? Because without, you know, without those kind of groundbreaking explorations we won't ... we won't discover, maybe, the things that make life easier to live.

5 **A:** You know what, NASA had a budget of 18 billion, not million, billion dollars last year.

  B: I don't believe it.

  A: It's incredible. And just think, the government could have used that money to ... well, help people in need for starters.

  B: Yeah, you're right, they could have. I mean, they could have put it into their international ... overseas aid for a start.

  A: International development, yeah.

  B: Yeah, and education in their own country, health.

  A: Yeah.

  B: I mean, it's mad, the whole system.

🔊 1.10–1.12

1 **A:** Hello.

  B: Hi, darling, it's me.

  A: Oh, hi, Dad.

  B: How are you?

  A: I'm really well. How are you?

  B: I'm fine. Listen, erm, are you doing anything on Sunday?

  A: This Sunday?

  B: This Sunday, yes.

  A: Yes, um, I'm actually tied up on Sunday. I've arranged to meet Sarah.

  B: Oh dear.

  A: I'm helping her move house.

  B: Oh dear. That's a shame because we're ... we're having a big family Sunday lunch.

  A: Oh no, I'm sorry, Dad, I really can't, I've sort of ...

  B: Your Aunty Rene's coming.

  A: Dad, it's been in the diary for ages and she's really relying on me.

Audioscript

B: Right, I understand. Listen, what about next Sunday? You doing anything then?

A: Let me see what I can do.

B: Oh that's great because Rene's down for a couple of weeks so she'll be here next Sunday and she'd love to see you.

A: And I'd love to see her, Dad. OK, well, why don't I give you a call back and, erm …

B: OK, but next Sunday is on, yes?

A: OK, Dad, next Sunday's on, next Sunday's on.

B: I'll tell your mother.

A: OK. I've got to go, Dad, erm so I'll speak to you soon.

B: All right darling, take care.

A: OK, love to Mum.

B: See you next Sunday.

A: OK, bye.

2 A: Hi Rob, it's Clare.

B: Oh, hi Clare.

A: I'm still on the coach at the moment.

B: Right.

A: I wondered if you could come and pick me up?

B: Er, what, from the coach station?

A: Yeah. My coach gets in at 4.30.

B: Er, what's the time now? It's about 3.15, that gives me an hour and … er yes, yes I can pick you up.

A: Erm, where do you want to meet me?

B: Oh, um, there's a meeting point in the coach station, by the clock. Um, if you can wait there, I mean, I don't know how long it'll take me to get there and I might get stuck in traffic or whatever, but I'll be there as soon as I can.

A: You'll probably be there before me 'cause it's pretty chocka on the motorway so um …

B: OK, um, right well, I'll do my best, but I'll certainly get there by 4.45.

A: OK, brilliant, that sounds great so it's the meeting place by the clock?

B: I'll see you there.

A: All right, see you then.

B: Bye.

A: Bye.

3 A: Hello, HRP.

B: Hello, is that Joanna Evans?

A: Speaking.

B: Hello, it's Geoff Parker.

A: Oh, oh thank you for getting in touch. We need to meet up.

B: Yes, um, is tomorrow any good for you?

A: Um, yes, I'm going to be working here until … one o'clock, ten to one. I could do lunch.

B: That's … that could work actually. I'm due in court at half past two so maybe between one and two would be good for me, then it would give me time to get there.

A: We could meet, um, on the corner, that Italian?

B: That sounds fine. I was going to be in that area anyway so … what time did we say, about five past one?

A: One o'clock. I'll book it.

B: Oh that's super. Thank you very much.

A: See you there.

B: Thanks, bye bye.

🔊 1.13–1.14

1 A: What are you up to at the weekend then?

B: Well, on Saturday I'm going down to my dad's in the countryside, erm, where I'm meeting up with my three brothers because it's his 70th birthday, my dad, so we're going to have a lovely meal in a restaurant. And, erm, Sunday we'll probably just go to the, you know, the nursery and, you know, buy some plants for the garden.

A: Lovely.

2 A: So, Ben, what are you doing this weekend? You got any plans?

B: I'm planning to go to London on Saturday. I've heard that there's a tennis tournament on so I thought I'd go and see what that's like and I might see if I can take some of my friends along. How about you?

A: Well, I think I'm just stuck at home really. We've got so many chores to do, I'm just going to basically paint the bathroom, which is getting really grotty, and after that I think if the weather is good I'll get into the garden 'cause it's looking a bit messy after the winter.

B: Oh lovely.

A: Yeah. Then I'm thinking of going and visiting my mother-in-law because I haven't seen her for a couple of weeks so I'll just check up and see how she's doing.

B: Maybe I'll do some gardening on Sunday as well if I'm free.

Unit 2

🔊 1.16

Woman with a Balance is one of Vermeer's finest paintings. As in so many of his interiors, the mood of gentle serenity is created by light streaming into a dimly-lit room from an external source and highlighting the most important details. Here, in the top left-hand corner, you can see a soft pale light emanating from a high window where the shutters seem to be half-closed. As it passes through the orange curtain it creates a warm golden glow, contrasting with the deep shadows around it, producing a faint reflection in the mirror, and then bouncing off the grey wall opposite to fall onto the table. Then our eyes follow the light as it shimmers on the edge of the table and, on the pearls which each gleam like single drops of light and finally rest on the woman's fingers and the balance in her hand. Then it's as if Vermeer creates an invisible line that draws us up to the woman's face and then down again as she contemplates the balance. It's a timeless moment as we gaze with her at the balance in the very centre of the painting, which itself is held in the balances of light and shadow, of grey and gold, in the surrounding canvas. What is she thinking? What is the meaning of the balance in her hand? Perhaps the painting of The Last Judgement in the background, and her clearly pregnant stomach are there to provide clues.

🔊 1.17

Woman with a Balance is one of Vermeer's finest paintings. As in so many of his interiors, the mood of gentle serenity is created by light streaming into a dimly-lit room from an external source and highlighting the most important details. Here, in the top left-hand corner, you can see a soft pale light emanating from a high window where the shutters seem to be half-closed. As it passes through the orange curtain it creates a warm golden glow, contrasting with the deep shadows around it, producing a faint reflection in the mirror, and then bouncing off the grey wall opposite to fall onto the table.

🔊 1.19–1.21

Through the Tunnel

In another four days, his mother said casually one morning, they must go home. On the day before they left, he would do it. He would do it if it killed him, he said defiantly to himself. But two days before they were to leave – a day of triumph when he increased his count by fifteen – his nose bled so badly that he turned dizzy and had to lie limply over the big rock like a bit of seaweed, watching the thick red blood flow on to the rock and trickle slowly down to the sea. He was frightened. Supposing he turned dizzy in the tunnel? Supposing he died there, trapped? Supposing — his head went around, in the hot sun, and he almost gave up. He thought he would return to the house and lie down, and next summer, perhaps, when he had another year's growth in him – then he would go through the hole.

But even after he had made the decision, or thought he had, he found himself sitting up on the rock and looking down into the water, and he knew that now, this moment when his nose had only just stopped bleeding, when his head was still sore and throbbing — this was the moment when he would try. If he did not do it now, he never would. He was trembling with fear that he would not go, and he was trembling with horror at that long, long tunnel under the rock, under the sea. Even in the open sunlight, the barrier rock seemed very wide and very heavy; tons of rock pressed down on where he would go. If he died there, he would lie until one day — perhaps not before next year — those big boys would swim into it and find it blocked.

He put on his goggles, fitted them tight, tested the vacuum. His hands were shaking. Then he chose the biggest stone he could carry and slipped over the edge of the rock until half of him was in the cool, enclosing water and half in the hot sun. He looked up once at the empty sky, filled his lungs once, twice, and then sank fast to the bottom with the stone. He let it go and began to count. He took the edges of the hole in his hands and drew himself into it, wriggling his shoulders in sidewise as he remembered he must, kicking himself along with his feet.

Soon he was clear inside. He was in a small rock-bound hole filled with yellowish-grey water. The water was pushing him up against the roof. The roof was sharp and pained his back. He pulled himself along with his hands — fast, fast — and used his legs as levers. His head knocked against something; a sharp pain dizzied him. Fifty, fifty-one, fifty-two … He was without light, and the water seemed to press upon him with the weight of rock. Seventy-one, seventy-two … There was no strain on his lungs. He felt like an inflated balloon, his lungs were so light and easy, but his head was pulsing.

He was being continually pressed against the sharp roof, which felt slimy as well as sharp. Again he thought of octopuses, and wondered if the tunnel might be filled with weed that could tangle him. He gave himself a panicky, convulsive kick forward, ducked his head, and swam. His feet and hands moved freely, as if in open water. The hole must have widened out. He thought he must be swimming fast, and he was frightened of banging his head if the tunnel narrowed.

A hundred, a hundred and one … The water paled. Victory filled him. His lungs were beginning to hurt. A few more strokes and he would be out. He was counting wildly; he said a hundred and fifteen, and then, a long time later, a hundred and fifteen again. The water was a clear jewel-green all around him. Then he saw, above his head, a crack running up through the rock. Sunlight was falling through it, showing the clean dark rock of the tunnel, a single mussel shell, and darkness ahead.

He was at the end of what he could do. He looked up at the crack as if it were filled with air and not water, as if he could put his mouth to it to draw in air. A hundred and fifteen, he heard himself say inside his head — but he had said that long ago. He must go on into the blackness ahead, or he would drown. His head was swelling, his lungs cracking. A hundred and fifteen, a hundred and fifteen pounded through his head, and he feebly clutched at rocks in the dark, pulling himself forward, leaving the brief space of sunlit water behind. He felt he was dying. He was no longer quite conscious. He struggled on in the darkness between lapses into unconsciousness. An immense, swelling pain filled his head, and then the darkness cracked with an explosion of green light. His hands, groping forward, met nothing, and his feet, kicking back, propelled him out into the open sea.

He drifted to the surface, his face turned up to the air. He was gasping like a fish. He felt he would sink now and drown; he could not swim the few feet back to the rock. Then he was clutching it and pulling himself up on to it. He lay face down, gasping. He could see nothing but a red-veined, clotted dark. His eyes must have burst, he thought; they were full of blood. He tore off his goggles and a gout of blood went into the sea. His nose was bleeding, and the blood had filled the goggles. He scooped up handfuls of water from the cool, salty sea, to splash on his face, and did not know whether it was blood or salt water he tasted. After a time, his heart quieted, his eyes cleared, and he sat up. He could see the local boys diving and playing half a mile away. He did not want them. He wanted nothing but to get back home and lie down.

In a short while, Jerry swam to shore and climbed slowly up the path to the villa. He flung himself on his bed and slept, waking at the sound of feet on the path outside. His mother was coming back. He rushed to the bathroom, thinking she must not see his face with bloodstains, or tearstains, on it. He came out of the bathroom and met her as she walked into the villa, smiling, her eyes lighting up. 'Have a nice morning?' she asked, laying her head on his warm brown shoulder a moment.

'Oh, yes, thank you,' he said.

'You look a bit pale.' And then, sharp and anxious. 'How did you bang your head?'

'Oh, just banged it,' he told her.

She looked at him closely. He was strained. His eyes were glazed-looking. She was worried. And then she said to herself, 'Oh, don't fuss! Nothing can happen. He can swim like a fish.'

They sat down to lunch together.

'Mummy,' he said, 'I can stay under water for two minutes — three minutes, at least.'

It came bursting out of him.

'Can you, darling?' she said. 'Well, I shouldn't overdo it. I don't think you ought to swim any more today.'

She was ready for a battle of wills, but he gave in at once. It was no longer of the least importance to go to the bay.

🔘 1.22–1.24

1   A: What do you think of it then?
    B: I really like it. This is why I came.
    A: Yeah.
    B: To see this.
    A: I think it's fantastic.
    B: Yeah, me too.
    C: Seriously? You came to see this exhibit?
    B: Yes.
    A: Something like this, you know, this is really rather special.
    C: It looks like my room when I haven't cleaned it for four weeks.
    B: Precisely.
    A: That's the point.
    B: It's about ...
    C: If I had wanted to see that I would have stayed at home. Why would I pay money to come see this?
    A: You know, I'm wondering the same thing, why didn't you stay at home?
    C: Oh ho ...
    B: It's the fact that it shows the artist's state of mind, it's the chaos.
    C: Oh it's these modern things, these modern exhibits which are ... they're ... anybody could have done and then they just put a huge price tag on it to pretend like it's a piece of art. This isn't art ...
    A: Well, the thing is ...
    B: ... it's just a mess.
    A: ... anybody could have done it, but only one person did and that's what's important.
    B: Absolutely. It is about somebody's idea, the originality of the piece.
    C: You see, I couldn't disagree with you more. Just because something is original doesn't mean it's necessarily good.
    A: Oh come on ...
    C: Oh come on yourself. Just because somebody went and painted a giant red line on the side of a building, nobody else may have done that, that doesn't make it art.
    A: You are denying all art since the 1920s.
    C: No, I'm not denying all art, but ...

2   A: And, of course, there's so much choice with university courses, aren't there?
    B: Yes, absolutely.
    C: Yes, perhaps too much.
    A: Yes, perhaps.
    C: And what we really lack is people who are studying the sciences.
    B: Yes, that's right, yeah.
    A: Proper science is about kind of pushing the limits forward, isn't it? Whereas ...
    C: Yes and research ...
    A: ... fine art could be seen as ...
    C: ... you know that's what we need ...
    A: ... enhancing, enriching life yeah, maybe.

C: ... we need, yes.
D: Yes, but if we thought like that then in the next 20 years we're going to need to have artists, you know, if we're sort of ...
B: Yeah.
D: ... moving ...
B: Absolutely.
E: I think a healthy balance is required.
A: But do you really think we need artists? I mean, we need scientists to help advance medicine ...
C: Yes, we really do ...
E: I see what you mean.
A: Do we need artists?
B: Well, we could survive without them probably, but ...
C: There always will be artists.
B: Always will be, yes. It's in our nature to create art.
C: But we should be encouraging the youth of today ...
B: Absolutely.
C: ... to, to work towards science and research, progress.
D: I'm sorry, I'm sorry ...
E: We shouldn't be dissuading them from creating.
D: I have mixed views about that because I think that, you know, we should be nurturing artists and there should be a lot more funding for them.
B: Nurturing artists and funding scientists.
C: Yes, I see what you mean.
E: And funding artists.
B: Yeah.
E: But, you know, art can't survive unfunded.
B: No.
D: Well, look at all the cuts they're making in the arts at the moment.
B: Exactly.
E: It's cutthroat.
A: Perhaps there needs to be a fine balance.
E: Yes.
D: That's certainly true.

3   A: I feel quite strongly about it. I don't think that people should study art subjects at university.
    B: Really ...
    A: Yeah.
    B: ... even though you did?
    A: Yeah, I think it's a waste of time quite frankly.
    B: Really.
    A: Yeah, I did it ...
    B: So you wish you'd done science?
    A: Um, well, I wish I'd done something slightly more scientific ... um ... than what I did do. I just think that you ... there's nothing that you can study on an arts subject that you can't do in your own spare time later.
    B: Yes, but isn't that the problem we have? We just think that everything to do with the arts is just a leisure activity and the only thing that counts is science, you know, hard facts.
    A: But Leonie don't you think that's true, it is a leisure activity really?
    B: It's not that scientists need to read books or, you know, read literature, it's just that the humanities make you into a fully rounded human being ...
    A: So three years at university reading novels, that does that, do you think so because to be honest when I was at university I wasted a lot of time, I wasted a lot of time, I could have been learning something valuable ...
    B: I agree ...
    A: ... that could have got me a better job, I could have made more money, I could have contributed to society ...
    B: Ah, but you see that's the two things, making money and contributing to society. You can contribute to society without being completely focused on making money or getting a good job straight away.
    A: But it would be nice to have some money, don't you think?

🔘 1.26–1.27

A = Giacomo; B = Caroline
Giacomo (Italy), Caroline (France)

A: Why do you think so many people are afraid of the dark?
B: Well, I think that's mainly because they can't see anything, so their other senses are kind of aroused and I think that imagination can arouse from, can be aroused from only the hearing because it leaves you the door to, like, imagine much more things so I think that's the main reason why. But what do you think?
A: Yes, I think these kind of things like mainly caused by imagination, yes, because when you are in the dark you really can't see and the sight is mainly the, for most of the people the most important sense that you have and so you always, like, base your ...
B: Sure.
A: ... behaviour and everything like your decisions on what you see. When you are in the dark you can't really see what's happening and you don't know what can happen.
B: But don't you think that sometimes people are kind of attracted by the darkness? For example, when you watch a scary movie the tendency of most people is, like, to, to switch off the lights, don't you think? Don't you do that? When you're ...
A: Yes, yes, it's true because you want to be more scared. Actually, I don't really like, personally, scary movies. Do you?
B: OK. Oh yeah, in fact when I was younger I was really after this kind of movies.
A: Really?
B: Yeah, and so I can remember that I had seen like all the horror movies from my video club.

B: And so I was in my room with my sister, actually in my room with my sister at the time, and so at some point I saw like the door opening, but I couldn't distinguish, like, what shape it was, it's a human one, and, and so we began to hear, like, kind of scratches against the desk ...
A: Really, scratches?
B: Yes, scratches and some, like, muffled sound and we couldn't, like, really say what it was. And so my sister, like, woke in panic so she ...
A: Was she screaming? Was she shouting?
B: No, no, she wasn't, but she was, like, 'Caroline stop!' because she, she ...
A: She thought it was you.
B: She thought it was me and I was, like, 'Oh no, I'm not doing anything!' so basically we also began to argue about this. And so she began to, like, run at the door and she hit, like, really violently and just, like, fell on the floor. And yeah just my father like got out of the desk and he was laughing like out loud. It was really crazy and then she was pretty mad at him for one week. Yep.
A: Nice for your father, I mean, so all your fear of the dark is because of your father and that night he came into your room.
B: Yes I think so.
A: Good.

Unit 3
🔘 1.29–1.31

1   Welcome to the Great Wall of China, one of the world's greatest national and historical sites and the longest man-made structure in the world. The Great Wall of China was built and rebuilt from the 5th century BC through to the 16th century and it was originally intended to protect the northern borders of the Chinese Empire against attacks by many different enemies.

The Wall stretches from Shanhaiguan in the east to Lop Nur in the west and along the southern edge of Inner Mongolia. Many people think it was built all in one go, but this isn't true. In actual fact it is a network, various segments were built at different times by different dynasties. The entire structure, with all its branches stretches for nearly 9,000 km. Of these

Audioscript

9,000 km, over 6,000 are actual wall, while nearly 3,000 kilometres consist of trenches and natural defensive barriers such as hills or rivers.

We will shortly be arriving at the most visited section of the Great Wall in Badaling. This section was built during the Ming Dynasty. Please remember to ...

2 This is one of the great natural features of the North American continent and of the planet itself. The Great Lakes – a chain of lakes in east-central North America comprising Lakes Superior, Michigan, Huron, Erie and Ontario. The combined area of the Great Lakes is some 94,850 square miles or 245,660 square kilometres, covering an area exceeding that of the United Kingdom. The Lakes contain about 84% of North America's surface fresh water and just over a fifth or 21% of the world's fresh water supply. Except for Lake Michigan, the lakes provide a natural border between Canada and the United States, a frontier that was stabilised by a boundary-waters treaty in 1909.

Individually, the lakes rank among the 14 largest in the world. They played a central role in the European colonisation and development of North America and for decades have attracted people and industry; Lakes Erie and Ontario and the southern portion of Lake Michigan are now ringed with large population concentrations. The lakes have not benefited from this development, however, and have been seriously affected by pollution. In the late 20th century, both the US and the Canadian governments began to investigate methods for reversing the consequences of years of misuse of the lakes' waters.

3 The Great Barrier Reef is one of the best places to visit in the world. One thing that you may not know before you plan your trip is you've got to really think about the size of the area and also really narrow down which part of the Great Barrier Reef you might want to visit. Did you know that there are actually over 900 islands? Not all of them you can visit, but a very large proportion of those. And the islands actually stretch over 2,600 kilometres so it's a much larger surface area than what people think. In fact, I think it actually works out at 344,400 square kilometres which is just massive. Most people don't realise that. I mean, obviously if you wanted to, you can take day trips to different islands so you don't have to choose just one. You could, for example, choose a couple of different ones which are close enough by each other. Sometimes it'll be a day trip, sometimes it's a longer trip, maybe a day or two. You can do overnights as well to visit the different islands, so that's a fantastic thing to do.

One thing to keep in mind though is that there are 2,900 individual reefs and the marine life is protected, so because of that the tours actually are only allowed to visit a small part of those areas, so before you make your choices, just really make sure you know which ones of those tours that you really want to go to.

Of course, once you make your choice you can do all sorts of activities on any of the islands. Outdoor activities are the main attraction. Snorkelling and scuba diving absolutely the principal things to do. If you are afraid you could also take the glass bottom boat.

🔊 1.32

1 two thousand eight hundred and forty square miles
2 62 per cent
3 2:1
4 six point two
5 22 square metres
6 1909
7 a hundred thousand
8 three point one four
9 a third
10 one million
11 2020
12 1:5
13 two-fifths
14 five per cent

🔊 1.34–1.37

1 When I was about seven or eight, um, it was Christmas morning, I remember coming down to this great pile of presents. But that day, the one thing that captured my imagination was this red box with a slinky in it. And basically, a slinky is, um, a spring, and for some reason this thing just captivated me and we had a good flight of stairs in our house, and after lunch when all the grown-ups had gone to sleep I started playing with this thing, and just, it felt like magic that it had a life of its own tumbling down the stairs. So then I started making obstacle courses for it and it didn't matter how steep the steps were, amazingly this thing would jump from one step to the other. And I had a friend with one as well and we used to race them down the stairs. It was such a simple toy and for all the technology that you can get today there was something about this that I absolutely loved.

2 I got my Rubik's Cube® in the 80s so I must have been about 13 and I got it from a friend who couldn't do it and she passed it on to me who ... I equally couldn't do it. And it was really frustrating at first because there're so many different ways to get all the different colours on the different faces, there're so many different routes to get there, that just when you think you've solved it there's one colour out and, ah, you just ... drove you mad with frustration and before you knew it you'd been doing it for like an hour. But in the end I actually just read about how to do it and, you know, followed the solution and there was no mystery left at all, and actually it made you think, 'How did I find it so hard?'. Which is exactly why I think that future kids won't play with toys like this because they just won't have the concentration or the patience and they will just be able to go on the internet pretty quickly, read the solution and solve it, so, there'll be no challenge.

3 Well, when I was a child I really loved LEGO® bricks. I had a huge boxful, you know, all different colours. I mean, it was just heaven. I spent hours, probably days, making all sorts of different buildings, people, animals, cars, everything – castles, actually one of my favourites was a castle. And I just see nowadays that modern LEGO® it's ... it hasn't really got the creativity. They come in kits so you kind of have to make a specific thing as opposed to just getting a box of bricks and making what you want. But it was just brilliant. The one thing that was very funny was when my mum and dad would come into my bedroom and, you know, they have bare feet or something and they'd tread on the LEGO® and it was like agony and that was something I constantly got told off for. But I just think it's something that's really stood the test of time and will probably be here forever. You know, it's so simple, you don't need batteries, you know, it promotes, you know, coordination, creativity, just everything about it is just such fun, such fun in these little different coloured blocks.

4 Oh, I had a red wooden yo-yo. I think they're all plastic or lightweight metal, aluminium or something like that now. But I remember being fascinated when I was a little kid, maybe about seven, because you could put them in your pocket and take on boring visits. And you could do tricks with them, the cradle or the swing or something I think they were called. I mean, you never played with a yo-yo for very long because they get a bit boring after a while. And when you get older they're not so interesting. But my nephew got one recently, very modern. It was all plastic with a ball-bearing system and they come back automatically and light up. I mean, is that cheating for yo-yo connoisseurs? I mean, they seem popular now. I don't know if a toy can reinvent itself further to appeal to kids in the future. I think the yo-yo has probably evolved.

🔊 1.40–1.41

1 A: Did I ever tell you about that time when Ben was on Port Meadow and wanted to borrow Tom's kite?

B: No.

A: Well, it was really funny. Grandad was there and he had bought a really nice kite for the twins and they were using it because they were a bit ... four years older than Ben and there was Ben aged five.

Tom was very happily flying this kite. Ben said 'Can I have a go, can I have a go?' and Tom said 'No, no' and finally Grandad persuaded him, 'Oh go on you ...'

B: Yeah, yeah.

A: ... and Tom said 'No, he'll let go of the kite,' and Ben said 'No, I won't.' 'Grandad said you won't, will you?' 'No, no won't let go', so they handed the kite to Ben and, of course, he let go ...

B: Oh no.

A: ... and the kite goes flying off into the air and we have a photograph of Ben with this very naughty smile on his face after this whole incident.

B: And what happened in the end then, what happened to the kite?

A: I think Tom probably had a tantrum and said 'You see, I told you he would.' The kite disappeared somewhere because it was a very windy day, just completely disappeared.

B: Oh you must have been so annoyed.

A: Yeah, funny as well.

2 A: Have I told you about the time that we lost Alastair?

B: No.

A: We were at a big open-air event at a park in Reading. There were quite a lot of people there. Alastair was only about three years old at the time.

B: Oh no. ...

A: ... and we were walking along and Alastair said 'Oh Mummy, can I run up this hill and I'll meet you on the other side?'. And I thought fine, it was just a small hill, so I let him run up and I went round to meet him on the other side and I waited and he never appeared ...

B: Oh no.

A: ... and I ... I was, you know, I started to get really anxious ...

B: Yeah, bet you did.

A: ... and I started looking around at the back of the hill, I went round the other way, I couldn't see him anywhere. I started asking all sorts of people, have you seen a little boy wearing whatever he was dressed in ...

B: You must have been so worried.

A: I was, I was absolutely terrified and getting really fearful about what might have happened to him and ... he was probably only lost for about 15 minutes, but I think it seemed like 15 hours ...

B: Yeah, it must have been awful.

A: ... yeah, but ... um ... eventually what happened was somebody did find me and ask me if I'd lost a child ...

B: What a relief.

A: ... and he, Ally, had got tired and lost himself in trying to find me and had gone and sat under a tree and was just crying under a tree ...

B: Oh poor little thing.

A: And I was so, so relieved ...

B: I bet you were, yeah.

Unit 4

🔊 2.01

The Myth of Mars and Venus

In a section of his book which explains how to ask men to do things, Gray says that women should avoid using indirect requests. For instance, they should not signal that they would like a man to bring in the shopping by saying, 'The groceries are in the car': they should ask him directly, by saying, 'Would you bring in the groceries?' Another mistake women make is to formulate requests using the word 'could' rather than 'would'. 'Could you empty the trash?', says Gray, 'is merely a question gathering information. 'Would you empty the trash?' is a request.

Gray seems to be suggesting that men hear utterances such as 'Could you empty the trash?' as purely hypothetical questions about their ability to perform the action mentioned. But that is a patently ridiculous claim. No competent user of English would take 'Could you empty the trash?' as 'merely a question gathering information', any more than they would take 'Could you run a mile in four minutes?' as a polite request to start running.

A friend once told me a story about the family dinners of her childhood. Each night as the family sat down to eat, her father would examine the food on his plate and then say to his wife something like, 'Is there any ketchup, Vera?' His wife would then get up and fetch whatever condiment he had mentioned. According to Gray's theory, he should have reacted with surprise: 'Oh, I didn't mean I wanted ketchup, I was just asking whether we had any.' Needless to say, that was not his reaction. Both he and his wife understood 'Is there any ketchup?' as an indirect request to get the ketchup, rather than 'merely a question gathering information'.

The more similar men and women become, the more they are in direct competition for the same kinds of rewards (jobs, status, money, leisure time). My parents never argued about who should take out the trash, pick up groceries, wash dishes, drive the car, or make important financial decisions. Nor were they ever in conflict about whose job came first or whose life had to be fitted around domestic commitments. These things were settled in advance by the basic fact of gender difference. [But] For many couples today, pretty much everything is up for negotiation. That has the potential to lead to arguments and conflicts.

⏺ 2.02

1 **A:** Great party!
   B: Yes, fantastic.
2 **A:** Have we met before?
   B: Yes, you look familiar – where do I know you from?
3 **A:** Hi, I'm Marina.
   B: Hi, I'm Laura. Nice to meet you.
4 **A:** May I join you?
   B: Please do.
5 **A:** Do you mind if I open the window?
   B: Actually, I'd rather you didn't if you don't mind.

⏺ 2.04–2.06

A = Mrs Higgins; **B** = Higgins; **C** = Parlour maid; **D** = Mrs Eynsford Hill; **E** = Clara; **F** = Eliza; **G** = Freddy

Pygmalion

A: Henry! What are you doing here to-day? It is my at-home day: you promised not to come. … Go home at once.

B: I know, mother. I came on purpose.

A: But you mustn't. I'm serious, Henry. You offend all my friends: they stop coming whenever they meet you.

B: Nonsense! I know I have no small talk; but people don't mind. … Besides, I've picked up a girl.

A: Does that mean that some girl has picked you up?

B: Not at all. I don't mean a love affair.

A: What a pity!

B: Why?

A: Well, you never fall in love with anyone under forty-five. When will you discover that there are some rather nice-looking young women about? … Now tell me about the girl.

B: She's coming to see you.

A: I don't remember asking her.

B: You didn't. I asked her. If you'd known her you wouldn't have asked her.

A: Indeed! Why?

B: Well, it's like this. She's a common flower girl. I picked her off the kerbstone.

A: And invited her to my at-home!

B: Oh, that'll be all right. I've taught her to speak properly; and she has strict orders as to her behaviour. She's to keep to two subjects: the weather and everybody's health – Fine day and How do you do, you know – and not to let herself go on things in general. That will be safe.

A: Safe! To talk about our health! about our insides! perhaps about our outsides! How could you be so silly, Henry?

B: Well, she must talk about something. Oh, she'll be all right: don't you fuss. I've a sort of bet on that I'll pass her off as a duchess in six months. I started on her

some months ago; and she's getting on like a house on fire. I shall win my bet. She has a quick ear; and she's been easier to teach than my middle-class pupils because she's had to learn a complete new language. She talks English almost as you talk French.

A: That's satisfactory, at all events.

B: Well, it is and it isn't.

A: What does that mean?

B: You see, I've got her pronunciation all right; but you have to consider not only how a girl pronounces, but what she pronounces; and that's where …

C: Mrs. and Miss Eynsford Hill.

B: Oh Lord!

D: How do you do?

E: How d'you do?

A: My son Henry.

D: Your celebrated son! I have so longed to meet you, Professor Higgins.

C: Miss Doolittle.

B: Here she is, mother.

F: How do you do, Mrs. Higgins? Mr. Higgins told me I might come.

A: Quite right: I'm very glad indeed to see you.

D: I feel sure we have met before, Miss Doolittle. I remember your eyes.

F: How do you do?

D: My daughter Clara.

F: How do you do?

E: How do you do? …

D: My son Freddy.

F: How do you do? ….

A: Will it rain, do you think?

F: The shallow depression in the west of these islands is likely to move slowly in an easterly direction. There are no indications of any great change in the barometrical situation.

G: Ha! ha! how awfully funny!

F: What is wrong with that, young man? I bet I got it right. … Here! what are you sniggering at?

G: The new small talk. You do it so awfully well.

F: If I was doing it proper, what was you laughing at? Have I said anything I oughtn't?

A: Not at all, Miss Doolittle.

F: Well, that's a mercy, anyhow. What I always say is …

B: Ahem!

F: Well! I must go. So pleased to have met you. Good-bye.

A: Good-bye. …

F: Good bye, all.

G: Are you walking across the Park, Miss Doolittle? If so, …

F: Walk! Not bloody likely. I am going in a taxi.

1 **A:** But you mustn't. I'm serious, Henry. You offend all my friends: they stop coming whenever they meet you.

   B: Nonsense! I know I have no small talk; but people don't mind. …. Besides, I've picked up a girl.

   A: Does that mean that some girl has picked you up?

   B: Not at all. I don't mean a love affair.

2 **B:** Well, she must talk about something. Oh, she'll be all right: don't you fuss. I've a sort of bet on that I'll pass her off as a duchess in six months. I started on her some months ago; and she's getting on like a house on fire.

3 **B:** Well, it's like this. She's a common flower girl. I picked her off the kerbstone.

   A: And invited her to my at-home!

   B: Oh, that'll be all right. I've taught her to speak properly; and she has strict orders as to her behaviour. She's to keep to two subjects: the weather and everybody's health – Fine day and How do you do, you know – and not to let herself go on things in general. That will be safe.

4 **F:** What is wrong with that, young man? I bet I got it right. … Here! what are you sniggering at?

G: The new small talk. You do it so awfully well.

F: If I was doing it proper, what was you laughing at? Have I said anything I oughtn't?

A: Not at all, Miss Doolittle.

⏺ 2.07–2.10

1 **A:** OK, so what does this button here do?

   B: OK, that actually turns the camera on right there. Once you've turned that on you're going to want to plug the cables into the back of the TV.

   A: So hang on, I have to plug that cable into the … into the television?

   B: Yes, right … right in the back of the television, right there. Once you've done that then you're going to need to take the television and put it to 'Input 1'.

   A: Sorry, you've lost me. Can … what 'Input 1' …?

   B: When you turn the television on there's a button on your remote that says 'Input' and you just keep pushing it until the picture comes up on the front.

   A: OK.

   B: So you don't … again you don't need to know 'Input 1', but just keep clicking it until it comes on and as long as you have it in the back then you should be fine.

   A: Fantastic.

2 **A:** Hi Nige.

   B: Hi Ben. You all right?

   A: Yes good mate, you?

   B: Not too bad thanks.

   A: Good.

   B: I've just had a call from Mark …

   A: Yeah.

   B: … he's told me … it's about footie practice on Thursday …

   A: Oh right, yeah.

   B: So he's changed the time of it.

   A: Right … from, to?

   B: It was going to be 6.45, it's now quarter past six.

   A: Right, so 6.45?

   B: Yeah, it was going to be 6.45, it's now quarter past six.

   A: Sorry, can you speak up a bit?

   B: Quarter past six.

   A: Sorry, I didn't catch that?

   B: Um, the footie practice is going to be at 6.15 on Thursday.

   A: Oh I'm sorry mate, this is a really bad line. I can't hear what you're saying. Just something about footie practice …

   B: Um, I'll ring you back in ten minutes.

   A: Sorry?

   B: I'll ring you back in ten minutes.

3 **A:** So, you want to join the gym?

   B: Ahm, yes.

   A: Right, well, if you want to be a monthly member, that costs £45, but if you want to be a yearly member, that's for 12 months, that's £350 and that's a much better deal.

   B: Sorry, could you repeat that, please?

   A: Right, for a monthly membership it's £45, for the year it's £350. Now that is the one you should really go for because you're saving yourself a lot more money that way.

   B: Right … er … sorry, how much is it for the one month?

   A: One month, £45, and all you have to do is fill out this little sheet of paper there, put your name at the top and all the relevant boxes, if you fill those out.

   B: Sorry, I have to do what?

   A: Fill in this form, and once you're a member then you can use all the facilities.

4 **A:** Oh well, hello Sally, thanks for coming.

   B: Oh you're welcome, hi.

   A: Sorry to have kept you, we're running a bit late. Yes, about Michael and Ellie.

   B: Yeah?

Audioscript

A: They're both doing really well.

B: Great.

A: There's no concern about Michael, it's just …

B: Oh.

A: … I'm just kind of flagging up …

B: Right.

A: … that his concentration is not quite as good as Ellie's. I mean, you might say she's doing a little bit better than him at the moment.

B: Right. Better?

A: Yes, um, simply in terms of being a bit more focused and a bit more enthusiastic about getting on with her tasks. Michael, you know, he just needs a little bit of a push now and again, um, especially with … his ability to sit down and hold a pencil and make small marks, you know, if you could encourage him, you know, perhaps to do a little bit of handwriting every day at home that would help.

B: So are you saying that he's disruptive?

A: No he's not … I'm not exactly saying that, he's not disruptive yet …

B: Because, you know, at home he's very active …

A: Yeah.

B: … but he is well-behaved.

A: Yes, it just depends …

B: He doesn't cause trouble.

A: … in a situation where we like them to sit and listen then he's finding that a bit difficult. I'm not saying there's actually a problem yet.

B: So are you saying that Ellie is basically much, much better in class?

A: Well, yes, more focused, more focused let's say.

2.12–2.15

Katsuya, Japan

I think probably not the easiest, but the most fun to learn was the pronunciation because, um, every time I find a phrase that I can't pronounce properly, um, I repeat saying the phrase while I am having a shower, like, you know, just singing a song in the shower room and stuff.

Carolina, Argentina

So I started learning English at high school, but I actually, I haven't studied formally English. I tried to pick up words and phrases from TV shows in English or from movies and ... but as I am a scientist we are currently exposed to articles written in English and we usually go to conferences in which the official language is English so you get the chance to practise a lot to, I mean, you need to, to find a way to express and to tell others about your work. You have to communicate your results so that's a really good opportunity to keep your level of English.

Miguel, Portugal

Well, I have been learning English since I am 12 and I studied one year abroad in Finland and all the university lessons were taught in English so I had to adapt and improve my English. It was really a necessity. If I have free time I tend to watch movies without subtitles because that way I am obliged to catch the accent and any vocabulary I may not know.

Rod, Gabon

Well, I started learning English at an early age when I was, since secondary school around the age of 12 years old, as you I mean. And I was really passionate in foreign languages, especially English, and tried to speak the language instead of speaking my native language, which is French, I mean, which is French. And I also use very much books in English, try to read, even if I didn't really understood what was going on in the book, but I use it at least to acquire new vocabulary, new words.

2.16–2.17

Rod, Gabon

Well, I would certainly encourage them, certainly encourage learners of English to go and engage in conversation with a native speaker if they can, if they can, I mean, if they possibly can do that. If they can't do that then use as much as possible, I mean, things like BBC, all the stuff you know which is really interesting.

Carolina, Argentina

Start speaking in English without thinking about the mistakes you might make. Because if you want to be perfect you will never speak English. I mean, you will never dare to speak English, you will be embarrassed and you won't do it and I think that you have to experiment and you have to try to relax and just let it, let it be and that's the best way of improving your English level in my opinion.

Unit 5

2.19

A = Interviewer; B = Justin Byworth

A: So can you tell me a little bit about World Vision and the kind of work you do?

B: Well, World Vision works in nearly a hundred countries in the world working with about 100 million people who face poverty and injustice, and we work through long-term community development, we work through humanitarian emergency relief and through campaigning for change in a situation of children's lives.

A: Can you tell me something about the kind of work that the charity has been doing recently?

B: So recently we've had several emergencies, several major emergencies, in Pakistan we've had floods affecting nearly 30 million people, in Haiti we've had an earthquake which brought, you know, huge amounts of death and devastation. But then we've got our work globally across the world through, you know, at community level where actually we're seeing some good things, some good news as well such as the number of children that die before their fifth birthday reduced from 8.8 million to 8.1 million a year, so every day 2,000 children less are dying of preventable diseases than they were this time last year and World Vision is a part of that, a small part of it, but we're part of that.

A: You mentioned disaster relief. Can you tell me a little bit more about what you do in disasters?

B: Well, because World Vision we are, you know, we work at community level in so many different countries in long-term development, when an emergency strikes, most places in the world we are working there already. So, you might remember the Tsunami in Asia back in 2006. Literally, within, within an hour in the south-east of India, community groups and local World Vision staff were responding, responding there with food, with water, with immediate medical care and things like that. So I think in an emergency situation, you know, one of the benefits of being a local organisation in those places is that you're there before and you're there after, kind of the media and the cameras come and go and so you can be there to help rebuild in the long term as well as providing immediate relief.

A: So you have staff locally? Or you have international staff?

B: World Vision has about 40,000 staff worldwide in nearly 100 countries of whom the vast majority are local to their own country, to their own communities, 95% or more. We do, of course, have some international staff going in, in some contexts as well … We also have thousands of volunteers that we work with.

A: And what sort of work do they do then?

B: Well, they're the kind of hands and feet of our work really. They are the people who often know best what the situation is whether it's an emergency or whether in longer-term development. And they often provide some of the most critical, you know, timely-critical, context-specific help and responses to, certainly to emergencies, but also to other things like, like diseases.

A: Can you give some examples of that?

B: Yes, one example from emergencies I'd say is, we had in Myanmar, Burma, a couple of years ago, a big cyclone, Cyclone Nargis which again, over 100,000 people died and thousands more were affected. Amazing. I heard from one of my colleagues there, a local volunteer there who had at the same time as her own house had collapsed, and in fact she didn't know where her six-year-old son was. He was out playing when the cyclone came or something like that and she sent her mum to go and look for her son while she went across town

to go to the World Vision office, which opened things up there with the staff there and actually get relief supplies out to one of the townships nearby where World Vision works. So just extraordinary to hear someone putting the needs of others before their own needs at a time of real hardship.

Another example in Haiti recently we had our staff working there out of the car park by the office, because the office had collapsed, and many, many staff there had lost or, either lost loved ones in their family or didn't know where they were. We had, one family I know there, who his wife and two kids were buried in a building all night long, in fact more than, for 24 hours, while he was having to help get on with the emergency response at the same time as trying to find his own family. So really shocking stories of, kind of, heroism really in the midst of tragedy. But then there are thousands more across the whole of sub Saharan Africa, there's probably hundreds of thousands, if not millions, of just normal people, often women who go out and care for families, and particularly for orphans, and for families that have been devastated by disease, such as TB or AIDS, and who just bring care when they're ill, but also help with food or with local livelihoods and things. So there's an army of those from local churches, from other faith groups and from community groups.

2.20

No seaman has ever seen anything like this. It's a war zone out there and, quite simply, the situation is out of control. It's not like before when they'd come on board and rob you. These days they hijack ships, take the entire crew hostage and demand huge ransoms. It's very primitive and very frightening. I come from a seafaring family, my father and brother are both merchant seamen and I'm in this job for nine years, doing seven months at a stretch on the high seas. I can tell you I'm scared. I have a young family, a wife who is expecting a baby and rightly she is beside herself with worry.

This month we've had to go through the Gulf of Aden twice. The first time we were totally unprotected and I felt so alone, so responsible for my crew and cargo. The second time we were able to join a convoy that was being escorted by a Russian frigate, but when another merchant ship about 30 miles south of us was suddenly attacked, the warship had to leave. More often than not the coalition warships that are meant to be patrolling the seas, warding off the pirates, are useless. A lot of the time they don't respond to distress calls and, anyway, the pirates are so quick. I'm now more afraid of piracy than storms and cyclones.

When they attack you – and so far the *Ellivita* has been lucky – the game is up quickly. In five to ten minutes the pirates surround you in speedboats; then using ladders they board the vessel and from that moment there's nothing you can do. They're the ones with the weapons and they've taken the crew hostage.

We're mariners not military men and our job is not to use guns against other people. But I also think we have reached a point where to protect ships we have to have security teams, or weapons, on board. Right now it really does seem as if it can't get any worse. But crews are also concerned that the next thing we'll be seeing are deaths, people being shot by pirates demanding ransoms.

2.21

I'm 42 years old and have nine children. I'm a boss with boats operating in the Gulf of Aden and the Indian Ocean. I finished high school and wanted to go to university, but there was no money. So I became a fisherman like my father, even though I still dreamed of working for a company. That never happened as the Somali government was destroyed in 1991 and the country became unstable. In Somalia, there are no jobs, and no rule of law because of the conflict. At sea we were often confronted by foreign fishing vessels who didn't want us there to compete. They would destroy our boats and force us to flee for our lives. I started to hijack these fishing boats in 1998. For our first captured ship we got $300,000. With the money we bought Automatic rifles and small speedboats.

I don't know exactly how many ships I've captured since then, but I think it's about 60. To get their attention we shoot near the ship. If it doesn't stop we use a rope ladder to get on board. We count the crew and find out their nationalities. After checking the cargo we ask the captain to phone the owner and say that we've seized the ship and we'll keep it until the ransom is paid. We make friends with the hostages, telling them that we only want money, not to kill them. Sometimes we even eat rice, fish, pasta with them. When the money is delivered to our ship we count the dollars and let the hostages go.

Our community thinks we're pirates getting illegal money. But we consider ourselves heroes running away from poverty. We don't see the hijacking as a criminal act, but as a road tax because we have no central government to control our sea. But we're getting new boats and weapons. We won't stop until we have a central government that can control our sea.

🔘 **2.23–2.28**

1 **A:** So would anyone like some more coffee?
    B: Oh I would love one thanks.
    All: Yeah yeah.
    B: Those cookies look nice.
    C: Just the one sugar, please. Thanks.
    B: It's very kind of you to invite us over and bake cookies ...
    D: They smell fantastic.
    B: Speaking of being kind, something amazing happened to my daughter last week. She was due to fly back from Hong Kong, where she'd been teaching, and she missed her flight because she misread midnight for midday ...
    E: Oh no, I've done that, yeah ...
    B: ... so she was ...
2 **B:** ... and he said oh I'll just ... I'll buy you another ticket, you know, this could have been my daughter on the other side of the world ...
    D: That's so kind ...
    E: Seriously?
    B: ... and he bought her a ticket ... um and ...
    E: To where she wanted to go?
    B: Yes, back home.
    E: Just like that?
    B: Yeah.
    E: That was it?
    B: And apparently he insisted on paying for it and didn't want to be paid back or anything, wouldn't give her his name or address.
    E: Oh that's really kind.
    C: Sorry to interrupt, but do you know that reminds me of a time I was in, I was in Italy and I'd left all my bags in the car and the car was broken into. I didn't have any money or any ID, anything, and the people at the car hire company lent me some money just to get through the weekend ...
3 **B:** ... so we had to pay an extra £200 each to get back.
    E: You've got to be very careful with these cheap flights really, because they're just not as cheap as you think they're going to be.
    B: No, they have ways of getting you, don't they?
    E: They do, they do.
    B: Luggage yes, luggage costs extra. Yeah.
    E: Oh luggage, that reminds me actually, once I was travelling abroad and I'd forgotten that we'd been for a picnic earlier in the day and I'd left my cutlery from the picnic at the bottom of my rucksack.
    B: Oh no.
    E: Yes, and it set off a big security alert and I was like no, I haven't got anything in here, I haven't got scissors, I haven't got a knife, nothing, I packed the bag myself, I swear, I swear. Completely forgetting about the picnic. And then ...
4 **B:** We had a funny thing happen once going through security. Again I thought I'd taken everything out that shouldn't be going through and ... um ... and suddenly they stopped me and pointed to the X-ray and said what's that in your bag and I looked and it looked like there was this huge knife in my bag, like a flick knife. So they started unpacking my bag and it wasn't a flick knife of course it was two metal objects. It was a comb in a

metal comb case next to a lipstick in a metal case and the lipstick looked like the handle and the comb looked like the blade.
    E: Oh my goodness, yeah ... On the subject of X-rays I had my results back, you know, for my knee operation.
    D: Oh yes.
    B: Is it all clear?
    E: Yes, it's fine, it's just ... och ... that I'm going to have to go back and have another operation.
    B: That's awful.
    D: It's always happening, isn't it? It happened to my neighbour.
    E: Yeah?
    D: Yeah, that reminds me of my neighbour because he ... he ... he was going to have his hip operation today and they just phoned him up and said that they can't fit him in, they're going to have to ... yeah ... put him a week later.
    E: It does affect your life ...
    C: Changing the subject completely though, you know, neighbours, I don't know how you get on with your neighbours but, you know, I hardly know my neighbours. I've lived there ...
5 **E:** I live in a block of flats and ... um ... I don't know, it's very friendly, very communal, I mean, we don't go in and out of each other's houses, you know, it's nothing like that ...
    C: Sure.
    E: ... but we all speak on the stairs, we know where the other people work, that kind of thing. It's quite a nice community actually.
    B: Yeah, people have been there a long time ...
    C: So do people help each other out and that kind of thing?
    E: Yeah I guess so. I mean, if we're locked out we can ...
    D: Sorry, can I just say something ...?
    E: Sure.
    D: ... you're wanted on the phone, Alexandra, um ...
    B: Oh right OK.
    D: Yes.
    B: OK fine.
    D: Sorry, do go on.
    E: No no it's OK, no problem, no problem.
6 **E:** You know, I'm so pleased I'm a homeowner now and that I'm not renting flats. I would not want to go through that again, no way. It's so good to have the control.
    D: Anyway, sorry, going back to my neighbour who's got this operation ...
    E: Aha. The hip one?
    D: Yeah. The problem is he's probably going to have to go into hospital next week ...
    E: Right, right.
    D: ... and, um, he's asked me whether I can take him, but I can't because, um, my ... my car's broken.
    E: Take him to hospital?
    D: Yeah.
    B: I could probably help out if you like ...
    D: Oh could you?
    B: ... depends which day it is. Do you know which day it is?

🔘 **2.29–2.34**

1 **All:** ... Yeah yeah.
    B: Those cookies look nice.
    C: Just the one sugar, please. Thanks.
    B: It's very kind of you to invite us over and bake cookies ...
    D: They smell fantastic.
    B: Speaking of being kind, something amazing happened to my daughter last week. She was due to fly back ...
2 **B:** ... and apparently he insisted on paying for it and didn't want to be paid back or anything, wouldn't give her his name or address.

    E: Oh that's really kind.
    C: Sorry to interrupt, but do you know that reminds me of a time I was in, I was in Italy and I'd left all my bags in the car and the car was broken into. I didn't have any money or any ID, anything, and the people at the car hire company lent me some money just to get through the weekend ...
3 **B:** ... so we had to pay an extra £200 each to get back.
    E: You've got to be very careful with these cheap flights really, because they're just not as cheap as you think they're going to be.
    B: No, they have ways of getting you, don't they?
    E: They do, they do.
    B: Luggage yes, luggage costs extra. Yeah.
    E: Oh, luggage, that reminds me actually, once I was travelling abroad and I'd forgotten that we'd been for a picnic earlier in the day ...
4 **B:** ... it wasn't a flick knife, of course, it was two metal objects. It was a comb in a metal comb case next to a lipstick in a metal case and the lipstick looked like the handle and the comb looked like the blade.
    E: Oh my goodness, yeah ... On the subject of X-rays I had my results back, you know, for my knee operation.
    D: Oh yes.
    B: Is it all clear?
    E: Yes, it's fine, it's just ... och ... that I'm going to have to go back and have another operation. ...
    B: That's awful.
    D: It's always happening, isn't it? It happened to my neighbour.
    B: Yeah?
    E: Yeah, that reminds me of my neighbour because he ... he ... he was going to have his hip operation today and they just phoned him up and said that they can't fit him in, they're going to have to ... yeah ... put him a week later. ...
5 **C:** ... So do people help each other out and that kind of thing?
    E: Yeah I guess so. I mean, if we're locked out we can ...
    D: Sorry, can I just say something ...?
    E: Sure.
    D: ... you're wanted on the phone, Alexandra, um ...
    B: Oh right OK.
    D: Yes.
    B: OK fine.
    D: Sorry, do go on.
    E: No no it's OK, no problem, no problem. ...
6 **E:** ... You know, I'm so pleased I'm a homeowner now and that I'm not renting flats. I would not want to go through that again, no way. It's so good to have the control.
    D: Anyway, sorry, going back to my neighbour who's got this operation ...
    E: Aha. The hip one?
    D: Yeah. ... The problem is he's probably going to have to go into hospital next week ...

Unit 6

🔘 **2.36–2.40**

1 The Silk Road was not, as the name suggests, a single road at all. It consisted of an extensive network of trade routes that criss-crossed China, parts of the Middle East and Europe, for almost 3,000 years from the first millennium BC until about 1500 AD. The starting point was in China, and the main land routes extended over a huge area of what is now modern day China, Turkey, Syria, Iraq, Iran, Afghanistan, Pakistan, India, Turkmenistan and Uzbekistan. And when goods arrived at the coast they were transported by sea to the major trading ports of Europe, northern Africa and Asia.

2 Since the transport capacity was limited, luxury goods were the only commodities that could be traded. As the name suggests, silk was the main commodity that was traded on the Silk Road. Silk was highly prized

and in great demand in the west, and the silk-making process was a secret that was closely guarded for centuries under punishment of death. Silk was ideal for overland travel as it was light, easy to carry and took up little space. It was manufactured in China, and was intricately decorated and embroidered, and when it arrived in Europe it was made into luxury goods such as book coverings, wall hangings and clothes.

3 Silk was by no means the only commodity exchanged by traders, however. Perfumes, precious stones and metals, and foodstuffs were exchanged in both directions. There was also a lucrative trade in spices from east to west; in fact one European town is on record as selling as many as 288 different kinds. In the west, people had to keep meat for a long time until it turned rancid, and spices were very useful for disguising the flavour. Some of the most valuable ones – ginger, nutmeg, cinnamon and saffron – were actually worth more than their weight in gold. Pepper was also extremely valuable, and caravans that carried it were heavily armed.

4 In addition to silk and spices, Europeans were eager to import teas and porcelain from China as well as Persian carpets. The Chinese, for their part, particularly appreciated coloured glass from the Mediterranean, and also imported such commodities as fine tableware, wool and linen, horses and saddles. Many of these goods were bartered for others along the way, and objects often changed hands several times. And it was not only goods that were exchanged on the routes, but also many important scientific and technological innovations; the magnetic compass, the printing press, paper-making and gunpowder all originated in the East, not to mention important intellectual developments such as algebra and astronomy. And in return, the West taught the East about construction techniques, shipbuilding and wine-making.

5 Life for traders along the Silk Road was often hard. As well as having to trek over some of the world's most inhospitable terrain, they also faced the ever present threat of bandits, not to mention wars, plagues and natural disasters. Between towns and oases they would often sleep in yurts or under the stars, or else would stop for rest and refreshment at one of the several bustling oasis towns that sprang up along the routes. Here they would stay at caravanserais, places which offered free board and lodging, as well as stables for their camels or donkeys. The caravanserai became a rich melting pot of ideas, used as they were not only by traders and merchants, but also by pilgrims, missionaries, soldiers, nomads and urban dwellers from all over the region.

🔊 2.41

By the end of the 14th century, as other trading routes were established, the importance of the Silk Road had greatly diminished. But it is no exaggeration to say that it had played a major part in establishing the foundations of the modern world. It had allowed the exchange not only of commodities, but also of music, arts, science, customs, ideas, religions and philosophies. In fact, there was so much cultural interchange over so many centuries that it is now often difficult to identify the origins of numerous traditions that our respective cultures take for granted. So we can say that, in its heyday the Silk Road was an early example of the political, economic and cultural integration that we know today as globalisation. And today, the Silk Road is again being used – not only by traders, but also for that most contemporary of international commodities – tourism.

🔊 2.43

1

The moment the slave resolves that he will no longer be a slave, his fetters fall. Freedom and slavery are mental states.

2

The danger of the past was that men became slaves. The danger of the future is that men may become robots.

3

The history of men's opposition to women's emancipation is more interesting perhaps than the story of that emancipation itself.

4

I disapprove of what you say, but I will defend to the death your right to say it.

5

To be free is not merely to cast off one's chains, but to live in a way that respects and enhances the freedom of others.

6

Freedom is never voluntarily given by the oppressor; it must be demanded by the oppressed.

7

Governments need armies to protect them against their enslaved and oppressed subjects.

8

Everything can be taken from a man but one thing: the last of the human freedoms – to choose one's attitude in any given set of circumstances.

🔊 2.44

For decades now as you know, large companies have been outsourcing information technology services as well as what we call 'back office services' – things like administrative duties and customer services. For companies, getting rid of these tasks, or passing on these office services, means lower costs, for one thing. But it also gives companies the chance to focus on their core business – manufacturing, sales, research, whatever business they're actually in. Up until the 1990s, American and British businesses tended to outsource these tasks to workers in their own country. But in the 1990s, company bosses realised that India had a large pool of technically literate workers who could work for a fraction of the cost. So many large companies started to take advantage of India's outsourcing companies in a big way.

The problem is that, now, India has just become too expensive. Firstly, there are no longer *enough* skilled English-speaking workers to cope with demand. So these workers have tended to move from company to company in search of the highest paid jobs. This has kept pushing up the cost of Indian salaries and therefore also pushed up the cost of outsourcing for American and British customers.

In addition, there's been a huge increase in property prices in cities such as Bangalore, Chennai and Pune. And infrastructure in these areas – things like transport and sanitation – has just not been able to keep pace with the growth of the outsourcing industry. Some Indian outsourcing companies have tried to move their businesses to rural locations in order to find a way round these issues. But, as you can imagine, there are usually fewer skilled workers in rural areas, so this isn't really a solution.

So basically, India has become a victim of its own success. What that means is that some American and British customers have started to outsource to lower-cost markets elsewhere instead – so places such as China, the Philippines, Brazil, Mexico, erm, eastern Europe. But there's also been a positive development and that is that some of the *Indian* companies which offer outsourcing services have begun to set up in business in other countries. So they're *re-exporting* outsourcing work to places with cheaper labour. Indian companies that used to be small firms providing services for global companies abroad have become important global companies themselves.

🔊 2.45–2.48

1 A: So is that really the best you can do?
    B: I'm terribly sorry sir, that's the absolute best price we can do.
    A: Well, I wasn't planning on paying that much, especially on a car that's done that mileage.
    B: Yes, I appreciate that sir. We have an older vehicle here if you'd rather that one, that's slightly cheaper.
    A: No, I'm not interested in the older one.
    B: No?
    A: This is the one I've got my eye on, but the price has to be ...
    B: I'm afraid that's absolutely the best we can do. We can throw in some cover if you'd like, but that's the best price we can offer.
    A: And the car mats, you'll throw those in?
    B: Absolutely, yes, but the price unfortunately is exactly the same.
    A: You won't budge on that at all?
    B: I'm afraid we can't sir. It wouldn't be worth my job.
    A: Well, I'm going to have to think about it, to be honest.

    B: OK, no problem, give me a call any time.
    A: OK, thanks for your help.

2 A: Good afternoon.
    B: Hello, Mr Akroyd. I just wanted to talk to you about the bank charges that I seem to have incurred. As far as I'm aware I was only ... I only went beyond my overdraft limit for a matter of 12 hours really and as far as I was aware I actually ... I put some money in at about quarter to five on the Wednesday.
    A: Yes, after the bank closed I'm afraid so it didn't clear in time. So you did actually go into overdraft for, you're right, for a few hours.
    B: Yes, but I mean, surely that ... that ... those few hours shouldn't have incurred such a hefty fine? I mean, I've been charged here £30.
    A: Well, it's a combination of the fine for going into overdraft without authority and also the interest that accrued as a result, but we ... I do understand it was for a short period of time so we could ... in this case, I do have to charge the interest, but I could actually waive the penalty fee.
    B: Thank you very much Mr Akroyd ...
    A: Is that all right?
    B: ... that's very kind.
    A: Thanks. If in future though, you must bear in mind that if the cheque hasn't cleared by the end of the day it can't be credited to your account.
    B: OK, thank you.

3 A: Sir, I'm afraid this, this flight is actually fully booked.
    B: But I have a ticket.
    A: I've just had a look at the computer and it's telling me, and I've just had it verified by my manager, that, um, this flight is fully booked and you will not be able to travel on this flight. I'm terribly sorry.
    B: Right, so what do you suggest?
    A: Um, well, there is another flight at 5.30 this afternoon ...
    B: That's too late for me, I have a meeting to get to.
    A: There is availability on this flight sir. I mean, in terms of getting you there we can, yes it will be later.
    B: But you do acknowledge that it's not my fault that I'm being bumped off this flight?
    A: You are absolutely right about that sir. What I can do is I can offer you an upgrade on the 5.30 flight. Would that be acceptable?
    B: To club class?
    A: Just one second. Yes, there is a seat in club class and I can put you on that straight away.
    B: Right, well, I mean ... it will have to do I suppose, but it's not a good way to treat frequent fliers. Is there anything else you can do for me?
    A: Sir, I could actually offer you a flight in the future if you wish and we can try to recompense you with vouchers for ...
    B: Well, I think that would be fair, don't you?
    A: Well, as I said, we will get you on the 5.30, we'll get you a club class seat, and I will offer you, we will offer you some vouchers for [your] next flight, to any destination in Europe flying with us ...
    B: OK, well, let's do that then.
    A: ... and I hope you continue to fly with us ...
    B: We'll see.

4 A: So my company could sell to you at a much cheaper rate than you're getting now because we are literally two minutes down the road. So we'll make a huge saving in petrol, which we can pass on to you in the unit price.
    B: Well, that does sound good, but we do have a long relationship with this other company. I mean, we'd, we'd need a pretty substantial discount in order to make it fiscally viable for us.
    A: OK, your unit price at the moment?
    B: It's about 70 per kilo.
    A: OK, well, we could do 50.
    B: Really?

A: Yeah.

B: OK, well, if you can do 50 ... um ... I'm actually ... I actually run about four different stores so what I can do if you can get ... tell you what ... if you can get it down to 45 then I can guarantee we would do at least four stores for you, rather than just one.

A: OK, 45 is pushing it, but if we can make it at least five, I've got to get one more than four to make, to make that viable.

B: OK, OK, we'll do five, five for 45.

A: Yeah.

B: OK, we can definitely do that.

A: Fantastic, it's a deal.

🔊 2.49

1 But you do acknowledge it's not my fault?
2 You did actually go into overdraft.
3 Well, that does sound good.

🔊 2.50

You said you'd deliver them today.
You did say you'd deliver them today.

I understand.
I do understand.

It seems like a good deal.
It does seem like a good deal.

I think that would be fair, don't you?
I do think that would be fair, don't you?

Have a seat.
Do have a seat.

You promised me a discount.
You did promise me a discount.

That sounds tempting.
That does sound tempting.

I appreciate that.
I do appreciate that.

🔊 2.51

A = Marion; **B** = Scott
Marion (The Netherlands), Scott (England)

A: I was in, um, I was in Holland over the weekend and went shopping with my mum and, um, it was really interesting because we went to, um ... generally I think the difference between The Netherlands and, and England isn't very big in terms of customer satisfaction or the way people meet and greet you in, in shops, um, but we were in a, a big department store and we were looking at children's socks and all of a sudden this woman came up to us and said 'Do you need help with anything?' and I thought 'We are in a department store', you know, 'looking at socks,' and it was just a really random sort of experience where she came up and said 'Do you need help with anything?' because they normally wouldn't do that.

B: I have had that experience in mobile phone shops before. You literally walk inside the door and then you get five people come up to you all at once and ask do you need help. You need a chance to actually look at the mobile phones to ascertain if you want to buy it or not so ...

A: Yes, and what you'd like.

B: ... a bit too intrusive I think, sometimes they need to stand back and let you decide on options ...

A: Let you decide.

B: ... before you want to buy.

A: Well, exactly, yes, absolutely.

B: I think certain industries are more intrusive ...

A: Yes.

B: ... when you go into ...

A: Yes, so ...

🔊 2.52

A = Lillian; **B** = Dominika
Lillian (Kenya), Dominika (Poland)

A: Well, um, Kenyans generally they are known for being hospitable and being nice to people, but sadly this

is not extended to the, to the low-class citizens. You know, they just have to tolerate being not treated well. But I must compare it to the UK, I find the British pleasant, very pleasant. I just recall the other day I went into Currys to buy an mp3 player. Now I'm not good in this electronic guidance ...

B: Me neither ...

A: ... but the gentleman there was very helpful. He explained to me, you know, the technical products, you know, how, how many songs the mp3 can hold, and he went out of his way and he took me to the counter, processed the payment, talked to me about the insurance, and I almost bought it, but I didn't ...

B: I hope he got fantastic commission?

A: Yes, but he was really, really helpful and I walked away feeling wow, that was good.

B: Did you have to wait for any staff to approach you or ...?

A: Actually, no, he saw me, he saw me looking at the area where the mp3s were kept and he walked over to me and asked me if he can help me which I thought was really nice because he took a personal interest in me.

B: Very good. Sometimes I have to say that I have need to wait for people to serve me. It happens quite often that two very young girls are just busy chatting to each other over the till rather than ... that's, that's the common thing. And that's something that wouldn't happen in Poland really. But yes the manner and, you know, saying 'thank you' and 'Is there anything I can do for you?' is very good.

Unit 7

🔊 3.03–3.05

A = Interviewer; **B** = Sue Gerhardt

A: So can you say something about how a baby's brain develops?

B: Yes, I think the most amazing thing to remember is that the brain is actually a social organ so it doesn't develop automatically; it actually develops in response to other people, especially in the first couple of years when the baby's brain is actually developing at the most rapid rate that it will ever develop. And in particular what's happening in the first couple of years is that the emotion systems are getting set up. And what I call emotion systems are in particular the stress response, what I would call the soothing response, and the pre-frontal area of the brain, which is the first bit of the higher brain to develop and really has a big impact on our emotions.

A: Can you say a bit more about the stress response and the soothing response?

B: There's a whole system which we call the stress response which is about triggering off a response to stress that kind of energises and focuses an individual to deal with a problem, or a threat, or a challenge of some kind. This stress response works by releasing Cortisol so that a challenge can be met. And then in infancy you actually need parents to do the soothing and to put things right so that the whole thing can come to a kind of conclusion and the Cortisol can be dispersed, it is not needed anymore. Unfortunately, one of the things that's emerged from all this scientific research of recent years is that if a young child has too much stress and therefore too much Cortisol, this Cortisol has a very toxic effect on all sorts of other systems. It also has a very toxic effect on the pre-frontal cortex and so it actually hampers growth of the pathways there.

A: So what should parents do to regulate their baby's stress or emotions?

B: In very early infancy it's really got a lot to do with very basic non-verbal things like the way a parent holds the baby, it's a lot to do with touch, tone of voice, eye contact, the sort of musicality of turn-taking between the adult and the child. As the baby gets bigger it sort of widens out into helping the baby do more and more for himself, or herself, and then helping the baby to regulate himself more and more. And one of the main tools there is also, it's about putting feelings into words, and that's a really important tool to help your baby to manage feelings.

A: Do you think a baby's temperament is due mainly to nature or to nurture?

B: We have all sorts of genetic predispositions which may or may not get realised in actual life, depending on what happens to the person. Genes don't, don't determine our lives in any automatic sense. They are there as a kind of store that we draw on as we have to deal with all sorts of different environments and circumstances which trigger off a genetic expression of a particular gene.
I mean, I'm certainly aware that every baby is different. My own two children are completely different. One was very cheerful and bouncy and the other was very sensitive and cautious. So yes, we definitely come with a temperament, but it's, you know, what the people around us trigger off, what the circumstances of our lives trigger off, that really matters.

A: What advice would you give to parents on how to bring up babies, the best way to shape their brain?

B: Attachment theory has really stressed how important it is for development that babies feel safe. The crucial thing is really to give your baby attention and to really notice, to really respond, and to realise that the baby can't manage his or her own feelings or emotions, or meet his or her own needs. It's up to the parents to do this for them in the early stages of life and that will help them.

🔊 3.08–3.11

A = Emily; **B** = Sarah; **C** = Receptionist

1 **A:** Sarah, I was wondering if you could do me a favour?

   B: Yeah.

   A: The thing is you see I've got an appointment at the hospital this afternoon and I was wondering, is there any way you could give me a lift?

   B: I would if I could, but I'm going to struggle this afternoon. The car is in for a service and I'm not entirely sure I'd be able to get back in time. Sorry.

   A: Oh, OK, well, I just thought I'd ask.

2 **C:** Good afternoon, St Michael's, Julie speaking, how can I help?

   A: Oh hello there. Um ... I'm afraid there's a slight problem. I've got an appointment this afternoon at 3.30. Would it be possible to change the appointment?

   C: What's your name, please?

   A: My name's Emily Watkins.

   C: OK. Ah yes, I see. Um ... hmm ... actually, let me just check something a minute.

   A: OK, thank you.

   C: Do you know, it's your lucky day. We've had a cancellation so that's not going to be a problem today.

   A: Great.

   C: So we will see you now at four o'clock.

   A: OK, yes, I think that should be all right.

   C: Will that be enough time?

   A: Mmm ... let's go for four o'clock, yes.

   C: OK.

   A: Thanks very much.

   C: We'll see you then.

   A: OK, bye.

   C: Bye bye.

3 **A:** Sarah, yes it all went fine actually. They saw me at four o'clock instead ...

   B: Great.

   A: ... and the only thing is ... um ... I don't suppose you could possibly pick up the prescription for me, it wasn't ready there and then, but they said it would be ready tomorrow morning. Would that be possible?

   B: Um ... yeah, no worries at all. And they're happy about me picking it up?

   A: Yeah, yeah. I said that you might be able to do that so that was fine for them.

   B: OK great.

   A: Great, thank you.

4 **B:** I've got an apology to make. I'm so sorry. You know I said I'd pick up the prescription?

A: Yes.

B: I didn't. I completely forgot. I'm so sorry.

A: Oh no.

B: I ... do you think it would be all right if I picked it up later this afternoon?

A: Yes, I'm sure that'll be fine. I'll give ... I'll give the hospital a call.

B: Yeah, do that and I'll pick it up this afternoon. I'm so sorry.

A: That's OK.

Unit 8

3.13

The Idea of Perfection

Douglas stood at his bedroom window in the Caledonia Hotel, Karakarook, looking out at the street. After a long period of stillness an old brown car appeared at the end of the street, came slowly along and parked tentatively alongside the hotel. A woman got out and stood looking up and down the street with her hands on her hips. She was a big plain raw-boned person, tall and unlikely, with a ragged haircut and a white teeshirt coming unstitched along the shoulder. It was a long time since she'd been young and it was unlikely that she had ever been lovely. She was not accessorised. There was no collar, no scarf, no beads, no earrings. Her head just came up sternly out of the teeshirt saying, here I am, and who do you think you are?

Douglas stood with the curtain in his hand, watching her across the road as she looked at Parnassus Road exposed under the sky. A salt of the earth type. The way the woman stood with her hands on her hips, looking down the street as if she owned it, he could imagine her life, a proper life anchored solid to the ground. There would be a big cheerful husband, uncomplicated children, fat red-cheeked grandchildren calling her Nanna. He could imagine the kitchen out on the farm, with the radio going, and the fridge door covered with magnets that said things like Bless this Mess. He let the curtain fall and stepped back from the window. Then he stood in the dim room wondering why he had done that.

3.14

Harley had seen him looking. She had seen him drop the curtain and move back from the window. She had forgotten how empty a country town could be, how closed, how you could feel looked-at and large. She walked further down the street and then, not looking where she was going, she walked straight into a man coming out of the doorway of the Caledonia. When they collided, he staggered backwards and nearly fell. She grabbed at a handful of his forearm, clutching at the fabric and the arm beneath, and he flailed out to steady himself, hitting her on the shoulder. Then they were both standing in the beer-smelling current of cool air from the doorway, apologising.

The man had a look of hysteria around the corners of his mouth. He wanted to blame himself.

My fault, he kept saying. Completely my fault. Stupid.

She had a feeling it was the man who had watched her from the window, but with his hat on it was hard to be sure.

Totally stupid. Not thinking at all.

So clumsy, Harley said. Me, I mean.

She did not look at him, but at the ground, where their shoes were arranged on the footpath like ballroom-dancing instructions.

Did I hurt you? Hitting you?

She looked at him, surprised.

Hurt me?

He pointed, but did not touch.

I hit you, he said, humbly. There.

No, no, she said, although now he had mentioned it, she could feel the place hurting.

She looked at her own hand, large and plain, that had clutched at him, and wondered if she should ask whether she had hurt him.

Well, he said, and laughed a meaningless laugh.

A moment extended itself into awkwardness.

Well, he said again, and she said it too at the same moment. Their voices sounded loud together. Harley felt as if the whole of Karakarook, behind its windows, must be watching this event that had burst into their silent afternoon: two bodies hitting together, two people standing apologising.

3.16–3.17

1 I like the industrial look. It's sort of that kind of inside out, you know, unique style. And I like it because it's not like any other building that I've ever seen. So if someone showed me a picture of it, or a postcard, I would know exactly where it was and what it represented. And I think because it's a building that represents modern art, you know, that sort of industrial, very sort of ... you know, those brightly coloured steel tubes, and that steel and glass, it's kind of modern, it's forward-thinking, it's a sign of our times you know, that's why I like it, because it reminds us of modern art.

2 Well, this building looks very modern, um, almost futuristic. It's like a giant dome which is half titanium and half glass with no straight lines, smooth and curved. Um, its nickname is the egg. It's surrounded by this man-made lake so that the light of the building reflects on the lake and makes it even seem bigger than it is. It's sort of silver in colour, but that can change depending on whether it's night or day and the light conditions. Um, it's a really amazing building. I love it.

3.18

A = Geoff; **B** = Grant; **C** = Man; **D** = Woman

A: Right, right. OK, shall we start? I'd like to welcome our speaker today Grant Fisher, who has very kindly agreed to come and talk to us about how to design your own website, which I know many of you are extremely keen to do. Grant is Head of IT at Ainsdale College, and I know his talk is going to be very practical and useful. So without further ado, I'll hand over to Grant.

B: Thanks Geoff, and thanks for inviting me to come and talk to you. It's a great pleasure to be here today. Maybe I could start by asking if any of you already have your own website? Could you raise your hands? One, two, three of you. Well done. And now, how many would like to have your own website, but don't have one simply because you haven't a clue how to go about it? Could you raise your hands? So that's the majority of you.

Well, the topic of my talk today is website design, and my aim is to take the mystery out of designing a website and I hope that by the end of it, you'll all go away fired with enthusiasm to create your own site, and as you'll see, you don't need to be an IT expert to design a simple site.

So, there are three parts to my presentation. I'm going to start by outlining the steps you need to take to set up a website. Then I'll look at some features of a good website, and I'll illustrate that with some slides of good and bad website design. And finally, I'll focus on troubleshooting, what to do when problems occur, as they inevitably will. If anything is not clear, please feel free to interrupt me as we go along, otherwise if you have any questions, I'll do my best to answer them at the end.

OK, so, let's think about the process of setting up a website, step by step. Any ideas about the very first thing you have to do? Yes, the gentleman at the back?

C: Get permission.

B: Get permission. Well, no not quite. Anyone else? Yes, the lady over there.

D: Get a name.

B: Get a name. Yes, yes, spot on. The very first thing you need to do is get yourself a domain name. What do I mean by 'domain name'? Well, a domain name is the name given to your website, the one you put into your search engine when you want to access a site. For example, designers dot com, or creativedesign dot org. Perhaps I should point out that the name you choose should be ...

Right, so, turning now to the features of a good website. If you'd like to take a look at the slide – can you all see there at the back? If not, there's a handout going round, I hope I've made enough. Well, as you can see on the slide, this is not a very user-friendly page. Just to elaborate on that, you can see that the graphics ...

Well, I'll skip this slide as we're running out of time. Yes, Geoff is telling me it's time to stop. So, just to conclude, I hope I've demonstrated that designing a website is not rocket science, and that actually it can be quite fun as well. Well, that's it, and thanks for listening. Does anyone have any questions?

3.19

It's a great pleasure to be here today. The topic of my talk today is website design, and my aim is to take the mystery out of designing a website. So, my presentation will be divided into three parts. I'm going to start by outlining the steps you need to take to set up a website. I'll go on to mention some features of a good website, and I'll illustrate that with some slides. And finally, I'll focus on troubleshooting. If anything is not clear, feel free to interrupt me as we go along, otherwise if you have any questions, I'll do my best to answer them at the end.

3.21

A = Beth; **B** = Tim

Beth (United States), Tim (Northern Ireland)

A: Have you ever been to the States?

B: I have.

A: Have you? Where did you visit?

B: I visited San Francisco, Los Angeles, Carmel, places like that. In fact, Yosemite National Park.

A: Oh that's beautiful.

B: And I went there in 1995 for my honeymoon.

A: OK. What did you think of San Francisco?

B: Superb. I thought the people were very warm as well. The whole city had a nice warm feeling to it. Very interesting architecture in terms of earthquakes and so forth. Apparently, a lot of the buildings are built on huge ball bearings so that they move ...

A: Really?

B: ... the foundations move when there's an earthquake.

A: Interesting.

B: Yes, it is fascinating.

A: Was there any building in particular that you enjoyed?

B: Um, I think probably the Museum of Modern Art was a beautiful, beautiful building.

A: What did you like about it?

B: What did I like about it? I liked the openness of the inside, the whiteness of it, the Yoko Ono exhibition was quite interesting, and the outside, there is a huge circle with red bricks on the other side like a triangle with a circle in the middle. It is so long ago I can hardly remember, but I remember being impressed by the sense of space. It was almost like being in the open air.

A: Really?

B: Because it was so, so airy and spartan, apart from the artworks. Have you been to York?

A: I have.

B: And seen York Minster?

A: That's one of my favourites. That's beautiful, and outside is just as pretty as inside because some of the cathedrals, they are quite ... just brick on the outside and there is not a lot ... the decoration is more inside, but that one was ... is both outside and inside are just full of sculptures and angles and arches and it's really pretty.

B: And what's the name of the window? There's a very famous window. I'm not going to remember the name of it.

A: I can't remember what it is ...

B: But it's ...

A: I do know what you are talking about.

B: Yes, it's all sort of greys and blues. It's not like your archetypical stained-glass multicoloured window. It's very, very subtle, very nice.

A: Yes, the whole ... actually the town of York, all the buildings are quite nice. I thought that they were all quite unique.

B: Yeah.

3.22

A = Silvia; B = Evgenia
Silvia (Catalonia), Evgenia (Belarus)

A: It is the Alhambra in Granada. And yeah, for like you said, as you said, it's also because of the air and the light and the water, these elements that make it a special place, like magic place.

B: What about water, how it works?

A: There are a lot of fountains and the reflections of the sun on the water and on the tiles, because it's very special for the tiles, Moorish style …

B: It's like a sunny place?

A: What do you mean …?

B: I mean, would you have a lot of sunshine there?

A: Yes, of course.

B: Because in Oxford it's like most buildings here are so beautiful, they are just beautiful, but when it's a sunny day, which is not that very often, especially in wintertime, it's just gorgeous. And it's like sunlight, just, you know, makes …

A: It makes a difference, yeah, and I think that is also why I like classical buildings because they really took into account the light and the air because there wasn't ventilation or artificial lighting so it was … they made the most of these elements. So, yeah.

Unit 9

3.23

When as a child, I laughed and wept,
Time crept.
When as a youth, I dreamt and talked,
Time walked.
When I became a full-grown man,
Time ran.
When older still I daily grew,
Time flew.
Soon I shall find when travelling on –
Time gone.

3.24

What is time? Does it move forward in a line from the past to the future, or does it go round and round in endless cycles? And how can we break it up into different parts or units? Different societies have always provided varying answers to these fundamental questions of life.

In the West, time is typically conceived of as linear, moving forward relentlessly. Events occur and cannot be repeated. This view of time is associated with ideas of progress and evolution, and in fact it is the dominant paradigm in times of economic prosperity and national confidence. Modern Western time has also been described as 'monochronic' time. In a monochronic view, time is quantifiable. This is the time of schedules, clocks and organisations – some have called it 'male' or 'public' time. It is divided into fixed elements: seconds, minutes, hours, days, weeks, and so on – in other words, into blocks of time that can be organised and timetabled. And it is only possible to 'do one thing at a time', as time itself flows swiftly past. People who operate with this view of time love to plan in detail, make lists, keep track of their activities, and organise their time into a daily routine. Punctuality and time management are important. Switching back and forth from one activity to another is not only wasteful and distracting, it is also uncomfortable.

In traditional agricultural societies, on the other hand, time is often experienced as cyclical, or spiral, slowly advancing in an endless cycle of birth, death and rebirth. And we can see this reflected in the Buddhist and Hindu concept of reincarnation. This view of time has been called 'polychronic' and is common in many parts of the non-Western world. Time is experienced as continuous, with no particular structure. It is like a never-ending river, flowing from the infinite past, through the present, into the infinite future. Polychronic time has also been described as more 'private' or 'female'. The pace of life in polychromic societies is typically less frenetic and more relaxed. Tasks are completed only 'when the time is right' rather than according to a strict agenda, and people may engage in multitasking, changing from one activity to another as the mood takes them. In such cultures, it is not important to be punctual, or to meet deadlines and it is acceptable to interrupt someone who is busy.

3.25

1 **A:** Oh no, it's raining again! If only I didn't have to walk home.
   B: I'm going home your way. Would you like me to give you a lift when I've finished these emails?

2 **A:** Do you mind if I smoke?
   B: Actually, I'd rather you didn't, if you don't mind. It's a non-smoking household.

3 **A:** It's time you had a haircut.
   B: Honestly! I'm old enough to decide for myself how I have my hair. I wish you wouldn't speak to me as if I were a child!

4 **A:** I was wondering if you'd like to go out tomorrow night – birthday treat.
   B: Sounds great. What did you have in mind?

5 **A:** Is Caroline coming?
   B: No, Stuart told me she went swimming on Tuesdays.

6 **A:** Would you mind working a couple of hours extra tomorrow?
   B: Actually, I was hoping I could take tomorrow off. It's my daughter's school play and I really wanted to see it.

7 **A:** I wish I hadn't agreed to work overtime. Evie will be so disappointed.
   B: Why don't you phone in sick? You need to be a bit more assertive, you know.

3.26

Part 1

Honeybee dancing is one of the most intriguing aspects of bees' biology. The dances are performed by a worker bee that has returned to the honeycomb with pollen or nectar. In essence, the dances constitute a language that 'tells' other workers where the food source is.

When a bee returns to the colony with nectar or pollen that is sufficiently nutritious to warrant a return to the source, she performs a dance on the surface of the honeycomb. The dancer 'spells out' two items of information – distance and direction – to the target food source. Other workers then leave the hive to find the nectar or pollen.

3.27

Part 2

When a food source is very close to the hive, a bee performs a round dance. She does this by first running around in narrow circles and then suddenly reversing direction to her original course. She may repeat the round dance several times at the same location or she may move to another location on the honeycomb to repeat it. After the dance she often distributes food to the bees following her. A round dance, therefore, communicates *distance* ('close to the hive' in this example), but not *direction*.

The waggle dance is performed by bees which are foraging at food sources that are more than 150 metres from the hive. This dance, unlike the round dance, communicates both distance *and* direction. A bee performing a waggle dance runs straight ahead for a short distance, returns in a semi-circle to the starting point and runs again through the straight course. Then the waggle dancer makes a semi-circle in the opposite direction to complete a full figure of eight circuit. The bee's body, especially the abdomen, wags vigorously from side to side during the straight-line course of the dance. This vibration of the body produces a tail-wagging motion, and at the same time, the bee emits a buzzing sound.

Although the representation of *distance* in the waggle dance is relatively straightforward, the method of communicating *direction* is more complicated. The orientation of the dancing bee during the straight portion of her waggle dance is significant because it represents the angle of the Sun. This indicates to the other bees where the food source is, relative to the Sun.

3.28

Part 1

A: So, Mrs Blackburn, thanks very much for coming today. Would you like to just take a seat?

B: Thank you.

A: And … um … yes, perhaps you could start by saying why you're interested in the job?

B: Well, I wanted to do a job which meant being involved with people, dealing with people, their problems …

A: Yes.

B: … responding to people's needs and I thought this job was really ideal, and that, you know, I was ideally qualified for it really.

A: And what previous experience do you have of this kind of work?

B: Well, I haven't actually done a receptionist's job before, but … um …

A: Right.

B: … I've done similar kinds of jobs, I mean, I used to teach actually before I got married …

A: Aha.

B: … and then, you know, I wanted to get back into a job that meant I would be, you know, dealing with people, but I just felt I didn't want to actually have to go back into the classroom, I wanted to be just using my people skills in a different context.

A: Right, well, in that case can you perhaps tell me about a problem you solved, or, or something you achieved in your last job, when you were teaching?

B: Well, I … you'd often have to be very tactful with the parents, you know, you might be telling them something that they don't really want to hear. I did a lot of that and then obviously, you know, when you're a mum, you know, you have to also, you know, juggle a lot of things, you have to be good at paying attention to lots of different things going on at the same time and people all having demands to make at the same time and so on …

A: Yes, so multitasking basically.

B: Multitasking, but also you know paying attention to several different people simultaneously …

A: Very good.

B: … without alienating anybody …

A: Oh right.

B: … and making them feel that you are actually responding to their needs.

A: Well, that all sounds very good, multitasking and diplomacy and tact. What other qualities do you think you can bring to this position?

B: Well, I have quite good IT skills. I understand there's a bit of IT work. You have to enter things on the computer, look people's records up and so on …

A: Yes.

B: … and I'm quite good at that, I, you know, spent years doing freelance work involving those skills so I thought that would be interesting too, you know, mix the two things together …

A: Um, let me see. Could you perhaps tell me about your strengths and weaknesses, as a person?

B: Let's see, well, I think I've already described my strengths, you know, I'm quite good at multitasking and I'm good at dealing with people.

A: Of course, yes.

B: My weaknesses, um, I find it a little bit difficult I suppose if people get very aggressive …

A: Understandably.

B: Yes, so … um … so yes, I obviously, that might, that could be a problem if I had to deal with a very difficult patient who was … who was violent …

A: And just to finish off with, what are your career goals, I mean, where do you see yourself going?

B: Well, I'd like to get into human resource management ultimately actually, but I just think that a job like this would … um … hone my skills a bit, you know, be a good place to start.

Audioscript

3.29
Part 2

A: Right, well, thank you very much Mrs Blackburn. Are there any questions you'd like to ask me?

B: Um, yes, well, what's the next stage in the process? I mean, will I get feedback from you, will I hear from you quite soon?

A: Well, we're going to, um, make our decision by the end of today, basically, and we'll be giving you a call tomorrow morning to let you know if you've been successful.

B: Oh that's wonderful, yes. OK, and if I were to get the job, is there any kind of mentoring to sort of see me into the job?

A: Yes, well, our current receptionist isn't going to be leaving for a month …

B: Oh that's wonderful.

A: Yes, so it would be very helpful if you could come in and work with her, shadow her, for a week.

B: Right, yes. And in … in, what would you expect of me in the job, you know, in the first six months or so, what would you be wanting me to do?

A: Well, obviously you'll receive a full job description so … but we wouldn't throw you completely in at the deep end, … we'd like you to become familiar with the main tasks and duties and then we'll build it up from there. There'll be some additional duties after the first initial, let's say, first two or three months …

B: Right OK.

A: … we'll increase the amount of work that you have to do.

B: Great, OK.

A: But we won't go over your 37.5 hours, we promise.

B: Right, so, yes, yes yes …

3.30

1 Perhaps you could start by saying why you are interested in the job?

2 What previous experience do you have of this kind of work?

3 Can you perhaps tell me about a problem you solved, or, or something you achieved in your last job?

4 What other qualities do you think you can bring to this position?

5 Could you perhaps tell me about your strengths and weaknesses, as a person?

6 Are there any questions you'd like to ask me?

3.31

1 Well, I have a close group of friends and we play golf on the weekend and I like to go swimming every morning before I come into work and seeing as this job starts in the afternoon I think that's … it's perfect for me there.

2 Well, I just don't feel like it was … I think it was constricting me, holding me back from what I could really achieve so to come here I feel would just give me that extra push.

3 I don't really think that far along … after five or six years I'm sure I'll start to think about the next step, but other than that I'm more than happy coming into this job here.

4 Well, we have several more people to interview and we will definitely get back in touch with you either by email or letter. There may be a second interview if we decide that we are interested in what you have to offer.

5 Yes, definitely, that usually happens for the first six months.

6 Just to continue with the smooth running of the establishment and to make sure that staff and customers are happy.

3.32

A: So tell me a little bit about what you like to do outside of work. What are your outside interests?

B: Well, I have a close group of friends and we play golf on the weekend and I like to go swimming every morning before I come into work and seeing as this job starts in the afternoon I think that's … it's perfect for me there.

A: Why did you want to leave your present job?

B: Well, I just don't feel like it was … I think it was constricting me, holding me back from what I could really achieve so to come here I feel would just give me that extra push.

A: Good. And do you have any particular career goals, like can I ask you where you see yourself in ten years' time?

B: I don't really think that far all … after five or six years I'm sure I'll start to think about the next step, but other than that I'm more than happy coming into this job here.

A: Well, thank you very much and do you have any questions for me?

B: Yes, I was just wondering, what's the next stage in this process? Will I receive feedback from this interview I've just done?

A: Yes. Well, we have several more people to interview and we will definitely get back in touch with you either by email or letter. There may be a second interview if we decide that we are interested in what you have to offer.

B: And when I first start will I be given a mentor to oversee my development?

A: Yes, definitely, that usually happens for the first six months.

B: And in terms of the first six months, for those six months to a year, is there anything specific that will be expected of me?

A: Just to continue with the smooth running of the establishment and to make sure that staff and customers are happy.

Unit 10

3.34–3.38

1 Yeah, it can be a bit of a hassle, eating, just because of my schedule with lectures, university and stuff, but I do a big shop at the supermarket once a week. Stock up on easy stuff really, ready meals and processed food, you know, pizza, lasagne and stuff. Stick it in the freezer. I do get some fruit, you know, just to nibble on between lectures, but I'm often on the move, moving from lecture to tutorial, so I'll eat on the move and just grab whatever I can really. I mean, I would like to eat more healthily, but just can't be bothered really sometimes.

2 I tend to buy my food from farmers' markets and local shops. I like to buy local and organic seasonal food from the area where I live. This can of course create problems sometimes because there's never enough data to actually tell you where the food was sourced from and also sometimes it can be difficult to stick to your principles, you know, when you're travelling, for instance, I was on a business trip recently and I had to, I had to buy … well, I didn't have to, but I did, I bought a coffee from a chain coffee shop and I had absolutely no choice really in the matter about where the coffee had come from and it had clearly travelled halfway around the world.

3 I'm not particularly picky about food. I mean, I eat most things, you know, like dairy and meat, but definitely no offal, I don't like offal. And all vegetables and fruit, well, most fruits, but not strawberries because I've got an allergy to them. I usually get a rash if I eat them and symptoms similar to a cold so like watery eyes and a runny nose. I mean, worst case scenario like my throat swells up if it's really bad and I have trouble breathing.

4 I haven't eaten meat or fish for over 20 years now and I love cooking. There's so much to choose from with vegetables and pulses. Not eating meat isn't a problem except when I'm travelling and I have to grab something quickly. That sometimes can be a bit problematic. I did consider becoming a vegan at one point, but that would have meant not eating cheese, milk, butter or any dairy and I didn't think I could go that far to be quite honest. I, at one point, toyed with the idea of not wearing any animal products, like wool from sheep for clothes, or leather for shoes. I even considered not eating any honey, but that I think is a little extreme so I'm quite happy as I am.

5 Absolutely, I mean, I agree that producers should get a better deal, be paid a fair price, to increase their

---

standards of living and get more control over their lives. That's what I think. I've always thought that and that's why I never buy chocolate or coffee, bananas, anything that doesn't display a *Fair Trade* logo. Look, the *Fair Trade* it enables producers to invest in more environment friendly practices and improve their lives so I want to be a part of that.

3.39

Football isn't only the world's most popular sport, but it's also probably the most positive symbol of globalisation in the 21st century. Never before has a single activity captured the hearts and minds of so many people. The South African 2010 World Cup final drew an estimated television audience of over half a billion people across the entire planet.

This event, held every four years, is a celebration. A celebration of a happier globalisation than the one we all know. It's a time when the countries of the world come together for a healthy contest between neighbours in the global village, with no single nation in charge. Not for nothing is it called the 'beautiful game'.

Even the former secretary of the United Nations, Kofi Annan, said the World Cup made the UN 'green with envy'. In Kofi Annan's words soccer 'is one of the few phenomena as universal as the UN. You could say it's even more universal.'

Football shows in a very tangible way the benefits of cross-pollination between peoples and countries. It is inconceivable that Brazilian, Cameroonian or Japanese doctors, computer scientists, factory workers or teachers could move from one country to another as Brazilian, Cameroonian or Japanese football players do. The rich football clubs, usually European, will search the world over for the best players. Teams such as England's Chelsea or Arsenal, Spain's Barcelona or Real Madrid or Italy's Juventus or AC Milan have the top players in the world and it means the quality of the game increases.

Now, one could talk about this as a drain on the talent and resources of the nations that have lost these players to the richest clubs. But in fact, football shows us that this is not necessarily the case for two reasons.

First, free movement has meant that good players from small leagues improve much more than they would had they stayed at home. A good Australian or Serbian player improves much faster if he joins Manchester United or Barcelona. Secondly, that improvement returns to national teams thanks to the international federation of football FIFA's rule requiring players to play only for their national team in international competitions. The Cameroonian player Eto'o can play for any Spanish, Italian or English club, but in the national competitions, he can play only for Cameroon. In other words, FIFA has introduced an institutional rule that allows small countries (in the football sense) to capture some of the benefits of today's higher-quality game.

In addition, more and more national teams now welcome coaches from other countries. These bring new ways of thinking and playing to the game. Not only do these players and managers help bring skills and knowledge acquired abroad back to their country, they also become heroes in their adopted countries, helping, as Kofi Annan said 'to open hearts and minds'.

In short, everybody benefits and standards rise.

The same process could be applied to other activities. Free movement of skilled labour could be accompanied by international requirements that migrants from poor countries should spend, say, one year in five working in their countries of origin. They would bring home skills, technology and connections that are as valuable as the skills that Eto'o, Essien or Messi bring back to Cameroon, Ghana or Argentina. Job placement would remain a problem, but the principle is sound: the world should learn from its most popular sport.

Let me now move on to the benefits in terms of investment in a country that has hosted the World Cup. Looking at the last five nations that have …

3.41

1 Rarely do we find out how decisions are made by FIFA.

2 Only recently have Asian countries joined the top teams of football.

3 No sooner had the 2010 World Cup finished when preparations started for the next one.

4   Only by paying huge amounts of money to FIFA, can a country host the World Cup.

5   Never again should we allow countries to spend so much money on a sporting event.

6   Not only is winning the World Cup good for a country's self-esteem, it also boosts its economy.

🎧 3.42

A: … typical, that's the last thing I need …

B: OK, thank you, thanks for this bit of hush, thanks, thanks everyone for coming today. I appreciate you being here. Now I've called this meeting to discuss the local government spending cuts, but in particular what they are suggesting now is that they close our local swimming pool … so has everyone got a copy of the agenda by the way?

All: … yeah … yeah … didn't get one … makes frightening reading …

B: OK, well, let's … let's without further ado, let's get started. So moving to item 1 of the agenda, erm, what proposals can we give to the council to counter what seems like a fait accompli that they close the pool? Anybody want to start us off on that?

C: Well, we could demonstrate …

B: Yes …

A: I think that's a good idea …

D: Yes, a really good idea, you know, let them know how we feel about …

C: It's easy to organise on the internet …

D: Absolutely.

C: … everyone's emails …

D: … yeah yeah yeah … very important for the kids …

C: … kids involved … community … yeah … daytime demonstrations … preferably a Saturday morning … well, I …

A: involve the schools …

B: I would just take issue with that from a safety point of view. If you're getting children involved on demonstrations things can …

E: Can I just clarify something here? I mean, they're asking us to supply them with a proposal, so something concrete, something realistic, so we need to really think about what the options are. In terms of the financials, right?

B: That's a good idea, Jean. Yes …

A: Yeah, but I would like to take issue with what Nigel just said about the kids not getting involved, not in protesting and, you know, rioting, throwing rocks and stuff, but, you know, getting in touch with their friends on, you know, the social networks and that's … that's the way to spread the word.

B: I don't think we should get too sidetracked by the whole demonstration thing, although I do take Kate's point that we should show that we mean business here, but …

C: Actually, I would like to endorse what Nigel has just said about health and safety as well.

A: Yes, we have to keep it within the …

B: OK, so what other proposals could we make to the council?

E: Well, it might be an idea, um, to reduce staff levels?

D: Yeah, maybe.

E: Then again that's health and safety issues come to the fore …

C: What about less hours?

B: Fewer hours?

C: Perhaps only opening three days a week?

E: So open for schools on maybe two days of the week and open weekends for the public?

B: But I agree that weekends are paramount. We all want to make sure that it's open as often as it was before on the weekends, but maybe we can reduce hours …

E: In the week …

B: … some weekday mornings.

E: Yes, definitely.

C: What about, just thinking about sort of income, perhaps we could have like a fundraiser?

B: Yeah … who would be willing to volunteer for the fundraiser, I mean, can we have a show of hands?

C: Well, yes, I'll certainly help organise …

A: And I know people who would help.

B: Great.

E: I know Martin would do it for sure.

B: Martin's brilliant, yeah.

D: Yeah, he's very good.

E: Very good …

B: So are we in agreement on this then? Yeah …

All: Yeah … so far? … I think so.

A: Good. Well, could we perhaps move on to item 2 on the agenda. Nigel?

B: … OK, so I'm sorry to wrap this up. Any other business from anybody because there's another group waiting to come in?

C: Can we just set a meeting …

D: I think we should set a date …

B: Very good idea.

C: … next Tuesday everyone?

E: I would like to propose that we meet up …

D: Next Tuesday …

E: … on Wednesday …

B: Yes, because I can't do Tuesday either.

C: OK.

A: Wednesday at six o'clock?

B: Six o'clock Wednesday.

C: Same place.

A: Fine.

D: Brilliant.

C: Thanks Nigel.

B: Superb. OK, well, that wraps it up for today and see you all again on Wednesday at six.

E: Excellent.

D: Thank you.

A: Well, that seemed to go …

C: Yeah …

E: Anyone want a lift?

🎧 3.44

Evgenia, Belarus

I am sorry, I am laughing because when you start to learn English like in Belarus there are like topics you are learning, or texts you are memorising, and one of the topics is, like, 'my native town' and you also have to prepare it for an exam. And it's like, you know, this text that you remember and write down, and it took ages and then learn and then repeat and I even suspect I had it in an exam because when you asked that the first thing was like this, there's the beginning of this text, like Vitebsk is found on the banks of three rivers and it is just like, you know, there, like a learned thing. I am feeling like I am back to school.

🎧 3.45–3.46

Harshula, Sri Lanka

Similarly, when I grew up, when I was growing up, I started schooling in the capital Colombo, but whenever I had holidays I used to visit Ratnapura because that was where I used to get the proper break and I remember whenever my parents asked where, what I wanted to do during the summer vacation or holidays I always used to say I want to go to my cousin's place in Ratnapura because that's where I rejuvenate and where I feel like I am living life because that was the proper break for me with the tea estates, the birds, the people, and even today when I am here in Oxford studying for my Masters in Law there are so many opportunities for me to stay back here and work for a London law firm, but I have decided very strongly to go back home. That is because of the experience I got from my home town I suppose, with the close, closeness I have with my people, the villagers, and the fact that I feel that I should do something for the community. So that's a very strong feeling.

Jiawei, China

My childhood memory is, as I mentioned earlier, my family used to live in, on the eastern side of the river, which is called Pudong these days. So I remember … so when we were living on the eastern side, which is the not so developed part, so my father always take me to visit the western side like the central Shanghai area on weekends.

At that time there runs a ferry, a very, very cheap ferry. When I remember it. The ferry was very old styled and it has this front of the boat like totally exposed to the weather. But at the front of the boat there is this, um, it's like a round structure, I would think that's almost like a part of the engine, but it's covered, totally covered, so it almost make a perfect sitting surface. So what I remember … what my father would do, is he would put me on top of that structure, which was about three or four foot tall. So when my father put me on that, and when I was sitting there, my father was just able to stand beside me, but his head, I remember, is at my eye level so we could continue talking, my father and I would ride back and forth on the same ferry, so we don't need to pay for the multiple trips, but we get to enjoy the view of the river, and also the architecture, the fantastic architecture, on the waterfront side, yeah. So that … because I guess it cost so little, but it gave me such immense happiness as a little child, it becomes a very fond memory of mine. Because nowadays I am sure Shanghai, like other parts of the world, or other parts of China, because of the economic development, people also got more materialised.

🎧 3.47–3.48

Harshula, Sri Lanka

Well, the town centre, I have noticed that it hasn't changed very much compared to other cities in the country because politically the town, and Ratnapura as a district, was neglected due to not many politicians coming up from the area. And even when they did come up to the national level, they were more involved in national level politics than the local politics so I would really say that Ratnapura as a district and as a major town in Sri Lanka has been neglected for two, three decades.

Jiawei, China

A lot of things have changed, like last year when I was back in China they had this Shanghai Expo, but the thing is they charge admission fee, right, and so it becomes a little bit different, it becomes like a commercial, it no longer … I think previously all the lighting, all the ferry boat in some way it feels like a public good, you know, you could enjoy it because it's almost free, but now like everything seems to have a price tag associated with it. Yes, like China is growing a lot, but I think in some way it lost that kind of simpleness that was previously associated with the city in, at least locals' mind. Yeah. Of course, the greater economic development, that is for everybody to see, yeah.

Irregular verbs

Infinitive	Past simple	Past participle
be	was/were	been
beat	beat	beaten
become	became	become
begin	began	begun
bend	bent	bent
bet	bet	bet
bite	bit	bitten
blow	blew	blown
break	broke	broken
bring	brought /brɔːt/	brought /brɔːt/
build /bɪld/	built /bɪlt/	built /bɪlt/
burn	burnt/burned	burnt/burned
burst	burst	burst
buy /baɪ/	bought /bɔːt/	bought /bɔːt/
can	could /kʊd/	(been able)
catch	caught /kɔːt/	caught /kɔːt/
choose	chose	chosen
come	came	come
cost	cost	cost
cut	cut	cut
deal /diːl/	dealt /delt/	dealt /delt/
dig	dug	dug
do	did	done
draw	drew	drawn
dream	dreamt/dreamed	dreamt/dreamed
drink	drank	drunk
drive	drove	driven
eat	ate	eaten
fall	fell	fallen
feed	fed	fed
feel	felt	felt
fight	fought /fɔːt/	fought /fɔːt/
find	found	found
fly	flew	flown
forget	forgot	forgotten
forgive	forgave	forgiven
freeze	froze	frozen
get	got	got
give	gave	given
go	went	gone/been
grow	grew	grown
hang	hung/hanged	hung/hanged
have	had	had
hear	heard /hɜːd/	heard /hɜːd/
hide	hid	hidden
hit	hit	hit
hold	held	held
hurt /hɜːt/	hurt /hɜːt/	hurt /hɜːt/
keep	kept	kept
kneel	knelt/kneeled	knelt/kneeled
know	knew /njuː/	known
lay	laid	laid
lead	led	led
learn	learnt/learned	learnt/learned
leave	left	left
lend	lent	lent
let	let	let

Infinitive	Past simple	Past participle
lie	lay	lain
light	lit	lit
lose	lost	lost
make	made	made
mean	meant /ment/	meant /ment/
meet	met	met
must	had to	(had to)
pay	paid	paid
put	put	put
read	read /red/	read /red/
ride	rode	ridden
ring	rang	rung
rise	rose	risen
run	ran	run
say	said /sed/	said /sed/
see	saw /sɔː/	seen
sell	sold	sold
send	sent	sent
set	set	set
shake	shook	shaken
shine	shone	shone
shoot	shot	shot
show	showed	shown
shrink	shrank	shrunk
shut	shut	shut
sing	sang	sung
sink	sank	sunk
sit	sat	sat
sleep	slept	slept
slide	slid	slid
smell	smelt/smelled	smelt/smelled
speak	spoke	spoken
spell	spelt/spelled	spelt/spelled
spend	spent	spent
spill	spilt/spilled	spilt/spilled
split	split	split
spoil	spoilt/spoiled	spoilt/spoiled
spread	spread	spread
stand	stood	stood
steal	stole	stolen
stick	stuck	stuck
swear	swore	sworn
swell	swelled	swollen/swelled
swim	swam	swum
take	took /tʊk/	taken
teach	taught /tɔːt/	taught /tɔːt/
tear	tore	torn
tell	told	told
think	thought /θɔːt/	thought /θɔːt/
throw	threw	thrown
understand	understood	understood
wake	woke	woken
wear	wore /wɔː/	worn
win	won /wʌn/	won /wʌn/
write	wrote	written

Macmillan Education
Between Towns Road, Oxford OX4 3PP
A division of Macmillan Publishers Limited

Companies and representatives throughout the world

ISBN 978-0-230-03327-6

Text © Lindsay Clandfield & Amanda Jeffries 2012
Additional material by Rebecca Robb Benne and Michael Vince
Design and illustration © Macmillan Publishers Limited 2012

First published 2012

Original design by Macmillan Publishers Limited
Page make-up by eMC Design Ltd
Illustrated by Jonathan Burton pp15, 39, 63, 79, 87, 111; Peter Cornwell p95;
Celia Hart pp59, 66, 68, 114, 116 and Piers Sanford pp30, 80.
Cover design by Macmillan Publishers Limited
Cover photograph used by permission of the Museum of the History of Science,
University of Oxford/Keiko Ikeuchi
Picture research by Sally Cole/Perseverance Works Ltd

Authors' acknowledgements
Amanda would like to thank all the team at Macmillan and her dedicated co-
authors for their hard work and commitment to quality. A special thank you also
goes to her family, friends and colleagues for their encouragement and support.
Finally, she would like to thank John Eckersley for giving her her first teaching
job, and for first kindling her interest in advanced English.

Lindsay would like to thank all his co-authors on the Global project, on the
Coursebooks, Teacher's books and eWorkbooks as well as all the other various
components. It's been a long, hard road but we have all made it intact at the other
end! I'm proud to be part of such a good writing team.

The authors and publishers would like to thank all the teachers and consultants
who have piloted and reviewed the material. Particular thanks go to the following
people: Andrea Córdova, Susana Flores (Anglo Multimedia School of English,
Haedo, Buenos Aires, Argentina); Ma. Cristina Maggi, Ma. Cristina Buero de
Chinton (Friends' School of English, Adrogué, Buenos Aires, Argentina); Mirta
Zampini, Aldana Anchorena, Elizabeth Rainieri, Ma. Soledad D. Mangiarotti,
Pamela Sabrina Pecorelli (IECI, Haedo, Buenos Aires, Argentina); Alejandro
Jorge Listrani (Cultural Inglesa de Palermo, Ciudad Autónoma de Buenos Aires,
Argentina); Lilian Itzicovitch Leventhal (Potential/Colegio I.L. Peretz, São
Paulo, Brazil); Ana Maria Miranda (Cultura Inglesa Ribeirão Preto, Ribeirão
Preto, Brazil); Magali de Moraes Menti (FACCAT - Escola Municipal Lauro
Rodrigues, Porto Alegre, Brazil); Simone Sarmento (PUCRS, Porto Alegre,
Brazil); Laura Lee Lehto (Cultura Inglesa, Fortaleza, Brazil); Viviane Cristine
Silva Grossklauss, Analice Sandovetti (Cultura Inglesa Jundiaí, Jundiaí, Brazil);
Celia Aguiar de Almeida Costa (Cultura Inglesa de Juiz de Fora, Brazil); Corina
Celia Machado Correa (Associação Alumni - São Paulo, Brazil); Jane Godwin,
(The Four, São Carlos, Brazil); Caroline Toubia (The Holy Family School,
Jesuite, Egypt); Amany Shawkey, Heidi Omara (Macmillan Publishers Ltd, Egypt)
Caroline Franz , Dana Jelinkova (MVHS Muenchner Volkshochschule, Munich,
Germany); Irene Rodriguez, Haydee Gutierrez Palafox, Antonio Morales de la
Barrera, Javier Ramos de Hoyos (The Anglo Mexican Foundation, Mexico City,
Mexico); Viviana Caruso de Curtius (freelance author and consultant, Mexico
City, Mexico); Emma Dominguez (Academic Studies Manager, The Anglo
Mexican Foundation, Mexico City, Mexico); Katarzyna Rogalińska-Gajewska
(Archibald, Warsaw, Poland); Małgorzata Woźniak, Dorota Pachwicewicz,
Agnieszka Kilanowska (Centrum Językowe 'Euroclub', Gdańsk, Poland); Fabiola
Georgiana Hosu (Little London School and Nursery School, Dimitrie Cantemir
University, Bucharest, Romania); Lydia B. Korzheva (Diplomatic Academy,
Moscow, Russia); Ludmila A. Pokrovskaya (Russian Academy of Foreign Trade,
Moscow, Russia); Olga S. Petrischeva (Moscow State University of International
Relations, Moscow, Russia); Albina Valieva (The international Language School
'Denis School', Moscow, Russia); Karen Dyer, Cathy Harris, Frank Hodgkins
(International House, Madrid, Spain); Carlos Trueba (E.O.I. Villaverde, Madrid,
Spain); Patricia Plaza Arregui, (E.O.I. Malaga, Spain); Maria Esther Álvarez Rico
(E.O.I. Sagunto, Valencia, Spain); Burcu Tezcan Ünal (Bilgi University, Istanbul,
Turkey); Dr. F. Ilke Buyukduman (Ozyegin University, Istanbul, Turkey); Sarah
Shaw (The British Council, Chiang Mai, Thailand); Aomboon Burutphakdee,
Nattinee Khuensri (Payap University, Chiang Mai, Thailand); Claudia Edwards
(London School of English, London, UK); Sally Jones (Regent Oxford, Oxford,
UK); Katherine Griggs (Community English School Oxfordshire Adult Learning,
Oxford, UK).

The authors and the publishers would like to thank the following for permission
to use their written material: Hilde Faber, Taru Kivilahti, Marina Jimenez
Morgado, Wenchao Li, Jose Manuel Roche, Alex Kuo, Chiara Letizia, Yu Tao,
Davide Volpi.

A special thank you to Oxford University Language Centre and to the following
for their help with Global Voices: Caroline Pierrey, Giacomo Perantoni, Evgenia
Ivanova, Silvia Xicola Tugas, Jiawei Wu, Harshula Seneviratne, Dominika
Kubicz-Macaulay, Lillian Ndinda, Katsuya Noguchi, Carolina Rezaval, Zaur
Mammadov, Miguel Fernandes Pereira, Rod Rembendambya; and also to Sue
Bateman, Ben Bateman, Leonie Caldecott and Sally Warner for their help with
Function Globally recordings.

The author and publishers would like to thank the following for permission to
reproduce their photographs:
AFP pp37(br), 47(br), 54(cl), 56(bl), 119(tr), 119(br); Alamy/Bon Appetit p116,
Alamy/Arcaid Images p110, Alamy/Aurora Photos p46(br), Alamy/BeeJay
Images p72(cl), Alamy/Cosmo Condina Concepts p34(br), Alamy/dbimages p36,
Alamy/I.Dagnall p94(bl), Alamy/D.Delimont p8(d), Alamy/R.Erol p103(br),
Alamy/Fresh Start Images p42 (bl), Alamy/Look Die Bildagenturder Fotografen
GmbH p8(c), Alamy/J.Sutton Hibbert p8(b), Alamy/T.Hyde p94(bc), Alamy/
ICP p117(cr), Alamy/N.Keevil p69(tl), Alamy/O.Maksymenko p121(tl), Alamy/
Moodboard p26, Alamy/Worldspec/NASA p12(cl), Alamy/Oxford Events
Photography p115(br), Alamy/M.Roper p21(br), Alamy/P.Scalia pp114(cl),
122, Alamy/StockImages p34(cl), Alamy/C.Thege p10, Alamy/Art Directors
& Trip p120(cl), Alamy/D.White p71(br), Alamy/J.Woodworth p115(c);
Archive Photos p85(tr); Bananastock p16; Michael Barkun p97(br); John
D Barrow/M.Alexander p90(br); Blend Images p103(tm); Brand X pp40(tr),
52(bl), 52(tr); British Library Images/The British Library Board p120(br);
Felicity Bryan/Alex Ramsay p115(bm); Bridgeman Art Library/Children
and Unicorn, 2003 (oil on canvas), Korsakova, Irina (b.1960) (Contemporary
Artist)/Private Collection/© Portal Painters p9(br), Bridgeman Art Library/
Then Scheherazade began her story, from 'The Arabian Nights', 1939 (colour
engraving), Broders, Roger (1883 1953)/ Private Collection/© DACS/Roger
Perrin p11(tr), Bridgeman Art Library/Woman Holding a Balance, c.1664 (oil on
canvas),Vermeer, Jan(1632-75)/National Gallery of Art, Washington DC, USA
p18(c), Bridgeman Art Library/Ulysses and his companions gouging out the eye
of the Cyclops Polyphemus, illustration from an antique Greek vase, 1887 (colour
litho), French School, (19th century)/ Bibliotheque des Arts Decoratifs, Paris,
France/Archives Charmet p54(br), Bridgeman Art Library/The Heart, facsimile
of the Windsor book (pen and ink on paper), Vinci, Leonardo da (1452-1519)
(after)/Bibliotheque des Arts Decoratifs, Paris, France/Archives Charmet p78(cl),
Bridgeman Art Library/William Shakespeare (1564-1616) c.1610 (oil on canvas),
Taylor, John (d.1651) (attr. to)/National Portrait Gallery, London, UK p81(cr),
Bridgeman Art Library/Juliet (oil on canvas), Waterhouse, John William (1849
1917)/Private Collection/By courtesy of Julian Hartnoll p81(tl), Bridgeman
Art Library/Portrait of Geoffrey Chaucer (c.1340-1400) c.1600, English
School, (16th century)/Private Collection/Photo © Philip Mould Ltd, London
p121(br), Bridgeman Art Library/Liverpool Docks from Wapping, c.1870, (oil
on canvas), Grimshaw, John Atkinson (1836-93)/Private Collection/Photo ©
Christie's Images p126; Christian Science Monitor p46(bl); Corbis/Atlantide
Phototravel p8(a), Corbis/Peace/Amanaimages p91, Corbis/Bettmann pp11(br),
49(tr), 79(bl), Corbis/J.Calder p117(tl), Corbis/R.de Chowdhuri/Reuters p56(cl),
Corbis/doc-stock p83(tr), Corbis/R.Yongrit/epa p82, Corbis/C.Felver p25(tc),
Corbis/K.Hackenberg p34(bm), Corbis/Image China p32(br), Corbis/Image
Source p34(c), 74, Corbis/W.Krecichwost p13(tr), Corbis/K.Sundelin/Photoalto
p14, Corbis/D.Zammit Lupi/Reuters p96(bl), Corbis/K.Motohashi/Aflo Relax
p19(t), Corbis/P.Macdiarmid/Reuters pp 3(tr), 18(tr), Corbis/D.Muench p32(cl),
Corbis/Ocean p6(A), Corbis/M.Pole p108(cl), Corbis/Science Faction pp6,
32(cr), Corbis/Sygma p34(bl), Corbis/J.Tarbell p68(cl), Corbis/D.Nunuk/Visuals
Unlimited p12(bl), Corbis/Yonhap News Agency p47(cr); Dialogue in the Dark/
Museo del Palacio de Bellas Artes in Mexico City and with the Fondo de Cultura
Económica in the Federal District of Mexico (2004) p22(bl); FLPA/F.Nicklin/
Minden Pictures p78(br); Flickr/H.Desplechin p23(tc), Flickr/P.Sharp p93(tr),
Flickr/D.Varney p92; Flickr Select/S.Gringauze p85(tm); Foodpix p31(br); Gallo
Images p93(tl); Harper Collins/Harper Perennial; New Ed edition (5 May 2004)

May 2004) p37(tr); **Getty**/ARS, NY and DACS, London 2011 p129; **Getty/ Blend Images** p48(bl), **Getty**/J.Blair p21(br), Getty/Y.Levy p66(B), Getty/Science Faction Jewels pp3(tl), p24; **Getty RF** p88; **Getty Images Entertainment** pp69(b),109(tr); **Getty Images News** p59(tr); **Hodder & Stoughton**, Hodder Faith, Headline Publishing Group & John Murray (Publishers) p69(tr); **Hulton Archive** pp19(cr), 25(br), 43, 44, 73(br), 130; **Image Bank** pp3(c), 38, 50(tl), 98, 104, 105(b); **Kobal**/Danish Film Institute/DR/Zentropa p128, Kobal/Nimbus Films p45(tl); **Lonely Planet Images**/H.Jones p71(tr); **Mary Evans Picture Library** pp55(br), 58(c); **National Geographic**/Winfield Parks p72(bl); **Nordic Photos** p105(bcr); **Panos Pictures**/G.M.B.Akash p118/Panos Pictures/Q. Shen p57; **Penguin Books** (6 Aug 2009) p107(tl), 107(cr); **Photoalto** p76; **Photographers Choice** p42; **Photolibrary**/B.Binzen p103(tr), Photolibrary/C. Bowman p106(br), Photolibrary/B.Brennan p78(clam), Photolibrary/Corbis pp33, 93(c), Photolibrary/R.Erwin p20(b), Photolibrary/Fotosearch pp70(bl), 109(tl), Photolibrary/F.Frith Collection p58(cl), Photolibrary/P.Harris p20(cl), Photolibrary/M.Runkel Hulger p20(cr), Photolibrary/W.Kent p112, Photolibrary/ Geophoto/A.Kuzin p37(c), Photolibrary/Imagebroker RF p84(cl), Photolibrary/ Imagestate p62, Photolibrary/Ingram Publishing p109(tml), Photolibrary/C. Kober p100, Photolibrary/V.McCormick p109(tmr), Photolibrary/L.Mouton p83(c), Photolibrary/I.Palacios pp66(C), Photolibrary/A.Penketh p21(tr), Photolibrary/The Print Collector p31(cr), Photolibrary/Radius Images p103(tl), Photolibrary/J. Rotman p48(cl), Photolibrary/C.Sanchez p78(shrew), Photolibrary/G.Zwerger-Schoner p13(br), Photolibrary/J.Sweeney p66(E), Photolibrary/TAO Images Ltd 94(br), Photolibrary/B.Yarvin p96(cl), Photolibrary/ Zoonar RF p35; **Photonica** pp22(cl), 93(tc), 106(cl); Profile Books, Gilgamesh, New English Version by Stephen Mitchell (6 Oct 2005) p55(tl); **Random House Publishers**/Black Swan (26 Feb 2009) p115(tr); **Reportage** p80(cl); **Rex Features**/D.Blair p119(tl), Rex Features/Fox Search/Everett p108(bl), Rex Features/Image Source p28, Rex Features/ITV p30(bc), 30(bl), Rex Features/A. Lentati/Evening Standard p73(cr), Rex Features/Sipa Press p93(br), Rex Features/ Creative Studio Heinemann/WestEnd61 p117(br); **Riser** p105(cr); **Ronald Grant Archive**/Gabriel Pascal Productions p49(tl), Ronald Grant Archive/United Artists p61(tl); **Science & Society Picture Library**/Library of Congress p127; **Science Photo Library**/L.Untidt/Bonnier Publications p108(tr), Science Photo Library/S.Horrell p121(tm), Science Photo Library/N.Kedersha p7, Science Photo Library/3D4Medical.com p84(bl); **Stanford University** p61(c); **Stock4B** p86; **Stock Image** p50(tm); **Stone** pp46(cl), 60, 73(c), 90(c), 97(sl); **Superstock**/ Marka p124; **Taxi** pp45(tr),102; **Time & Life Pictures** p94(cl); **Topfoto**/The Granger Collection p58(cr); **The Trustees of the British Museum** p55(tl); **Win Initiative** p23(br).

Commissioned photography by Joshua Gross/Joshua Tree photography: pp27, 51, 75, 99, 123.

The author(s) and publishers are grateful for permission to reprint the following copyright material:
Spiked for an extract abridged from "Is Wikipedia part of a new 'global brain'?" by Theresa Clifford, 14 February 2007, www.spiked-online.com/ copyright © Spiked; Wikipedia: Five Pillars, http://en.wikipedia.org/wiki/Wikipedia:Five_pillars, granted under the GNU Free Documentation License (GFDL); Professor Ken Arnold for interview material, reproduced with permission; Penguin Books (UK) Ltd for an extract from *The Arabian Nights Tales of 1001 Nights Volume 1* by Malcolm C Lyons, pp.7-11. Reproduced by permission of Penguin Group (UK) Ltd; NASA for an extract from 'Science Fiction or Science Fact?', source NASA, www.nasa.gov; Dr. Diana C. Issidorides for an extract from 'Dialogue in the dark: An exhibition to discover the unseen' by Diana Issidorides, copyright © Dr. Diana C. Issidorides; Jonathan Clowes Ltd for an extract from *Through the Tunnel* by Doris Lessing, copyright © 1953, Doris Lessing. Reprinted by kind permission of Jonathan Clowes Ltd., London, on behalf of David Nobbs; Trip Technologies Inc. for material from 'My 3 top travel experiences' by Ricki www.tripbase.com reproduced with permission; Encyclopaedia Britannica, Inc. for an extract adapted from 'The Great Lakes' frp, *Encyclopaedia Britannica 2007 Ultimate Reference Suite*. Adapted with permission from Encyclopaedia Britannica, © 2007 by Encyclopaedia Britannica, Inc.; David Godwin Associates for an extract from *The God of Small Things* by Arundhati Roy, 1997, pp.10-11, copyright © Arundhati Roy, 1997; Oxford University Press for extracts from *Myth of Mars & Venus* by Deborah Cameron, copyright © Oxford University Press 2008; Time Out Magazine Ltd for the film review of 'Italian for beginners' by GM, www.timeout.com, reproduced with permission; The Society of Authors for an extract from *Pygmalion*, Act 3 by George Bernard Shaw. Reproduced by permission of The Society of Authors, on behalf of George Bernard Shaw Estate; Profile Books for an extract from *Gilgamesh, A new English Version* translated by Stephen Mitchell, pp.121-124, Profile Books. Reproduced with permission; Justin Byworth, World Vision Charity for interview material, reproduced with

permission; The Guardian for extracts abridged from "I'm more afraid of piracy than cyclones" by Helena Smith, *The Guardian* 22/11/2008; and "We consider ourselves heroes: a Somali Pirate Speaks" by Xan Rice and Abdiqani Hassan, *The Guardian*, 22/11/2008. Copyright © Guardian News & Media Ltd 2008; Extract from 'QED' by Robert Matthews copyright © Telegraph Group Limited 2004, first published in The Daily Telegraph 06.01.04, reprinted by permission of the publisher; Headline Publishing Group Limited and Penguin Group Canada for an extract from *The Long Song* by Andrea Levy, pp.92-95, copyright © 2010 Andrea Levy. Reproduced by permission of Headline Publishing Group Limited and Penguin Group (Canada), a Division of Pearson Canada, Inc.; Encyclopaedia Britannica, Inc. for an extract adapted from 'Bangalore' from *Encyclopedia Britannica 2007 Ultimate Reference Suite*. Adapted with permission from Encyclopaedia Britannica, © 2007 by Encyclopaedia Britannica, Inc.; Extract from 'The New Golden Age' interviews by Yasmin Alibhai-Brown, copyright © *The Independent* 2010, first published in The Independent 19.05.10, reprinted by permission of the publisher; James Peto for an extract from "The Beating Heart" by Ted Bianco in *The Heart* by James Peto 2007, pp.181-182, reproduced with permission; Oxford Mindfulness Centre, University of Oxford Dept. of Psychiatry (MBCT) for an extract from 'Mindfulness based cognitive therapy' http://mbct.co.uk/about-mbct, reproduced with permission of Professor Mark Williams; 'Extract from 'Taming the monkey mind' by Kathy Phillips, copyright © Telegraph Group Limited, first published in The Sunday Telegraph, reprinted by permission of the publisher; Sue Gerhardt for interview material, reproduced with permission; The Random House Group Ltd and WW Norton & Company, Inc. for an extract from *One Hundred Essential Things You Didn't Know: Maths Explains your World* by John D. Barrow, published by Bodley Head, pp.18-19, 2008. Reprinted by permission of The Random House Group Ltd and W.W. Norton & Company, Inc.; Barbara Mobbs Literary Agency for an extract from "The idea of perfection" by Kate Grenville, pp.2-9, 1999. Reproduced with permission; The University of California Press for an extract from *A Culture of Conspiracy: Apocalyptic Visions in Contemporary America* by Michael Barkun, copyright © 2004 by the Regents of the University of California. Published by the University of California Press; Forbes Media LLC for an extract from "The World's Hardest Working Countries" by Parmy Olsen, 21 May 2008, www.forbes. com. Reprinted by permission of Forbes Media LLC, copyright © 2011; The Four-hour Day Foundation, Inc. for an extract from 'The Four-Hour Day: 'The Idea' by Gabe Sinclair, www.fourhourday.org/. Random House Inc,: Penguin Books Ltd for an extract from *Traffic: Why We Drive the Way we Do (and What it Says about Us)* by Tom Vanderbilt, pp.3-4, 6, Penguin Books, 2008, copyright © Tom Vanderbilt, 2008. Reproduced by permission of Alfred A. Knopf, a division of Random House, Inc. Penguin Books Ltd; Penguin Group (USA) Inc. for an extract from *The Secret Life of Bees* by Sue Monk Kidd, copyright © 2002 by Sue Monk Kidd. Used by permission of Viking Penguin, a division of Penguin Group (USA) Inc.; The University of Chicago Press for an extract adapted from "Isolarion: A Different Oxford Journey" by James Attlee, pp.xv-xvi, viii, copyright © The University of Chicago Press. Reproduced with permission of The University of Chicago Press and James Attlee.

Printed and bound in Thailand

2016 2015 2014 2013 2012
10 9 8 7 6 5 4 3 2 1